LINKAGES

LINKAGES

A Content-Based Integrated Skills Text

PATRICE CONNERTON

FRANCES REID

The George Washington University

HEINLE & HEINLE PUBLISHERS
A Division of Wadsworth, Inc.
Boston, Massachusetts 02116 U.S.A.

The publication of *Linkages* was directed by the members of the
Heinle & Heinle ESL Publishing Team:

Erik Gundersen, Editorial Director
Susan Mraz, Marketing Manager
Kristin Thalheimer, Production Editor

Also participating in the publication of this program were:

Publisher: Stanley J. Galek
Editorial Production Manager: Elizabeth Holthaus
Associate Editor: Lynne Telson Barsky
Project Manager: Cindy Funkhouser
Manufacturing Coordinator: Mary Beth Lynch
Photo Coordinator: Carl Spector
Interior Designer and Compositor: Paola Di Stefano
Illustrator: Carol O'Malia
Cover Illustrator: Vanderbyl Design
Cover Designer: Bortman Design Group

Linkages: A Content-Based Integrated Skills Text

Manufactured in the United States of America.

Library of Congress Cataloging-in-Publication Data

Connerton, Patrice.
  Linkages : a content-based integrated skills text / Patrice
Connerton and Frances Reid.
        p.   cm.
      ISBN 0-8384-3955-1
        1. English language—Textbooks for foreign speakers. I. Reid,
Frances. II. Title.
PE1128. C6943 1993   92-41831
428.2'4—dc20   CIP

ISBN: 0-8384-3955-1

10 9 8 7 6

CONTENTS

CHAPTER 12   **Selling to the New America**   **236**

OVERVIEW

Linkages is a content-based, integrated skills text for high-intermediate ESL students who plan to study at an American college or university. The readings in the text form the base for the presentation of content. For the most part, they are authentic and include material from college texts, general audience texts, periodicals, and literary works. Lectures, discussions, and other communicative activities, as well as writing tasks help to expand the students' understanding of the content and to develop their language skills. The topics presented are drawn from the fields of American history and culture, psychology, sociology, and business.

RATIONALE

Students can learn a second language more efficiently and successfully when they are responsible for learning new information about academic topics of interest to them. This content-based approach offers several advantages.

1. The content-based approach easily lends itself to the development and integration of all language skills.

2. The focus on learning content increases students' motivation.

3. In this approach, the tasks and student-teacher interaction help to prepare students for success in mainstream academic classes.

4. The thematic grouping of the content-based lesson facilitates the natural recycling of vocabulary, concepts, and discourse styles.

SPECIAL FEATURES

Linkages has several features that make the program particularly well suited for students at the high-intermediate level. These are:

■ authentic, substantive readings that challenge students

■ extended readings that help students to face the reality of an academic reading load

■ rich selection of topic-related vocabulary that is recycled throughout the program

■ lectures that assess and expand students' knowledge of topics

■ tasks that develop students' critical thinking skills

■ study aids such as charts, timelines, and marginal notes to help develop students' study skills

■ readings for pleasure such as poems, folktales, and autobiographical selections

WHAT DOES THE TITLE MEAN?

The title *Linkages* was chosen for several reasons. First, the learning of content and language are linked. Second, the content of the readings and lectures in each unit is closely related, allowing students to build a body of knowledge on the subject. Finally, through this program's approach, students connect their prior knowledge with the new information and ideas presented in the text.

COMPONENTS OF THE PROGRAM

Supplementary materials include video cassettes of the lectures and audio cassettes of the lectures and dictations. Also included is an Instructor's Manual containing lesson tips, samples of student writing, a sample test, an answer key, and lecture transcripts.

ACKNOWLEDGMENTS

We wish to give thanks to the many people who helped in the production of this book. They are: the supportive staff at Heinle & Heinle; Kathleen Ossip, formerly of Newbury House; our reviewers; and the EFL program, colleagues, and students at The George Washington University. We give special recognition to those who volunteered their time for the videotaped lectures: Peggy Bangham, Belle Tyndall, Shirley Thompson, Jim Fry, Robert Werckle, Mary Catherine Holden, Bob Adamson, Sharon Ann O'Brien, and Frank Meeks. Finally, the time spent with our families and close friends, though so little, has meant so much to us over the many months.

Patrice Connerton
Frances Reid

Linkages is a content-based textbook. This means that one important objective in studying this book is to learn new and interesting information or content. In Unit One, you will learn about four historic American cities; in Unit Two, about psychology in everyday life; in Unit Three, about the American family at work; and in Unit Four, about the entrepreneur or businessperson. After you complete a unit, you will have learned a large body of knowledge on the topic of that unit.

Linkages is also an integrated skills textbook. This means that a second important objective in studying this book is to practice and develop each of the four language skills: reading, writing, listening, and speaking. If you look at the Contents, you will see that each unit consists of three chapters. Each chapter begins with a reading selection accompanied by a set of activities: a pre-reading discussion, a reading check, comprehension exercises, topics for discussion and writing, vocabulary exercises, and a journal writing assignment.

In addition to the reading selection, most chapters have a communicative activity, a lecture, and/or a reading for pleasure. For example, look at Chapter 3 in the Contents. Besides the reading selection, what other kinds of activities are there? As you can see from these activities, you will be practicing and developing all four language skills in this book.

Vocabulary is an important concern for many intermediate and high-intermediate students. In *Linkages*, you may find that many words are new for you and that the reading selections are longer than those you are used to reading. Don't worry; you can succeed. With regular practice, you will learn that when you read you don't have to know every word in order to understand the writer's most important ideas.

Finally, we want to share with you the reaction of our former students who have used *Linkages*. Most have said that the book is interesting and challenging and that it has helped them to improve their language skills and gain confidence in English. We hope that you have a similar positive reaction to the book.

Jazz on Bourbon Street in New Orleans, Louisiana.

A busy marketplace in Boston, Massachusetts.

Above: *Historic houses along the waterfront in Charleston, South Carolina.*

Riding a cable car in San Francisco, California.

UNIT ONE
Historic American Cities

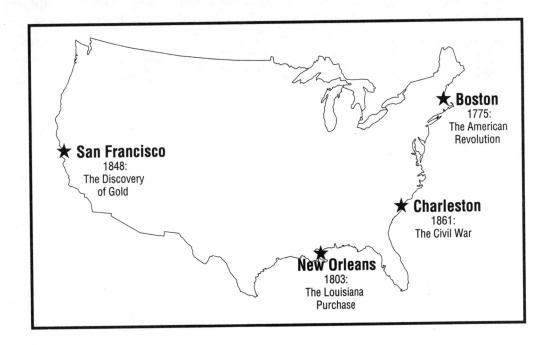

In this unit, you will learn about the four American cities on the map above. Look at the photos on the previous page that show a tourist attraction in each city. What are these tourist attractions? Have you visited any of these cities?

Before learning more about these cities and the United States, let's learn more about where each person in the class is from. To help you do this, draw a map of your country and the surrounding region and bodies of water. Mark the capital of your country, your hometown, and your favorite vacation spot in your country. Now use the map to introduce your country and the region where you are from. Describe to the class your favorite vacation spot and the things you like to do there.

These four events are historic because they represent important stages in the development of this country. For example, the American Revolution, which began in Boston in 1775, marks the beginning stage in the development of this country: ***the birth of this nation.***

In 1803, the U.S. government bought the city of New Orleans and a large area of land west of the Mississippi River from the French. This event, which is called the Louisiana Purchase, represents a second stage in the development of this country: *the growth of the nation.*

In 1848, gold was discovered outside the small town of San Francisco. Soon hundreds of thousands of Americans from cities in the East and Midwest left their jobs and their families and headed west with dreams of getting rich quick. San Francisco and other small towns in California grew overnight into cities as large as those in the East and Midwest. Thus, the discovery of gold represents a third stage of development: *a nation united from east to west.*

In 1861, the American Civil War began in Charleston, South Carolina. This event represents a fourth stage in the development of this country: *a nation divided.*

As you learn about these historic events and the role each played in the development of this country, you will begin to understand why these cities are interesting places to visit.

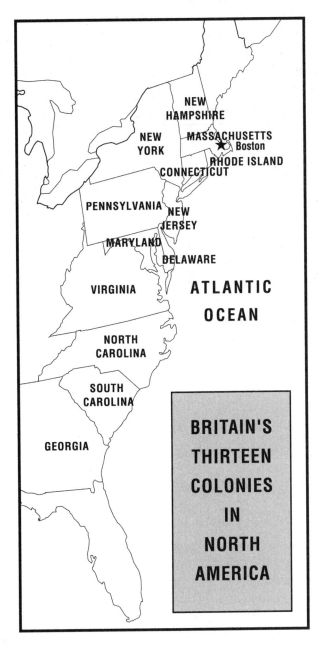

In this reading, you will learn about Boston during the colonial period, that is, when Massachusetts was one of 13 British colonies in North America. You will learn about the role Boston played in the events that led to the American Revolution against Great Britain. Boston and the colony of Massachusetts represent the first stage in the development of this country—the birth of the United States of America.

READING SELECTION

PRE-READING DISCUSSION

Getting into the Topic

■ What is a colony? Can you give your own example of a colony?

■ Where in North America did Great Britain establish colonies? Before the British settled this region, what group of people was already living there?

■   Trade between the mother country and her colonies was very important. Many British goods were shipped to the colonies, and natural resources from the colonies were shipped to Great Britain. Lumber from trees was one of these natural resources. What do you think another one was? Think about the location of the colonies.

■   What words come to mind when you hear the word "revolution"? What do you already know about the American Revolution?

Getting an Overview of the Reading Selection

The reading selection is divided into several **sections.** Each section has its own title called a **heading.** Below is an outline of the title and headings in this reading. Look at the sections in the reading to complete the outline.

BOSTON, MASSACHUSETTS: THE BIRTH OF A NEW NATION

1.   The Thirteen British Colonies in America

2.   Parliament Taxes the Colonies

3.   Protests Against Taxation Without Representation

4.

5.

6.

■   A *protest* is an expression of strong disagreement. Based on the outline, what were the colonies protesting against? How can people protest against unfair taxes?

■   Look at the illustrations in the reading selection. What do you think the word "massacre" means? Why do you think British soldiers were shooting at Bostonians? Was the Boston Tea Party actually a party or a protest?

READ THE SELECTION: FIRST TIME

Read to get a general understanding of each section. Do not stop to look up words in the dictionary. Some unfamiliar words are explained in the margin.

THE THIRTEEN BRITISH COLONIES IN AMERICA

settle: go and live in

merchants: businessmen

British Empire: group of countries and land under the control of the British government

royal stamp: stamp of the king

consent: permission; approval

1   In the 1400s and 1500s, European explorers claimed land in North America for the kings of France, Spain, and England. Much of the land along the Atlantic coast was claimed for the king of England. However, it wasn't until the 1600s and 1700s that the British came to settle this land as colonies of Great Britain. In total, 13 colonies were established.

2   These colonies were very important to England for trade reasons. The colonies were new markets where British merchants could sell their goods, and the land was rich in natural resources that they could sell to the mother country.

3   Although Great Britain controlled colonial trade, she did not control everyday life in the colonies. She found it almost impossible to govern her colonies from across the ocean. Therefore, each of the 13 colonies elected its own assembly, a group of men that governed the colony and made laws.

4   The relationship between Mother England and her colonies in America seemed to be a fairly happy one; in fact, Englishmen in the colonies seemed to have more independence than Englishmen back in Great Britain.

PARLIAMENT TAXES THE COLONIES

5   In 1740, a war broke out between Great Britain and France. This war was fought both in Europe and North America. Part of the reason for the war was over territory in North America. In 1763, when the British finally defeated the French, France had to give up most of her territory in America. Now the British Empire in North America was larger than ever.

6   With this new territory came new problems. Britain needed to protect her new territory from the French and the American Indians who fought on their side. Leaving 10,000 British soldiers in the territory would require money. People in Britain were already heavily taxed, so Parliament had to think of a way to make the American colonists help pay for the soldiers.

7   In 1765, Parliament passed the Stamp Act. This law required that all newspapers, magazines, and legal papers in the colonies have a royal stamp. Because the stamp increased the price of these items, the colonists considered it a tax.

PROTESTS AGAINST TAXATION WITHOUT REPRESENTATION

8   That same year, colonists in Boston protested against the Stamp Act. They sent letters to Parliament, protesting that it did not have the right to tax the colonists because they did not have any representation in Parliament. "No taxation without representation!" they shouted. What did the colonists mean by "no taxation without representation"? They meant that since they did not have members of Parliament in London, they did not see why Parliament should have the right to decide their taxes.

9   Bostonians argued that if Parliament could tax newspapers without the colonists' consent, it could tax books. Moreover, if Parliament could tax books

without the colonists' consent, it could eventually tax everything without their consent. They believed that the colonial assemblies, not Parliament, had the right to make laws for them.

10   However, in 1767, Parliament passed another law. This one required that the colonists pay import taxes on a long list of British goods. Once again, the colonists in Boston protested and demonstrated against taxation without representation. A group of Bostonians called the "Sons of Liberty" organized a boycott. They got all 13 colonies to agree not to buy glass, tea, and other British imports that were taxed.

This picture of the Boston Massacre did much to make the colonists angry against the British.

THE BOSTON MASSACRE

11   Protests continued in Boston and in other colonial towns. In 1768, Bostonians set fire to the homes of British tax collectors. Following this violence, 4,000 British soldiers were sent to Boston to quiet the leaders of the Sons of Liberty and to protect the tax collectors from attacks.

12   Bostonians resented the taxes and the presence of British soldiers in their town. On March 5, 1770, a group of angry protestors carrying rocks and stones surrounded a much smaller group of British soldiers guarding the tax building. No one knows for sure what caused the soldiers to fire at the demonstrators, killing five citizens and wounding six others. As news of the "Boston Massacre" spread throughout the colonies, resentment toward Parliament and British soldiers grew stronger.

demonstrated: showed strong feelings publicly by marching and carrying signs

Disguised as Indians, the Sons of Liberty threw English tea into the Boston harbor.

THE BOSTON TEA PARTY

13   Largely because of the colonial boycott, Parliament decided in 1772 to repeal all of the import taxes, except one. The tax on British tea was kept as a symbol of Parliament's power to make laws for the colonies. Although the tea tax was small, "no taxation without representation" was an extremely important issue to the colonists. When tea was unloaded from British ships, colonial merchants refused to buy it or sell it in their stores. In Boston, townspeople would not even allow the tea to be unloaded. On the night of December 16, 1773, the Sons of Liberty disguised themselves as Indians, boarded three British tea ships in the Boston harbor, and threw all their tea into the water. Later, other towns held their own tea parties.

symbol: sign which represents an idea

issue: important point

14   When the king of England and Parliament heard about the "Boston Tea Party," they decided it was time to punish the unruly colonists. They decided to make Boston an example. In 1774, they closed the port of Boston, took away the power of the Massachusetts assembly, and put the colony under the control of British soldiers. As Bostonians saw it, their town was under military occupation!

15   The other 12 colonies united to support Boston and the colony of Massachusetts. They were afraid that if Parliament could punish Massachusetts, it could punish them, too. The colonial assemblies met and wrote a letter of protest to the king. In this letter, they expressed their hope that the relationship between Mother England and her colonies would improve. Most colonists had no desire to go to war against the mother country and the most powerful empire in the world! At the same time, the letter also warned the king that all trade with Britain would stop until Parliament reopened Boston port and restored the power of the Massachusetts assembly.

16   However, the relationship between Mother England and her colonies did not improve. In 1775, fighting broke out between British troops and Bostonians. This was the first fighting of the American Revolution. Shortly afterwards, Parliament closed all colonial ports. The colonists now felt they had no choice but to declare themselves independent from the mother country. This happened on July 4, 1776. To the colonists, this day marked the end of the colonial period and the birth of a new nation—the United States of America.

declare: state officially

17   Although the new nation had declared its independence in 1776, it had to fight long and hard to win its freedom. The American Revolution lasted until 1783. After being defeated, Great Britain officially recognized the independence of her former colonies and also gave up the territory she had won from France. The United States was not only young and independent, but it was now much larger in size.

recognized: accepted as being lawful

READING CHECK

A. Matching: Names and Terms

In your reading, you came across the names and terms in the matching exercise below. Match them with the explanations on the right. If you can't recall one of them, *scan* the reading to find its meaning. *To scan* means to look back at a selection you have already read to quickly find a specific piece of information.

b **1.** Parliament _____ b **a.** protest against the tea tax

f **2.** Stamp Act _____ f **b.** British lawmakers

d **3.** import taxes _____ d **c.** killing of protesters by British soldiers

g **4.** Sons of Liberty _____ g **d.** taxes on certain British goods shipped to the colonies

h **5.** colonial boycott _____ **e.** war the colonists fought to win independence from Great Britain

c **6.** Boston Massacre _____ **f.** tax on newspapers and other everyday colonial items

a **7.** Boston Tea Party _____ a **g.** group of Bostonians who organized a boycott

e **8.** American Revolution _____ e **h.** protest against import taxes by refusing to buy certain British goods

B. Guessing the Meaning from Context

Before doing this exercise, refer to **Appendix 2: Vocabulary Strategies for Unfamiliar Words.** Then look carefully at the context of the underlined words below. Try to guess their meaning. Use the context clue(s) suggested to help you and be prepared to explain your answer. (**P1** = Paragraph 1)

1. Each of the 13 colonies elected its own <u>assembly</u>, a group of men that governed the colony and made laws. (**P3**)

    ASSEMBLY _____
    context clue: definition provided by writer

2. Bostonians <u>resented</u> the taxes and the presence of British soldiers in their town. On March 5, 1770, a group of angry protesters carrying rocks and stones surrounded a much smaller group of British soldiers guarding the tax building. (**P12**)

    RESENTED _____to feel angry_____
    context clues: cause and effect relationship; SEED

3. No one knows for sure what caused the soldiers to fire at the demonstrators, killing five citizens and <u>wounding</u> six others. (**P12**)

    WOUNDING_____
    context clue: familiar situation

4. Largely because of the boycott, Parliament decided in 1772 to <u>repeal</u> all of the import taxes, except one. The tax on British tea was kept as a symbol of Parliament's power to make laws for the colonies. (**P13**)

    REPEAL _____
    context clue: contrasting relationship

5. The king of England and Parliament closed the port of Boston, took away the power of the Massachusetts assembly, and put the colony under the control of British soldiers. As Bostonians saw it, their town was under <u>military occupation</u>. (**P14**)

    MILITARY OCCUPATION _____
    context clues: similar words; SEED

READ THE SELECTION: SECOND TIME

Read more carefully to get a better understanding of each section. Use the dictionary, only if necessary.

A. True or False

Write true or false and the number of the paragraph(s) that supports your answer. Be prepared to explain your answer.

False / __1__   **1.** Most of the land in North America was claimed for the king of England.

false / _____   **2.** Great Britain saw her American colonies only as a place where British merchants could sell their goods.

3   _____ / _True_   **3.** The American colonies were mostly self-governed, except in trade matters.

5   _____ / _True_   **4.** In 1763, Britain gained new territory in America as a result of winning a war against France.

False / _____   **5.** To raise money to protect Britain's new territory in America, Parliament increased taxes in Britain.

_____ / _True_   **6.** Bostonians felt that because the colonists did not have representation in Parliament, Parliament did not have the right to tax them.

False / _____   **7.** Only Bostonians joined the boycott of British imports that were taxed.

_____ / _True_   **8.** The protests against taxation without representation grew increasingly violent.

False / _____   **9.** After Parliament took away the power of the Massachusetts assembly, the other 12 colonial assemblies wrote a declaration of independence.

false / _____   **10.** July 4, 1776, is the date when the American colonies finally won their independence.

B. Timeline

A timeline is a good way of organizing historic events. In the timeline on the facing page, some of the major events of the American colonial period have been given. Complete the timeline. Give brief answers (as few words as possible). Then answer the questions that follow.

THE AMERICAN COLONIAL PERIOD

Date	Major Event
1400s–1500s	European explorers claimed land
1600s–1700s	_____
1740–1763	War between Great Britain and France; Britain won
1765	Stamp Act
1767	_____
1768	Bostonians burned tax collectors' homes; British soldiers were sent to Boston
1770	_____ Boston massacre _____
1772	_____ accept the tea tax _____
1773	Boston Tea Party
1774	Punishment of Boston
1775	_____ beginning of the revolution _____
July 4, 1776	_____ independent _____
1783	_____ end of revolution _____

■ When do Americans celebrate their independence?

_____

■ When is your country's national day or independence day?

_____

C. Timeline

This timeline focuses on the major events in Boston that led to the American Revolution and the date of each event. Complete the timeline by listing the cause of each event. Give brief answers (as few words as possible). Then answer the questions that follow.

BOSTON AND THE AMERICAN REVOLUTION

Date	Major Event	Cause of the Event
1765	Bostonians protested against taxation without representation	parliament passed Stamp act
1767	Sons of Liberty organized a boycott	_A_ new import taxes
1768	British troops were sent to Boston to quiet the Sons of Liberty and protect tax collectors	Bostonian attack the tax collector collectors from attacks
1770	Boston Massacre	A group of angry protectors carry Surrounded
1773	Boston Tea Party	The tea Tax was time to push the duty colinits.
1774	Punishment of Boston	Boston tea parties
1775	British soldiers and Bostonians fought	Boston British is very bad

■ Based on the timeline, what was the *major* issue that led to the American Revolution?

_____

_____

■ Why does colonial Boston represent the first stage in the development of this country—the birth of a new nation?

_____

_____

TOPICS FOR DISCUSSION AND WRITING

Before doing this exercise, refer to **Appendix 3: Guidelines for Small Group Discussions.**

1. The American colonists were protesting against taxation without representation. What does "without representation" mean? Give a modern-day example of a group that is protesting because it is without fair representation.

2. List three different ways the colonists protested. Do you think they were all suitable forms of protest? Explain.

3. The dictionary meaning of "to boycott" is "to refuse to do business with, attend, or take part in." A modern-day example of a boycott is when a group of college students do not attend classes for one day as a protest against an increase in tuition. Give another modern-day example of a boycott. Explain who organized it and why.

4. You learned that the general meaning of "massacre" is "a killing." What is the dictionary meaning of this word? Was the event of March 5, 1770, actually a massacre? Explain. Who do you think used this word— Bostonians or British soldiers? Why did they use it?

5. Look up the subject "Attucks, Crispus" in an encyclopedia. After you read about this man, go back and take notes on two or three interesting points about him. Be prepared to tell the class what you have learned.

6. Imagine that you were one of the soldiers guarding the tax building. Describe what actually took place on March 5 and what caused you and your fellow soldiers to fire.

7. Taxation without representation was an important issue during the colonial period. Today, Americans are concerned about other issues: how to control crime, how to reduce unemployment, and how to clean up the environment. What issues are people in your country concerned about today?

VOCABULARY EXERCISES

A. Word Forms

Choose the correct word form that completes each sentence. The base form of the word is in **bold.** For nouns, use singular or plural forms. For verbs, use appropriate verb tenses and passive voice where necessary. (**P1** = Paragraph 1)

(**P1**)   1.   **colony,** colonist *n*   to colonize *v*   colonial *adj*

    a. Great Britain established 13 ___colonies___ in North America.

    b. Much of the land along the Atlantic coast ___was colonized___ by the British because of its rich natural resources.

    c. The ___colonist___ in America had more self-government than Englishmen in Great Britain.

    d. The Declaration of Independence marked the end of the ___colonial___ period.

(**P4**)   2.   (in)dependence *n*   **to depend on** *v*   (in)dependent *adj*
                         to be dependent on *v*

    a. Because the colonies were across the ocean from the mother country, they had to ___depend on___ themselves for many things.

    b. The colonists ___depended on___ trade for a living.

    c. The colonies declared themselves ___independent___ after Parliament closed all of the colonial ports.

    d. The American Revolution is sometimes called the American War of ___independence___.

(**P8**)   3.   representation, representative *n*   **to represent** *v*

    a. The immediate cause of the American Revolution was the closing of colonial ports, but the underlying cause was the issue of taxation without ___representation___.

    b. The colonists felt that Parliament ___represented___ only the economic interests of Great Britain.

c. Why wasn't each colony allowed to send one ___representative___ to the Parliament in London?

(P10) 4. demonstration, demonstrator *n*   **to demonstrate** *v*

    a. Why were the colonists ___demonstrating___ against Parliament?

    b. Were these ___demonstrations___ mostly peaceful?

    c. Were the soldiers who fired at the ___demonstrators___ in Boston ever punished?

(P12) 5. resentment *n*   **to resent** *v*

    a. Bostonians ___resented___ the large number of British troops in their town; to them, their town was under British military occupation!

    b. Their ___resentment___ was directed toward the British government, not British people.

B. Other Useful Words

Complete the sentences with an appropriate word from the list. For nouns, use singular or plural forms. For verbs, use appropriate verb tenses.
(**P1** = Paragraph 1)

merchant (**P2**)	to govern (**P3**)	unruly (**P14**)
military occupation (**P14**)	to organize (**P10**)	eventually (**P9**)
Parliament (**P6**)	to protest (**P8**)	
revolution (**P17**)	to restore (**P15**)	
territory (**P5**)	to settle (**P1**)	

1. When did Englishmen begin to ___settle___ the Atlantic coast of North America?

2. The colonists mostly ___governed___ themselves through their assemblies.

3. The Sons of Liberty ___protested___ against the import taxes by ___organizing___ a boycott against certain British goods.

4. The boycott had a serious economic effect on British _____merchants_____.

5. As a result, British merchants put political pressure on _____Parliament_____ to repeal the import taxes.

6. Because of this political pressure, Parliament _____inventually_____ repealed all of the import taxes, except one.

7. British newspapers described the Sons of Liberty as _____unruly_____, but colonial newspapers described them as patriotic.

8. What did the other 12 colonies do when they heard the colony of Massachusetts was under _____military_____?

9. The colonies agreed to stop all trade with the mother country if Parliament did not _____restore_____ the power of the Massachusetts assembly.

10. When the American _____revolution_____ ended, Great Britain not only officially recognized the independence of her former colonies but also gave up the _____teritory_____ it had won from France.

C. Vocabulary Oral Practice

Practice using the underlined words by answering the questions below. (**P1** = Paragraph 1)

1. Parents <u>punish</u> their children for doing something wrong. What do you still remember getting <u>punished</u> for? What kind of <u>punishment</u> did you receive? (**P14**)

2. In your country, can young couples get married without their parents' <u>consent</u>? Why or why not? Do you have friends who have gotten married without their parents' <u>consent</u>? Why didn't they <u>consent</u> to the marriage? (**P9**)

3. What do flight attendants <u>warn</u> airline passengers to do or not to do? What might happen if passengers do not pay attention to these <u>warnings</u>? (**P15**)

4. Both things and people can be <u>symbols</u>. The tax on tea was a <u>symbol</u> of Parliament's power over the colonies. Crispus Attucks became a <u>symbol</u> of the colonists' struggle for representation. Can you think of other <u>symbols</u>? What idea do they <u>symbolize</u>? (**P13**)

D. Dictation

Study the spelling of the words in the previous vocabulary exercises. You will have a dictation of sentences that contain these words.

JOURNAL WRITING

Topic 1

Most of you have left behind your parents, brothers and sisters, and friends to study in the United States. Since you have been in this culture, you have experienced a greater sense of independence. In your journal, describe how this independence has been a learning experience for you. Include some interesting personal examples.

Topic 2

When people from other cultures come to the United States to visit or study, they are often amazed by the independence or freedom that Americans have to say and do almost anything. What are some personal observations that you have made about freedom in this country or about the freedom that American students seem to have? What is your opinion of this freedom? Explain your ideas.

NEW ORLEANS, LOUISIANA: THE GROWTH OF A NATION

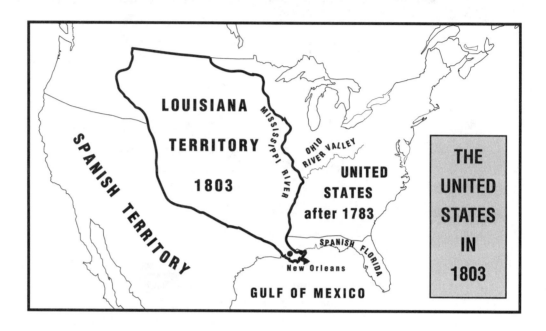

In this reading, you will learn about New Orleans and its role in the growth of the United States. In 1803, the United States bought the Louisiana Territory from France. At this stage of development, the country doubled the size of its land and different cultural groups began to influence the new American culture.

**READING
SELECTION**

PRE-READING DISCUSSION

Getting into the Topic

■ What comes to mind when you think of New Orleans?

■ Find New Orleans on the map and describe where it is located. In the 1700s and 1800s, New Orleans' location was considered especially advantageous. Can you suggest reasons for this? Think about where it is located on the Mississippi River and how goods were transported at that time.

Getting an Overview of the Reading Selection

Scan the reading to complete the headings in the outline.

NEW ORLEANS, LOUISIANA: THE GROWTH OF A NATION

1. The Early History of New Orleans and the Louisiana Territory

   a. The Settlement of New Orleans

   b.

   c.

2.

   a.

   b.

   c.

■ During the first 100 years of its history, the city of New Orleans was under the control of three different countries. Name these three countries.

■ How do you think these changes in power influenced the culture and language?

■ Now, look at the illustrations in the reading. What do they tell you about New Orleans?

READ THE SELECTION: FIRST TIME

Read to get a general understanding of each section. Do not stop to look up words in the dictionary. Some unfamiliar words are explained in the margin.

READING	New Orleans, Louisiana: The Growth of a Nation

1   After winning the Revolution, Americans slowly began to settle the new land they had gained in the Ohio River Valley. In 1803, however, there was a major expansion of land westward when the United States purchased a vast, mostly undeveloped area known as the Louisiana Territory. This territory, located west of the great Mississippi River, doubled the size of the United States. The expansion not only changed the size of the United States but also began to change the culture of the country in some ways. A city that played a role in the territorial expansion and cultural diversity of the country at that time was New Orleans.

THE EARLY HISTORY OF NEW ORLEANS AND THE LOUISIANA TERRITORY

The Settlement of New Orleans

2   New Orleans, founded in 1718 by a French-Canadian named Bienville, was part of the great Louisiana Territory, that had been claimed by France in 1682 and named in honor of King Louis XIV of France. When Bienville began the settlement, it consisted of only a few small, wooden houses built on swampy, delta land.

due to: because of

3   The development of New Orleans and the Louisiana Territory was due to the efforts of a trading company sponsored by the king of France. The leader of the company, John Law, was a brilliant man, but a man without good princi-

principles: rules of good behavior

ples; he had made his fortune gambling. To encourage settlement in Louisiana, Law falsely reported that it had gold and silver mines and that it had a mild climate and easy living. Some French settlers were attracted, but to get enough people for the settlement, prostitutes and criminals in French prisons were forced against their will to this new land. When these settlers arrived in New

shocked: unpleasantly surprised

Orleans, they were shocked to find a land of tropical heat, humidity, floods, hurricanes, and mosquitoes, not to mention the biggest cockroaches in the land. Despite the poor conditions, the settlement developed slowly and survived. John Law's trading company did not.

4   During this early period, the first half of the 1700s, New Orleans was often described as an unruly city. Some considered it a city without religion, without justice, and without order.

Spanish Control

5   French control of New Orleans ended in 1762 when King Louis XV of France made a gift of New Orleans and the territory west of the Mississippi to his cousin King Charles II of Spain. The French king did this to keep Louisiana from falling into the hands of the British. At that time, England controlled the eastern part of the North America (except for French Canada and Spanish Florida) and was preparing to take over the Canadian land that belonged to France.

6   During the period of Spanish rule, the population of Louisiana doubled and its farm economy grew. Plantations along the Mississippi produced large crops of sugar cane, rice, tobacco, indigo, and cotton. Work on the plantations

slave: person "owned" by another person

was done mostly by black slave labor and of the nearly 43,000 people living in the Louisiana Territory in 1787, more than half were slaves.

7   Despite Spanish control, the French culture continued to dominate Louisiana and several new groups of French-speaking immigrants arrived.

expelled: forced out

There were the French Canadians (called Cajuns) expelled from Canada by the British, the wealthy upper-class French escaping the French Revolution in Europe, and the French-speaking Santo Domingans (today known as Haitians) fleeing political trouble in the Caribbean. These groups helped to keep the French culture as the dominant culture in New Orleans and Louisiana, even though the territory was ruled by Spain.

Louisiana Purchase ceremony in New Orleans.

Return to French Rule and the Louisiana Purchase

Spain returned Louisiana to French rule by a treaty in 1801. This treaty, however, was kept so secret that the people of Louisiana only learned about the change when the new French governor arrived in New Orleans on November 30, 1803. Then within just 20 days, on December 20, 1803, French and American representatives met in New Orleans to sign papers which sold the Louisiana Territory to the United States. The United States paid France $15 million for the territory, not a very great sum of money considering the vast amount of land it included. It became known as the Louisiana Purchase.

PEOPLE AND CULTURE OF NEW ORLEANS

The Creoles and the Anglos

After the Louisiana Purchase, English-speaking people (Anglo-Americans) first arrived in New Orleans. The French-speaking people there, most of whom were Creoles, were not pleased with the change in power. For some time, there was dislike and competition between the two groups, with each living in different sections of the city. Eventually, through intermarriage and business interaction, New Orleans began its process of Americanization.

initially: at first, in the beginning

10   Initially, the term *Creole* referred to the white descendants of the old French and Spanish families, the original settlers of Louisiana. Later, it referred to any person born in Louisiana, whether black or white or of mixed blood. Today, it most often refers to French-speaking natives of New Orleans and Louisiana as well as to their music and food. Whenever Americans hear the word "Creole," they are reminded of the French cultural influence in this part of the country.

11   As mentioned before, the Creoles and the Anglos did not get along with each other initially. A comparison of these two cultures at that time shows sig-

nificant differences, and these differences obviously contributed to their difficulties. First of all, they spoke different languages. French was the language of the established community, but the newcomers, who also represented the new government, spoke English. Next, although both groups were Christian, the Creoles were mainly Catholic and the Anglos were mainly Anglican. Concerning integration of cultures, most Creoles were a mixture of "different" blood, whereas most Anglos were of only "English" blood. As for behavior, the Anglos were more organized, businesslike, and paid attention to such matters as being on time, while the Creoles were more easy-going, pleasure-loving, and relaxed. The Creoles wanted to enjoy "la bonne vie," the good life, and part of this good life can be seen in their cultural traditions of music (jazz) and merrymaking (Mardi Gras) in New Orleans.

traditions: cultural customs and beliefs passed down from the past to the present

Jazz

12   New Orleans is generally considered the birthplace of jazz. The origin of this unique form of music is found in African folk music, slave work songs and Negro spirituals, and in the music of the Creoles. Jazz was first heard in the late 1800s being played by black funeral music bands. On the way to the burial, the bands would play sad and mournful music. On the way back, the musicians would try to make the mourners forget their sadness by playing happier music. Although the basic melody stayed the same, the musicians would improvise while they played by adding extra musical notes and making the rhythm livelier. This improvised music was not written down, so their jazz music was probably never played the same way twice. It was a liberating music that did not follow the traditional rules. From New Orleans, jazz spread to Chicago and then to New York, where it reached its golden age in the 1920s. Today, jazz is considered one of America's cultural contributions to the world.

improvise: make changes at the last minute

Mardi Gras

13   Another famous cultural tradition of New Orleans is Mardi Gras, a time for merrymaking. This two-week celebration in February was originally held so that Catholics could eat well and enjoy themselves before they began a 40-day

carnival: public merry-making, usually outside, with drinking, food, dancing, and parades

costumes: special clothing, like those worn by actors

14

happy-go-lucky: care-free

period of fasting and sacrifice. Today, strict fasting is no longer required by the Catholic Church, but the citizens of New Orleans still enjoy their Mardi Gras. It is a carnival at which everyone can drink a lot, eat a lot, and have a good time. There are parades all over the city, and people wearing costumes and masks walk along the streets of the old section called the French Quarter. Mardi Gras is also known for its nightly parties and dancing balls throughout the city. Good music and good times are part of the tradition of this city.

New Orleans has a special place in American history and culture. By its history and its people, the city of New Orleans can represent the mixture of French, Spanish, African, Caribbean, and English cultures, and in many ways, the happy-go-lucky, easy-going, somewhat unruly part of American culture.

READING CHECK

A. Matching: Names and Terms

Match the names and terms on the left with the explanations on the right. If you can't recall one of them, scan the reading to quickly find its meaning.

1. Bienville   ___3___   **a.** French people from Canada

2. John Law   ___1___   **b.** founder of New Orleans

3. Cajuns   6   ___6___   **c.** agreement by which the United States bought land from France

4. Creoles   ___11___   **d.** New Orleans' celebration with parades and dancing parties

5. Anglos   ___9___   **e.** different cultures

6. Louisiana Purchase   ___2___   **f.** leader of trading company that developed New Orleans

7. Americanization   ___10___   **g.** special music started in New Orleans

8. territorial expansion   ___7___   **h.** process by which people become part of American culture

9. cultural diversity   12 ___   **i.** land purchased from France

10. jazz   ___4___   **j.** people of mixed blood (of French, Spanish, African and/or Caribbean origin)

11. Mardi Gras   ___8___   **k.** adding new land

12. Louisiana Territory   ___5___   **l.** English-speaking people

Read more carefully to get a better understanding of each section. Use the dictionary, only if necessary.

COMPREHENSION EXERCISES

A. True or False

Write true or false and the number of the paragraph(s) that supports your answer. Be prepared to explain your answer.

True / 2   **1.** The Louisiana Territory was first claimed by the French.

false / 2   **2.** The early settlers of the Louisiana Territory were very satisfied with their new home.

F   True / 5   **3.** The king of France gave New Orleans and the land west of the Mississippi to the king of Spain because France owed Spain money.

True / 5   **4.** During the period of Spanish rule, Louisiana experienced a growth in its economy and population.

False / 5   **5.** Under Spanish control, the cultural diversity of New Orleans and Louisiana began to disappear.

T   False / 9   **6.** Later, Spain secretly returned the Louisiana Territory to France.

True / 10   **7.** Today the word Creole helps keep alive the idea of the French influence in the city of New Orleans.

False / 12   **8.** Jazz is a lively, happy music that was first heard at black weddings in New Orleans.

True / 13   **9.** Mardi Gras is an occasion for eating and drinking and having a good time.

True / 14   **10.** In American history, New Orleans can represent a city where there was a mixture of many cultures including French, Spanish, African, Caribbean, and English.

B. Timeline

Complete the timeline of the history of New Orleans and Louisiana. Write either the date or the event. For the date, give either the specific period of time (for example, 1910 or 1900–1950) or the general period of time (for example, the second half of the 1900s or after 1960). For the event, give a brief answer (no more than six words). Then answer the question that follows.

THE HISTORY OF NEW ORLEANS AND LOUISIANA

Dates	Major Events
1. _French_	France claimed Louisiana Territory
2. 1718	_religion , Catholic Anglican_
3. _Cuilture Englis blood_	Period when New Orleans was unruly
4. _behavious_ (the first)	France gave Louisiana Territory to Spain
5. From_____to_____	Period of Spanish control
6. 1801	_____
7. 1803	a. _____ b. _____
8. _Easy going_	a. English-speaking people arrived b. New Orleans started process of Americanization

■ Based on the timeline, list the countries that controlled Louisiana and New Orleans during the first 125 years. Include the period of time that each country controlled this area of land.

_____

_____

_____

_____

C. Chart

The reading identifies several points of comparison (or you might say contrast) between the Creole and the Anglo cultures and then tells how the two groups are different on each point of comparison. Complete the chart. Give brief answers. Then answer the question that follows.

COMPARISON OF CREOLE AND ANGLO CULTURES		
Points of Comparison	**Creoles**	**Anglos**
1. Language	16 82	
2. New Orlan	found by	Benville
3. 1700	Mixture of "different" blood	
4. 1769	1801	More organized, businesslike, paid attention to time

■ You have read that these two groups did not get along well initially. From the four points of comparison on the chart, identify the one that you think was the strongest reason for their not getting along well. Explain your choice. From the reading, tell what happened to improve their relationship.

_____

_____

_____

_____

_____

_____

TOPICS FOR DISCUSSION AND WRITING

1. The reading compares the cultural behavior of the Creoles and the Anglos. Is your own cultural behavior similar to one of these two types of cultural behavior? Or is your cultural behavior a combination of both types? Explain.

2. The reading discusses the cultural diversity of New Orleans. Name another city or country that you know which has cultural diversity and describe it. Does living in a culturally diverse community have both advantages and disadvantages? Explain.

3. Find a book in your library that contains pictures of New Orleans and the surrounding area. Look especially for pictures of the French Quarter (the old section of the city). Typical photos include buildings with fancy iron-work balconies and gates, churches, above-ground cemeteries, Mardi Gras parades, and Bourbon Street with its nightclubs and jazz music. Bring the book to class and talk about the pictures.

4. The reading describes jazz as lively, improvised, and liberating. What do these three words mean? To understand this description better, listen to several pieces of jazz, either the more traditional early jazz or the more modern jazz of today. For traditional music, listen to the music of the Preservation Hall jazz bands, Louis Armstrong, or Al Hirt, and for modern jazz, listen to the music of Wynton Marsalis or Chick Corea. How do you feel as you listen to the music? Do you like jazz? Why or why not?

   It is said that the spirit of jazz is similar to the spirit of New Orleans. Reread the description of jazz in Paragraph 12 and the description of New Orleans in Paragraph 14. Compare the two.

A. Word Forms

Choose the correct word form that completes each sentence. The base form of the word is in **bold.** For nouns, use singular or plural forms. For verbs, use appropriate verb tenses and passive voice where necessary.

(Title) 1. growth *n*   **to grow** *v*   growing *adj*

    a. During the period of Spanish control, French influence in New Orleans continued to be strong because of the _____ growing _____ number of French-speaking immigrants.

    b. The _____ growth _____ of the sugar industry in the Louisiana Territory helped the economy of the area.

    c. The popularity of jazz _____ grew _____ as this new form of music spread from New Orleans to Chicago and then to New York.

(P1) 2. development *n*   **to develop** *v*   (un)developed *adj*

    a. At the time of the Louisiana Purchase, most of the Louisiana Territory remained _____ undeveloped _____ .

    b. The transportation of goods on the Mississippi River helped to _____ develop _____ the Louisiana Territory.

    c. With the _____ development _____ of the Louisiana Territory, John Law expected to make a lot of money for himself and for the government of France.

(P7) 3. domination *n*   **to dominate** *v*   dominant *adj*

    a. The king of France gave the Louisiana Territory to his cousin, the king of Spain, to prevent this land from coming under the _____ domination _____ of Great Britain.

    b. Which culture _____ dominated _____ New Orleans when it was under Spanish control?

    c. Was the _____ dominant _____ language of the Creoles French or Spanish?

(P11) 4. difference *n*   **to differ** *v*   different *adj*
                           to be different *v*

   a. Do you know how jazz _____ *differs (is different)* from other forms of music?

   b. The European settlers found that the climate of New Orleans _____ *different differed* from what had been reported.

   c. Did the French-speaking immigrants who came to New Orleans have similar or _____ *different* _____ reasons for leaving their home?

   d. In the early 1800s, the French-speaking people and the newly arrived English-speaking people in New Orleans disliked each other. What were the _____ *differences* _____ between these two groups?

(P12) 5. **origin** *n*   to originate *v*   original *adj*
                                              originally *adv*

   a. Who _____ *originally* _____ claimed the Louisiana Territory?

   b. Who were the _____ *original* _____ settlers of New Orleans?

   c. Do you know what kind of music jazz _____ *originates* _____ from?

   d. Do you know the _____ *origin* _____ of Mardi Gras?

B. Other Useful Words

Complete the sentences with an appropriate word from the list. Use the same form of the word as given in the list.

comparison (**P11**)	control (**P5**)	major (**P1**)
competition (**P9**)	diversity (**P1**)	unique (**P12**)
contribution (**P12**)	mixture (**P11**)	vast (**P1**)

   1. New Orleans is considered a _____ *unique* _____ American city because of its special cultural traditions.

   2. Initially, there was business _____ *competition* _____ between the French and English-speaking groups in New Orleans.

   3. By the Louisiana Purchase, the United States gained a _____ *vast* _____ area of land west of the Mississippi.

4. For three years, from 1801 to 1803, the citizens of New Orleans did not know that the city was again under the ___control___ of France.

5. Creoles can be a ___mixture___ of French, Spanish, African, and/or Caribbean.

6. In making a ___comparision___ of the Anglos and Creoles in New Orleans in the 1800s, what points would you consider?

7. The French had a ___major___ influence on the culture of New Orleans.

8. In addition to New Orleans, what is another American city that shows cultural ___diversity___?

9. Soul music is another ___contribution___ by blacks to American music.

C. Vocabulary Oral Practice

Practice using the underlined words by answering the questions below.

1. When you <u>initially</u> arrived in the United States, how did you feel? **(P10)**

2. The settlers in New Orleans eventually began the process of <u>Americani-zation</u>. Have you become <u>Americanized</u>? If so, in what ways have you become <u>Americanized</u>? In what ways have you not? **(P9)**

3. The Creoles of New Orleans can be described as <u>easy-going</u>. Describe an <u>easy-going</u> person. Which students in this class do you think are <u>easy-going</u>? **(P11)**

4. What is the most famous <u>cultural tradition</u> in your country? **(P11)**

5. Sometimes people don't <u>get along with</u> each other; for example, neighbors might not <u>get along with</u> each other. What could be the reason for this? Give another example of people who might not <u>get along with</u> each other and explain the reason why. **(P11)**

6. In the United States, Halloween is <u>celebrated</u> on the last day of October. On this day, children wear <u>costumes</u> and go trick or treating at neighbors' houses. Describe a <u>celebration</u> in your country that is for children. Do the children wear <u>costumes</u> for this <u>celebration</u>? **(P13)**

D. Dictation

Study the spelling of the words in the previous exercises. You will have a dictation of sentences that contain these words.

JOURNAL WRITING

The reading briefly describes Mardi Gras, the major cultural event celebrated each year in New Orleans. In your journal, write about the celebration that you like the most in your country. Describe the celebration and tell why you enjoy it the most.

COMMUNICATIVE ACTIVITY

Sharing a Cultural Tradition of Your Country

You have learned about two cultural traditions of New Orleans: jazz and Mardi Gras. Now, it is time for you to share with the class a cultural tradition of your country.

Below are some of the cultural traditions that other students have spoken about:

TAIWAN	traditional **custom**	celebrating adulthood
THAILAND	traditional **holiday**	*Song Karn*
MEXICO	traditional **dishes**	tacos and burritos
KOREA	traditonal **game**	*Yut*
ARGENTINA	traditional **dance**	tango
UNITED ARAB EMIRATE	traditional **sport**	camel racing
JAPAN	traditional **art**	origami
SAUDI ARABIA	traditional **instruments**	lute and drums

Procedure:

1. Choose a cultural tradition that you can describe simply. For example, if you are explaining how to prepare a traditional dish, choose one with only a few ingredients that can be prepared in no more than five steps.

2. Make an outline for yourself. For example, if you are explaining how to prepare a dish, your outline may have three major parts.
   a. origin of dish
   b. ingredients
   c. steps how to prepare dish

3. Decide what kind of visual (or audio) aid to bring. For instance, if you are explaining how to prepare a dish, bring the ingredients and a sample of the dish to class. In the case of a very simple dish, you may show the class the preparation steps and have them make the dish themselves. Your visual or audio aid can be a photo, drawing, object, or tape of music. Make sure all visuals are large.

4. If you have any questions, ask your instructor for advice.

LECTURE San Francisco, California: A Nation United

Miners panning for gold in a mountain stream.

Like New Orleans, San Francisco represents a stage in the development of the United States. During this stage the West was settled almost overnight. The event that led to the rapid settlement of the West was the discovery of gold near San Francisco. With the settlement of the West, the United States was now a nation united from coast to coast.

LISTENING STRATEGY

Organization of a Lecture

Most academic lectures are organized in a structured way to help students better understand the information and take notes on the most important information. The organization of an academic lecture has three parts. In the **introduction,** the major points to be discussed are listed. In the **body,** each of the major points are developed through explanations, examples, description, and other kinds of specific information. In the **conclusion,** the most important idea(s) in the lecture are restated briefly.

The lecture on San Francisco begins with some background information about the gold discovery. The two major points of the lecture are the travel adventures of gold-seekers who rushed to San Francisco to get rich quick and the effects of the gold discovery.

[handwritten margin notes: false advertising / →1849 / Gold Rush / native guides / 1848 - 14,000 / 1854 - 25 million]

TERMS USED IN THE LECTURE*

the Gold Rush
forty-niners
false advertising
overcrowded
tropical jungle
to hire native guides
to (over)charge

tropical diseases
wagon trains
froze to death
migration of people
iron pans
transcontinental
railroad system

* These terms are defined or made clear from context in the lecture.

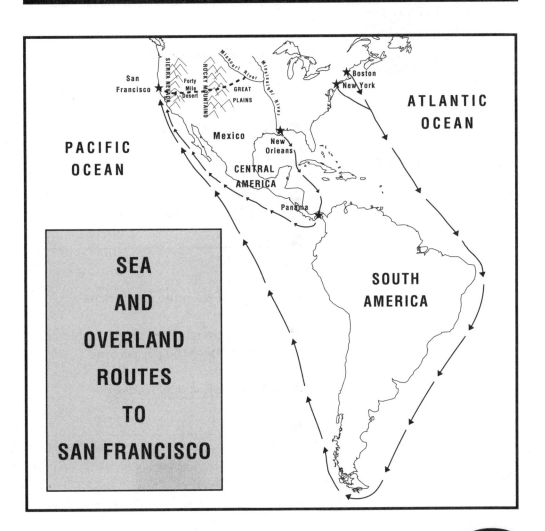

SEA AND OVERLAND ROUTES TO SAN FRANCISCO

1. Listen to the lecture. Follow the outline below as you listen. Do not write anything at this time.

2. Listen again and complete the notes. Write only key words or phrases. After the lecture, compare your notes with a classmate's. You may want to listen to the lecture again to confirm any points that you missed.

3. After completing your notes, discuss them with the class.

Outline of Lecture on San Francisco: A Nation United

1. Background information about gold discovery

   When and where: _____

   How: _____

2. Travel adventures of the gold-seekers

   a. Difficulties of sea route around tip of South America

      ■ long—took 6 months

      ■ _____

      ■ _____

      ■ _____

   b. Difficulties of sea route via Panama

      ■ Natives overcharged to guide gold-seekers overland, $10—$50—$100 per person

      ■ _____

      ■ _____

c. Difficulties of overland route

■ Rocky Mts.—danger of falling off side of mts. and getting caught in snowstorm

■ _____

_____

3. Effects of the gold discovery

a. _____

_____

b. _____

_____

c. _____

_____

DISCUSSION QUESTIONS

1. For most of the gold-seekers, it was their first big trip away from home. Describe your first big trip away from home. How old were you? Where did you go and with whom did you go?

2. Describe one of your most memorable travel adventures. You can describe an adventure you had traveling to or visiting a particular place.

3. Explain how the discovery of gold helped to unite this country. Then describe a past event or a more recent one that has had a positive effect on your country.

CHAPTER 3

CHARLESTON, SOUTH CAROLINA: A NATION DIVIDED

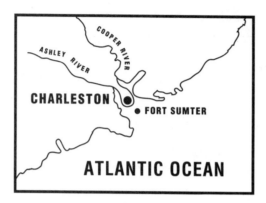

In this reading, you will learn about the small southern city of Charleston and the life of its citizens, both black and white. The focus on Charleston leads to three larger issues facing the nation: civil unrest, civil war, and civil rights. At this stage of development, the country was facing the greatest test of its young life thus far.

READING SELECTION

PRE-READING DISCUSSION

Getting into the Topic

■   Describe Charleston's location on the map. In your description, use the word "peninsula." 3 phía
bán đảo

■   In the early days of this country, why did many blacks live in Charleston? (Remember Charleston is a port.) Why did many blacks live in the South?

■   The three issues mentioned in the introduction each have the word "civil." What does "civil" mean? Look it up in the dictionary, if you don't know. What do the phrases, "civil unrest," "civil war," and "civil rights" mean? Can you give an example of each?

■   What do you know about the U.S. Civil War? When was it fought? Who was president at that time? Can you give one cause of the war? Who won the war, the North or the South?

Getting an Overview of the Reading Selection

Scan the reading to complete the headings in the outline.

CHARLESTON, SOUTH CAROLINA: A NATION DIVIDED

1.

2.

3.

4.

■ What information do you expect to learn from the reading after looking at each heading?

■ Look at the illustrations in the reading. What information do they give you?

READ THE SELECTION: FIRST TIME

Read to get a general understanding of each section. Do not stop to look up words in the dictionary. Some unfamiliar words are explained in the margin.

READING   **Charleston, South Carolina: A Nation Divided**

1   As the nation expanded from coast to coast, more and more states were added to the Union. When California joined in 1850, it became the 31st state. However, as the nation was growing, trouble was also growing, especially in the South. The trouble centered around two major issues: states' rights and slavery. Although forbidden in the North, slavery played an important role in the economy of the agricultural South, and many Southerners worried that they would be forced by the central (or federal) government to change their way of life and give up slavery. They were so worried that they wanted to leave the Union. The resulting civil unrest between the Northern and Southern states led to the American Civil War, which lasted from 1861 to 1865. A city that represented the Southern way of life at that time and also played a role in the Civil War is the small historic city in South Carolina named Charleston.

CHARLESTON, A HISTORIC CITY

2   Charleston, South Carolina, was founded in 1670 by English settlers. It had originally been named Charles Town in honor of King Charles II of England. Located on a narrow peninsula between the Ashley and Cooper rivers, Charleston is a port city with a fine harbor along the Atlantic coast.

3   Today, Charleston is especially well known for the preservation of its historic buildings and the old sections of the city. The past remains alive there with its many houses, churches, and other buildings that date from the 1700s and 1800s. Some of the historic houses with side porches and flowering gardens behind ironwork fences were built by wealthy plantation owners who

restored: repaired to the original condition

auctioneers: people who sell things in public to whoever offers the most money
factor: something that actively contributes to bring about a result

used to come with their <u>families</u> to the city in the summer. Their plantations, beautifully restored today, are found along the riverbanks north of the city. On one Charleston street stands the Old Slave Mart Museum. In the past, this was the office of slave auctioneers; now it is a museum for African-American arts and crafts.

4   Two factors contributed to the preservation of Charleston. The first resulted from the effects of the South's defeat in the <u>Civil War</u>. During the war, Charleston had suffered much physical damage, but in the post-war period, its economy was too weak for reconstruction. Charlestonians, although still proud, were too poor to rebuild their city. So, the city remained unchanged for several decades and this helped to preserve its historic character.

5   However, around 1920, new wealth from outside the city arrived and the rich outsiders began to modernize the old <u>neighborhoods</u>. This did not please Charleston's citizens, so they joined together in a historic preservation movement. This movement was the second factor that helped to preserve the city. It not only protected the old and historic sections of the city from modernization but also helped to restore their former beauty. Because of the continuing efforts of the citizens' movement, the historic sections of Charleston are still preserved today.

CHARLESTON AND SLAVERY

6   Since its earliest days, Charleston had accepted the practice of slave labor. Only five months after the city was settled in 1670, the first slave arrived, and after some time, Charleston became the South's major slaveport. Indeed, the economy, great wealth, and way of life of the city depended on slavery.

7   Slaves in Charleston worked both in the city and in the fields of the surrounding plantations and they contributed greatly to the economy of South Carolina. In the 1700s, slaves labored in the rice and indigo fields and in the 1800s, they worked in the cotton fields. Eventually cotton replaced rice and indigo as the major crop and chief export of South Carolina, and cotton became king in the South. Because of the growing demand for cotton in the world and the invention of the cotton gin in 1793, the need for slaves increased. As the cotton crop spread to more and more plantations, the demand for more slave labor on the plantations spread as well.

cotton gin: machine that separates seeds and other unwanted material from cotton

8   In the city, slaves were better off than those on the plantations. Their general standard of living in Charleston was far superior. They had much better food, health care, clothing, and working conditions. Many worked as house servants; others worked as carpenters, bricklayers, blacksmiths, porters, bakers, and cigar makers.

9   As slaves, blacks did not have the same rights as whites. It was illegal to teach them to read or write. It was also illegal for them to marry. However, in some cases, a black man and woman did form a lasting relationship and raise children, if their white master permitted. This "marriage" could be destroyed at the sudden change of mind or the death of the master. More than one black family in Charleston was torn apart when the master sold the husband to one person and the wife and children to another.

10   One activity that whites wanted blacks to participate in was religious worship. From the colonial period, blacks were encouraged to attend religious services in white churches where they most often sat separately. Around 1850, when the black section of churches became too crowded, the whites themselves established separate black churches. Religion became a special source of strength for black Americans then, and it has continued to be a strong part of their culture ever since.

CHARLESTON AND THE CIVIL WAR

11   The Civil War, or the War Between the States, (1861–1865) was different from most civil wars in which two or more groups within a country struggle to take control of the federal government. In this case, 11 Southern states fought to become an independent nation, and 21 Northern states (and 2 Western states) fought to preserve the Union.

12   The two major issues that divided the North and South in 1861 were states' rights and slavery. States' rights are those powers that individual states have; other powers belong to the federal government. The principal disagreement about states' rights between the North and South was whether or not a state had the right to leave the Union. The North believed a state did not have this right; the South believed it did. The states' rights issue was related to the second issue, slavery.

13   In the United States at the time of the Civil War, slavery was legal in 15 states in the agricultural South; the states in the North and West were free

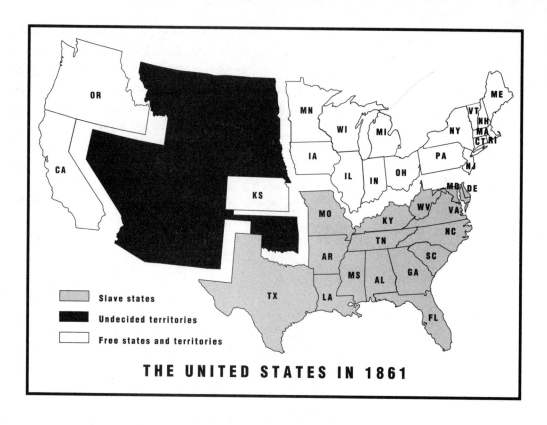

THE UNITED STATES IN 1861

Map legend:
- Slave states
- Undecided territories
- Free states and territories

textile mills: factories that turn cotton into cloth
abolishing: stopping

states. For the South, slavery was necessary to preserve its way of life. Its economy depended on cheap slave labor and it did not want any restrictions on slavery. Although the industrial North with its factories and textile mills favored abolishing slavery, it did not necessarily want to end slavery in the South. What the North wanted was to prohibit the spread of slavery into new states entering the Union, namely, those in the Midwest and West. The South, on the other hand, wanted to allow the spread of slavery. It held that states' rights would allow the use of slaves in these states. The disagreement over these issues eventually led to the Civil War.

14   As a strong believer in slavery and states' rights, Charleston played a role in the Civil War. The war began there on April 12, 1861, when soldiers from the South attacked federal government troops at Fort Sumter in the city's harbor. On that day, the United States became a nation divided.

Fort Sumter: federal government military base located on an island in Charleston harbor

15   Before this attack and the start of the war, there had been, as mentioned above, increasing disagreement between the North and South over the issue of slavery. In fact, since the early 1800s, there had been growing opposition to the practice of slavery, and some efforts to abolish it had begun. When Abraham Lincoln ran for president, he expressed his antislavery views and his opposition to the growth of slavery in the West.

16   After Lincoln was elected president in November 1860, many whites in Charleston and throughout the South feared that slaves would begin to revolt and demand freedom, and so they gathered in Charleston to discuss this. At their meeting on December 20, 1860, South Carolina became the first state to leave the Union; other Southern states followed. Four months later in April 1861, the war began in Charleston harbor. Four years after that in April 1865, it ended in Virginia when the North defeated the South.

emancipation: act of making socially, politically, and legally free

17   Before the end of the Civil War, however, President Lincoln signed a legal document freeing all slaves living within the rebellious Southern states. This famous document is known as the Emancipation Proclamation of 1863. After the war, the freedom of slaves and the protection of their civil rights became part of the U.S. Constitution in the form of amendments. In late 1865, the states approved the 13th Amendment to the Constitution which abolished slavery. The 14th Amendment, approved in 1868, guaranteed blacks the rights of all citizens. These rights include life, liberty, ownership of property, and equal protection under the law. The 15th Amendment, approved in 1870, protected the right of blacks to vote.

discrimination: treating people differently because of race, sex, etc.

18   These three amendments were only the beginning of the movement to protect the civil rights of blacks and other minorities and to fight against discrimination in the United States. In fact, it took another 100 years of struggle for the rights given in the 14th and 15th Amendments to be enjoyed by all its citizens. Charleston, like other Southern cities, was slow in bringing about changes in civil rights for blacks. Unlike other Southern cities, Charleston has succeeded in bringing about changes without violence. The civil rights movement has advanced slowly. It still continues to this day.

READING CHECK

A. Matching: Names and Terms

Match the names and terms on the left with the explanations on the right. If you can't recall one of them, scan the reading to quickly find its meaning.

b **1.** Abraham Lincoln _____

2. minorities _____
    Small part of group
    thici so?

3. U.S. Civil War _____

4. civil rights _____

d **5.** slavery _____

6. states' rights _____

7. civil unrest _____

a. powers belonging to the state

b. president of the United States during the Civil War

c. organized group that works to keep historic places from destruction

d. practice by which one person can be "owned" by another person

e. war fought between the North and South

f. people who are not members of the largest group in a society

g. changes to the laws of a country

C   **8.** historic preservation   _____   **h.** citizens' dissatisfaction which leads to
        movement   protest

   9. civil rights movement   _____   **i.** another way of saying "the United
                                                 States" in the late 1800s

   10. constitutional   _____   **j.** organized group that works to protect
         amendments   the rights of citizens

   11. the Union   _____   **k.** political/social privileges guaranteed to
                                                 all citizens regardless of race, sex,
                                                 religion, or national origin

B. Guessing the Meaning from Context

Look carefully at the context of the underlined words below. Try to guess
their meaning. Use the context clue(s) suggested to help you and be prepared to
explain your answer.

1. Eventually cotton replaced rice and indigo as the major crop and chief
    export of South Carolina, and cotton became <u>king</u> in the South. (**P7**)

    KING _____ major _____
    context clues: similar words; cause and effect relationship

2. In the city, slaves <u>were better off</u> than those on the plantations. Their gen-
    eral standard of living in the city of Charleston was far superior. They had
    much better food, health care, clothing, and working conditions. (**P8**)

    WERE BETTER OFF _____ had better life _____
    content clue: SEED

3. More than one black family in Charleston was <u>torn apart</u> when the master
    sold the husband to one person and the wife and children to another. (**P9**)

    TORN APART _____ separate each other _____
    content clues: SEED; cause and effect relationship

4. What the North wanted was to <u>prohibit</u> the spread of slavery into new
    states entering the Union, namely, those in the Midwest and West. The
    South, on the other hand, wanted to allow the spread of slavery. It held
    that states' rights would allow the use of slaves in these states. (**P13**)

    PROHIBIT _____ to forbid _____ illegal ____ allow
    context clue: contrasting relationship

5. President Lincoln signed a legal <u>document</u> freeing all slaves living within the rebellious Southern states. **(P17)**

DOCUMENT_____*important peper*_____

context clue: familiar situation

READ THE SELECTION: SECOND TIME

Read more carefully to get a better understanding of each section. Use the dictionary, only if necessary.

COMPREHENSION EXERCISES

A. True or False

Write true or false and the number of the paragraph(s) that supports your answer. Be prepared to explain your answer.

3 / ~~2~~ ___True__/_____ **1.** Charleston has preserved many of its historic buildings, so today old sections of the city look similar to the way they looked in the 1800s.

5 ___True__/_____ **2.** The historic preservation movement helped to modernize the old neighborhoods of Charleston.

6 ___True__/_____ **3.** Charleston had slaves since the early days and became the center for Southern slave trade.

6 ___True__/_____ **4.** Charlestonians depended on cheap slave labor to preserve their way of life, support their economy, and help build their great wealth.

8 ___False_/_____ **5.** The slaves who worked on the plantations had a better life than the slaves who lived in the city.

10 ___True__/_____ **6.** For a period of time, slaves were allowed to attend religious services in the white churches.

12 ___True__/_____ **7.** The two related issues that caused the Civil War were states' rights and slavery.

16 ___False_/_____ **8.** Abraham Lincoln was elected president because he believed in slavery.

16 False / _____   **9.** The first state to officially leave the Union was Virginia.

16 False / _____   **10.** The Civil War ended in Charleston.

17 True / _____   **11.** Before the end of the war, Abraham Lincoln freed the slaves in the states that had left the Union by signing the Emancipation Proclamation.

17 True / _____   **12.** The 13th, 14th, and 15th Amendments to the U.S. Constitution guaranteed the freedom of the slaves and the protection of their civil rights.

B. Listing

Answer these questions by making lists. A heading is given for each list. Write the points in the list as briefly as possible. Numbers are used when listing.

1. List the two factors that helped to preserve the historic sections of Charleston.

   The two factors that helped to preserve Charleston were:

   1. Too poor to rebuild after the Civil War _____

   _____

   2. historic Preservation _____

   _____

2. Charleston played a role in the Civil War. In time order, list two important events that happened in Charleston at that time.

   Two important events in Charleston at that time were:

   1. 1860 South Carolina was the first State to leave the Union

   2. 1861 Civil War began in Charleston _____

   _____

C. Timeline

Complete the timeline with the appropriate information. Then answer the questions that follow.

ISSUES AND EVENTS THAT LED TO THE CIVIL WAR

Dates	Issues and Events
1. Since early 1800s	Growing disagreement between the North and the South over the issues of _The state rights_ and _Slaver_
2. November 1860	Election of _Abaham Licoln_
3. _1861_	Southern states met in _Charleston_ and decided to _leave Union_
4. _April 12 / 1861_	Southern troops fired on Fort Sumter and the Civil War began. The South fought to _invelopment_ _____; the North fought to _preserve the Union_ _____.

■ From the reading, tell how Lincoln's election led to the Civil War.

he opposed slavery

slavery and states' rights

firing on fort sumter

■ Based on the chart, identify the underlying cause of the Civil War and the immediate cause of the Civil War.

_____

_____

_____

D. Chart

During the Civil War and immediately after, legal actions were taken to improve the status of blacks and advance their civil rights. Complete the chart with information on these legal actions. Then answer the questions that follow.

	LEGAL ACTIONS TO IMPROVE THE STATUS OF BLACKS AT THE END OF THE 19TH CENTURY		
	Date	Name of Legal Action	Purpose of Legal Action
1.	_1863_	_Proclamation Emanicaption_	_freed all the slaves_
2.	_1865+_	13th Amendment	_Abolish slavery_
3.	_1868_	_14th Amendment_	To guarantee blacks the rights of all citizens
4.	_1870_	_15th Amendment_	_to ciprotest the right of back to vote_

■ If the 14th Amendment guaranteed blacks the rights of all citizens, then it included the right to vote. So, why do you think the 15th Amendment was necessary?

_____

_____

indentured servant

■ Which of these legal actions made a more immediate change in the lives of the blacks at that time? Which of them took much longer to make a change in their lives?

_____

_____

TOPICS FOR DISCUSSION AND WRITING

1. Black slaves were not allowed to marry and they were not allowed to learn to read or write. What do you think the reasons for this were?

2. The two major issues of the Civil War were states' rights and slavery. A more general way of looking at these two issues is in terms of economics and politics. How do you think states' rights and slavery relate to economics and politics? Explain each relationship more fully.

3. At the time of the Civil War, the economy of the South was based on agriculture and the economy of the North was based on industry, so these two regions were dependent on each other. Explain how they were interdependent. (Think about the major crop of the South and the industry in the North that used this crop.) On a larger scale, give examples of how the world is interdependent.

4. Why do you think the civil rights movement in the United States has advanced so slowly in the past 100 years? Think about people's attitudes and human nature.

5. First, with a partner, write your own definition of discrimination. Then make a list of as many types of discrimination as you can think of that are found in the world. In this reading, for example, we saw discrimination because of race. Compare your definition with others in the class. Then write the different types of discrimination on the board and discuss each.

6. Look up the subject "slavery" in an encyclopedia and read about the history of slavery in pre-modern times. Find out when slavery began, what

parts of the world had the greatest numbers of slaves at that time, how a person became a slave, and what work these slaves did. Take notes on slavery and be prepared to tell the class about what you have learned.

7. You have read about the 13th, 14th, and 15th Amendments to the United States Constitution. Look up the subject "amendment" or "constitution" in an encyclopedia. Find the 26th amendment (XXVI) and find out what issue it deals with and when it was ratified (approved). New amendments can be proposed by either the Congress or the state governments. However, to become a law, they must be ratified by the states. Find out how many states must ratify a new amendment in order for it to become a law. Take notes and be prepared to tell the class about what you have learned.

VOCABULARY EXERCISES

A. Word Forms

Choose the correct word form that completes each sentence. The base form of the word is in **bold**. For nouns, use singular or plural forms. For verbs, use appropriate verb tenses and passive voice where necessary.

(P12) 1. (dis)agreement *n* **to (dis)agree (with)** *v*

    a. Do you think that all whites in the South _agreed with_ the practice of slavery?

    b. Before the Civil War, there was growing _disagreement_ between the North and South about slavery.

(P13) 2. restriction *n* **to restrict** *v* restrictive *adj*

    a. After the 15th Amendment was approved, there should have been no _restriction_ to the voting rights of blacks.

    b. However at that time, many Southern states passed _restrictive_ laws that attempted to prohibit blacks from voting.

    c. For many years, blacks _were restricted_ from voting by such methods as having to pass a literacy test or pay a special tax.

(P15)   3. opposition *n*   **to oppose** *v*   opposing *adj*

     a. Abraham Lincoln _____opposed_____ the spread of slavery to the Western territories.

     b. In a civil war, it can happen that members of one family find themselves on _____opposing_____ sides in the war.

     c. There was strong _____opposition_____ in Boston to paying a tax on tea.

(P18)   4. advancement *n*   **to advance** *v*

     a. The 19th Amendment, which was approved in 1920, _____advanced_____ women's rights by giving them the right to vote.

     b. The _____advancement_____ of civil rights in the United States applies to all minority groups.

B. Other Useful Words

Complete the sentences with an appropriate word from the list. For nouns, use singular or plural forms. For verbs, use appropriate verb tenses and passive voice where necessary.

crop (**P7**)	modernization (**P5**)
demand (for something) (**P7**)	preservation movement (**P5**)
discrimination (**P18**)	slave labor (**P6**)
factor (**P4**)	to abolish (**P13**)
federal government (**P11**)	to prohibit (**P13**)

    1. The citizens of Charleston protected the historic buildings from destruction and _____modernization_____ by organizing a _____preservation_____.

    2. The expansion of the cotton crop in the South in the 1800s increased the _____demand_____ for _____slave labor_____.

    3. Slavery _____prohibited_____ in the North.

    4. One reason for the war between the North and South was that the _____federal government_____ would not allow the slave states to leave the Union.

5. President Lincoln _____to abolished_____ slavery by signing the Emancipation Proclamation in 1863.

6. Cotton and tobacco are two major _____crop_____ in the South today.

7. What _____factor_____ have caused the civil rights movement to advance so slowly?

8. Today, civil rights leaders continue to fight against _____discrimination_____.

C. Vocabulary Oral Practice

Practice using the underlined words by answering the questions below.

1. Slaves in the city <u>were better off</u> than the slaves on the plantations. Think of two fields of study, for example, political science and engineering or law and music. Which student <u>will be better off</u> when (s)he graduates, the student majoring in political science or the one in engineering, the one majoring in law or the one in music? Why? **(P8)**

2. Religion is <u>a source of strength</u> for many African-Americans. What is <u>a source of strength</u> for an international student at an American university? **(P10)**

3. The U.S. Constitution <u>guarantees</u> certain rights to all citizens. When you buy certain products, the manufacturer usually <u>guarantees</u> the product. Name some products that usually have a <u>guarantee</u>. What does the manufacturer <u>guarantee</u> about the product? **(P17)**

4. What are some <u>minorities</u> in the United States? Which is the largest <u>minority</u> group? What group in the United States is not part of the <u>minorities</u>? Do you have <u>minorities</u> in your country? Tell about them. **(P18)**

D. Dictation

Study the spelling of the words in the previous exercises. You will have a dictation of sentences that contain these words.

JOURNAL WRITING

In the Topics for Discussion and Writing, you talked about discrimination. Now, in your journal, write about your thoughts on discrimination or write about one specific type of discrimination and give an example(s).

After the end of the Civil War, the movement to advance the civil rights of blacks and other minorities began. Many citizens contributed to the movement; some played a major role and others a minor role. One person who played a major role was a courageous black woman named Rosa Parks. In this lecture, you will hear the story of Rosa Parks. You will learn about what she did and what the effects of her action were.

Sequence of Events

This lecture tells about the events in a person's life and is organized in time order. The story begins in December 1955 and ends less than one year later in November 1956. Near the beginning of the lecture, however, the speaker departs from the story to explain some events that happened before 1955. For the most part, the events develop in a cause and effect relationship. The story takes place in Montgomery, Alabama. As you listen, pay attention to the sequence of events and find out how one event led to another event.

Rhetorical Questions

Also, in this lecture, you should pay attention to the speaker's use of questions. From time to time, you will hear the speaker ask a question. For example, you could hear "What happened to Rosa Parks when she went to court?" The purpose of the question is not to get an answer but to signal that a new point is coming. The question is a transition signal. It announces the new point and prepares you to listen for it. This type of question is called a rhetorical question.

TERMS USED IN THE LECTURE*

seamstress
segregation laws*
Jim Crow laws*
"separate but equal"*
bond money

NAACP = National Association for the Advancement of Colored People (established in 1910)
Montgomery Improvement Association (the MIA)

* These terms are defined in the lecture.

SIMPLIFIED DIAGRAM OF THE U.S. COURT SYSTEM

Lower Court or Local Court	→ appeals to →	Higher Court or District Court	→ appeals to →	Highest Court or Supreme Court

1. Listen to the lecture. Follow the outline below as you listen. Pay attention for rhetorical questions. Do not write anything at this time.

2. Listen again and take notes in each part of the outline. Write only key words or phrases. After the lecture, compare your notes with a classmate's. You may want to listen to the lecture again to confirm any points that you missed.

3. After completing your notes, discuss them with the class.

Outline of Lecture on Rosa Parks

and the Civil Rights Movement

1. Some background information

   a. Rosa Parks

   _____

   _____

   _____

   _____

   b. Jim Crow laws in the South

   _____

   _____ *laws always require back* _____

   _____

   _____

   _____

   _____

   _____

bus, restaurant
hotel

2. Sequence of events

   a. Rosa Parks' action on the Montgomery bus

   _____

   _____

   _____

   _____

   _____

   b. Immediate response of the black community

   _____

   _____

   _____

   _____

   _____

   c. Rosa Parks at court / decision to appeal

   _____

   _____

   _____

   _____

   d. Further response of the black community

   _____

   _____

   _____

   _____

   high school indelation _____

   _____

e. Supreme Court decision

_____

_____

_____

DISCUSSION QUESTIONS

1. Describe Rosa Parks. From this description, do you think she was a typical protester? Explain.

2. Protesters have both a reason for their protest and a way to show their protest. What was the cause of Rosa Parks' protest and what action did she take to show her protest?

3. Protesters usually plan their actions in advance. Do you think Rosa Parks had planned her protest in advance? Explain.

4. A protest can lead to a sequence of results or effects. What were the various effects of Rosa Parks' action? Give these effects in time order.

5. This story shows how the action of one person can make a difference in the lives of many others. How did Rosa Parks' action make a difference in the lives of other people? Think of another person, whether well known or not and perhaps from your country, who made a difference in the lives of other people. Tell what this person did.

From the reading on Charleston and the lecture on Rosa Parks, we have learned about racial discrimination. In the two poems that follow, the African-American writer and poet Langston Hughes presents situations in the first half of the 20th century in which blacks faced discrimination. The specific situation described in each poem can represent the larger, more general picture of segregation and racial inequality in society at that time. The first poem is about a young boy and the second is about a young man.

BIOGRAPHICAL SKETCH: LANGSTON HUGHES (1902–1967)

Langston Hughes was a prolific writer. He wrote novels, plays, biographies, histories, essays, and songs, but his primary work was poetry. The general theme of his poems was the common person of that time, more specifically the black and his pleasures, joys, and sorrows.

Hughes' strong sense of black pride came initially from his mother. As a young boy, he would listen to his mother's stories of black freedom fighters during the Civil War. She would tell him about her first husband, Lewis Leary, who was killed during the war while fighting at Harpers Ferry, West Virginia. Hughes' own father abandoned his wife and son soon after he was born.

At 19, Hughes attended Columbia University in New York City, and while there, first became acquainted with Harlem, a section of the city that was the center for black music, art, and theatre at that time. After one year, he left Columbia and began the first of his extensive travels overseas. At different times during his life, he lived in Europe, Africa, and Russia. In these places, he continued to write his poetry and stories.

At home in the United States, Hughes held various jobs during his lifetime. As a young man, he worked in Washington, D.C., as a busboy at an elegant hotel. In his late twenties, he finished his undergraduate studies at Lincoln University, a small school near Philadelphia. In his thirties, he worked as a newspaper columnist in Chicago. Later he founded theatres in Harlem, Chicago, and Los Angeles. During all this time, he continued his writing and eventually become known as the Poet Laureate of Harlem.

Where is the Jim Crow section

On this merry-go-round,

Mister, cause I want to ride?

Down South where I come from

White and colored

Cannot sit side by side.

Down South on the train

There's a Jim Crow car.

On the bus we're put in the back—

But there ain't no back

To a merry-go-round!

Where's the horse

For a kid that's black?

DISCUSSION QUESTIONS

1. The speaker in this poem is a "colored child." What does "colored" mean? Where is the speaker, in the North or the South? How do you know?

2. Briefly tell what happens in the poem.

3. The situation described in this poem would not happen today. Name someone who helped to change the situation for blacks. What did this person do?

4. Hughes ends his poem with a question and when the poem is read aloud, this question is not spoken by a child but by an adult in a forceful and angry voice. Think about why Hughes ends his poem with a question spoken in this way. Do you think he wants an answer to the question? Or do you think he uses the question to state a point of view? If so, what is the point of view?

5. A theme is the central idea of a piece of literature. It is a statement about life. What is the theme of this poem?

I, too, sing America.

I am the darker brother.
They send me to eat in the kitchen
When company comes,
But I laugh,
And eat well,
And grow strong.

Tomorrow,
I'll be at the table
When company comes.
Nobody'll dare
Say to me,
"Eat in the kitchen,"
Then.

Besides,
They'll see how beautiful I am
And be ashamed—

I, too, am America.

DISCUSSION QUESTIONS

1. Who is speaking in the poem? How do you know?

2. How does the speaker feel about himself? How do you know this?

3. The first line of the poem says, "I, too, sing America" and the last line says "I, too, am America." "Too" in these sentences indicates there is another person. Who is the other person?

4. Briefly tell what happens in the poem.

5. The places where the speaker eats have a special meaning in the poem. What are these two places? When does he eat in the kitchen? Which place represents equal rights? What does the other place represent?

6. What are the two time periods in the poem? What change(s) in society must take place for the second period to come about?

7. The title and first line of the poem are "I, too, sing America." The song that Hughes refers to is the well-known patriotic song, "America," that was first sung in Boston on July 4, 1831. Here is the beginning of the song.

   My country, 'tis of thee,   [thee = you]
   Sweet land of liberty, Of thee I sing.
   Land where my fathers died!
   Land of the Pilgrims' pride!
   From ev'ry mountainside,
   Let freedom ring!

   Which words/phrases in this song do you think would be especially important for the speaker in Hughes' poem? Why?

8. What is the theme of this poem?

COMMUNICATIVE ACTIVITY

Getting to Know More About the United States

In the introduction to this unit, you shared information about your country, including a popular vacation spot. Then, during the past weeks, you have "visited" four historic cities that are popular vacation spots in the United States.

In this activity, you will learn more about the United States by talking with Americans about their favorite vacation spot. If you already know an American, you can talk with this person. If you don't know an American, this will be a good opportunity to meet one. Americans (and almost everyone) love to talk about vacation. If you would like, you and a classmate can work together on this interview activity.

Procedure:

1. Introduce yourself to an American, explain your assignment, and ask permission to interview the person.

   Example: "Excuse me. In my English language class, we are studying about the United States. I have an assignment to interview Americans about their favorite vacation spot. May I interview you?"

   Note: If the person does not have the time or ignores you, just say, "Thank you, anyway." Then try someone else! If the person agrees to the interview, thank him or her before you begin the interview.

2. Ask the person what his or her favorite vacation spot is. Then ask why. Don't write anything down at this point.

3. Let the person know if you don't understand something.

   Example: "I'm sorry...I don't know what 'snorkeling' is. Can you explain this to me?"..."Oh, I understand now. It's like diving. This sport is also popular in my country."

4. Ask at least two questions about his or her favorite vacation spot.

5. Don't forget to thank the person again for his or her time.

6. Write down what you have learned in the list that follows and share this information with the class.

INFORMATION ON INTERVIEW

■ Brief description of person interviewed:

_____

■ His or her favorite vacation spot and where it is located in the United States:

_____

■ What he or she likes to see and do there:

_____

_____

_____

■ New words I learned from the interview and their meaning:

_____

_____

■ My reaction to the experience of talking with an American—positive or
negative and reason why:

_____

_____

_____

Places I Would Like to Visit

Things I Would Like to Do

How about the area or region where you are now living and studying?
What are some places you would like to visit and things you would like to do?
Write down as many of these as you can and share them with the class.

■ _____

■ _____

■ _____

■ _____

■ _____

■ _____

UNIT TWO
Psychology in Everyday Life

Questions like the ones below are studied by psychologists. They deal with situations in everyday life. Read the three questions and give your own answers.

1. Why does one person learn a foreign language faster than another?

2. How do people feel when their plane is delayed because of bad weather and they won't be able to catch the connecting flight to their favorite vacation spot? How do they react in this situation?

3. How does TV advertising affect the thinking and behavior of children?

In this unit, you will learn possible answers to these questions. Here are the titles of the three chapters in the unit.

Chapter 4	Attitudes
Chapter 5	Language-Learner Traits
Chapter 6	Frustration

From these titles, tell which chapter relates to which question above. Explain your choices.

Now write your own definition of psychology and compare it with others in the class.

Psychology is the study of _____

_____.

This reading selection is taken from an introductory psychology textbook.
It gives a basic explanation of the term "attitude" as it is used by psychologists.

Getting into the Topic

CONSIDER ATTITUDES TOWARD ANIMALS

■ How do you feel about animals? Do you like animals? Do you dislike them? What kinds? Why?

■ How does Amy Kirkland feel about cats? Why?

Whenever Amy sees a cat, her first thought is to get away from it. She believes that cats will attack a person for no reason and that they cannot be trusted. When Amy was little, she was scratched by a cat. After that, her mother, who has always had a great fear of cats, would not let her touch one, so she became afraid of them too. Amy has a strong dislike for cats.

■ How does Jeff Hall feel about animals? Why?

Jeff has both a dog and a cat and enjoys watching the squirrels and birds busily gathering food or building a nest in his backyard. When he was growing up, his family always had pets, mostly dogs and cats, and his mother always fed the birds outside. Jeff believes that animals and people can get along with each other. He says that an animal will not hurt a person unless something or someone threatens it. If he sees an animal that needs help, his first thought is to try to help it. Jeff really likes all kinds of animals.

These examples show different attitudes toward animals. Now write your own definition of an attitude and compare it with others in the class.

An attitude is _____

_____.

A Psychologist's Definition of Attitude

As you will see in the first paragraph of the reading, the writer gives this definition of an attitude. An attitude is:

a readiness to act that involves both thinking and feeling

The definition has three key ideas. Circle these three ideas.

To analyze these ideas, complete the chart on the next page. In the chart, Amy's attitude toward cats is given. Fill in Jeff's attitude toward animals. Then answer the question that follows.

ANALYSIS OF THREE KEY IDEAS IN DEFINITION OF ATTITUDE

Three Key Ideas in Definition	Amy's Attitude Toward Cats	Jeff's Attitude Toward Animals
1. Thinking = what you believe (Cognitive Element)	Believes cats attack people for no reason; cats cannot be trusted	animal won't hurt the person person unless something animal and people can get along with each other
2. Feeling = what you like or dislike, making you feel afraid, happy, nervous, angry, etc. (Emotional Element)	Afraid of cats; has strong dislike of cats	
3. Readiness to act = being prepared to act, NOT the act itself (Behavioral Element)	Ready to get away from cats	

■ Psychologists tell us that attitudes develop from influences. Who or what influenced the attitudes of Amy and Jeff toward animals?

_____

_____

Scan the reading to complete the headings in the outline.

ATTITUDES

1. *influences attitudes*

2. Attitudes and Behavior

3. Positive and Negative Attitudes

4. *changing attitudes*

   a. *Beginning to change attitudes*

   b. *changing attitudes or to time*

5. Determining Attitudes

◼ The last heading, "Determining Attitudes," means getting to know (or finding out) a person's attitudes. For example, in American culture, you might get to know a person's attitude by a clue such as a smile. What else can help you get to know a person's attitude?

READ THE SELECTION: FIRST TIME

Read to get a general understanding of each section. Do not stop to look up words in the dictionary.

READING	Attitudes

1   Probably nothing is more fundamental to what you are and to what you do than your attitudes. An attitude is a readiness to act that involves both thinking and feeling. It is a readiness to act or respond in a particular way to an object, a person, a group, or an idea. A person can hold many attitudes, and these attitudes can be favorable or unfavorable. Even if a person does not care about something, this lack of interest is still an attitude and it is called apathy.

have a tendency to , tend to: are likely to

2   We have a tendency to believe we are more rational, or thinking, than we probably are. In other words, most of us tend to think that we use our minds more than our feelings in responding to other people, situations, and events. However, thinking and feeling are interrelated. What we think affects how we feel, and how we feel affects what we think. An attitude or a reaction may seem to be based on thinking, but it may be based largely on an emotion such as fear or jealousy. In fact, what we feel can become so closely linked to what we think that we may be unable to explain clearly our own reaction to a particular person, event, or thing.

controversial: involving disagreement
capital punishment: punishment by death

accurate: correct

3   In a discussion of a controversial issue such as capital punishment, you would probably hear such statements as "I think deliberately killing another person is always wrong" or "I feel each state should have the right to make its own laws." People often use the expressions "I think" and "I feel" interchangeably when expressing their attitudes. However, it would be more accurate to say, "My attitude is...." This would indicate that both the ideas and the feelings of the speaker are involved.

INFLUENCES ON ATTITUDES

4   The many attitudes you now have were learned. They were acquired over a period of time, and they were influenced by at least four different factors: your family, your peers, your experience, and your culture.

inherit: receive at birth

5   You did not inherit your attitudes from your parents even though the members of a family often have similar ideas and beliefs. For example, the members of a family may have similar attitudes about exercising or about watching television. This happens because children learn their attitudes from their parents. Of course, parents do not sit the children down and say, "Today we are going to teach you an attitude about television." Instead, attitudes develop in a more gradual and subtle way. Neither the child nor the parents may even be aware that an attitude is being taught. Suppose, for example, that the parents say things like, "I'm too busy to watch the junk on television. It rots your mind." From these words, their child will learn a different attitude about television than if they say, "I really enjoy watching television after a hard day. It gives me a break and helps me to relax."

imitating: copying the behavior of another person

6   So children learn by watching and imitating. If parents and older children hold strong attitudes about something, a young child is likely to develop similar attitudes. Many attitudes are learned in the home. Your feelings about spending or saving money or about treating older people politely are likely to be influenced by your family. Your family is also particularly influential when it comes to religious and political attitudes.

seldom: not often
adolescence: young teenage years
values: standards considered desirable

7   Although your family will undoubtedly have a lasting effect on how you think and feel about many things, it is seldom the only strong influence on your attitudes. By the time children reach adolescence, other people their own age—their peers—become an important influence on their attitudes and values. Young people during these years are psychologically breaking away from their families. Being accepted by peers becomes extremely important. Thus, the attitudes of most young people are affected at least for a while by friends and acquaintances of their own age.

8   Your own personal experience also influences your attitudes. If you have had many bad experiences in a particular situation, you are likely to develop a negative attitude toward it. For example, if Roger has had poor luck fishing on Perch Lake several times, he is likely to have a negative attitude toward fishing there. On the other hand, if Louise has had a good time whenever she visited her friend in Denver, she will undoubtedly develop a favorable attitude toward that city as well as toward her friend.

9   Another influence on your attitudes is the culture in which you grow up. For example, the Eastern and Western parts of the world have different attitudes toward death. Particular attitudes might also be found in different sections of a country or might differ in rural areas and in cities. People in different places are likely to have different attitudes about such subjects as work, leisure time, family relationships, and public transportation. In general, your attitudes are affected strongly by how you live and where you live.

ATTITUDES AND BEHAVIOR

10   It is valuable to understand attitudes, your own and others, because of their close relationship to behavior. By understanding attitudes, you can control your own behavior better. You can also understand the behavior of others better, and thus can better predict what someone else might do in a particular situation. Finally, by understanding your own attitudes, you can see how others are trying to change your attitudes in order to influence your behavior.

11   Even though attitudes usually precede behavior, they can also result from behavior. Behaving or acting in a certain way can lead you to develop a particular attitude. For example, if you make a special effort to accept other people by saying hello and talking to them—though they have characteristics quite different from yours—this may cause you to develop a more tolerant attitude toward them. Similarly, by acting enthusiastic about your work or some other activity, even though you may not feel that way at first, you can develop an enthusiastic attitude.

tolerant: accepting or allowing beliefs or behavior different from one's own

12   However, attitudes and behavior do not always agree. What you say and do may contradict what you think and feel. A phrase as simple as "thank you" can be sincere or can express sarcasm and discontent. Your facial expressions and gestures may emphasize or contradict the actual words you are using. Thus, you may agree to work on your day off, even though you think the request is unfair and you resent it.

facial expressions: looks on a person's face
gestures: body movements, esp. hands, that express meaning

POSITIVE AND NEGATIVE ATTITUDES

13   A common way of classifying attitudes is to think of them as positive or negative. People who habitually show negative attitudes toward their jobs and the world are called pessimists. Those who see the brighter, more positive side of life are optimists. Both types of people may be reacting to the same experience, but they perceive it differently. Thus, a pessimist might consider a job transfer to be an undesirable change that probably would cause disappointments and problems. An optimist, however, would see the situation as a new opportunity and challenge. In both cases, attitudes would affect the person's way of perceiving the situation.

perceive: see; think about
job transfer: move to new place of work by company

14   In fact, a job transfer probably would cause some problems, such as finding a new place to live. An optimist would focus on the desirable aspects of such a situation, and a pessimist would pay more attention to the negative aspects. Interestingly, very few people view themselves as pessimists. Most people tend to believe that they are viewing the situation as it really is.

15   An appropriate theme for attitude improvement might be "Accentuate the positive; eliminate the negative." Accentuating the positive makes you feel better. You are also a more interesting person when you have a positive attitude. People like to work with you, to be on your team in sports, or to attend social events with you. Examples of positive attitudes are tolerance, enthusiasm, optimism, confidence, and conscientiousness. Examples of negative attitudes are revengefulness, pessimism, suspicion, apathy, and uncooperativeness.

16   Writer Elwood Chapman in his book, *Your Attitude Is Showing,* tells us that:

When you are positive you are usually more energetic, highly motivated, productive, and alert. Thinking about negative things too much has a way of draining your energy. Put another way, a positive attitude opens a gate and lets your inner enthusiasm spill out. A negative attitude, on theother hand, will keep the gate closed.

CHANGING ATTITUDES

17   If we were not able to change or to influence attitudes, we would be much less concerned about them. However, people do change their attitudes, and they change them only after they perceive situations differently. This doesn't ordinarily happen easily or quickly.

Changing attitudes toward food: brown bread.

Beginning to Change Attitudes

18   If a change in either attitude or behavior is desired, where does one begin? Most often it is suggested that attitudes be changed first, since they tend to result in certain kinds of behavior. However, some people say that attitude changes should begin with a behavior change. This, they say, will encourage a more natural, permanent behavior change. Consider the approach taken by Daryl J. Bem in his book, *Beliefs, Attitudes, and Human Affairs:*

evidence: proof

conventional wisdom: generally accepted good sense or judgment

> There is now sufficient evidence to suggest that under certain conditions, one of the most effective ways to "change the hearts and minds of men" is to begin by changing their behavior. In fact, this may even be easier than first trying to change their attitude. For example, conventional wisdom suggests that promoting goodwill toward minorities may convince people to discriminate less. However, there is better evidence that suggests making people discriminate less may convince them to feel goodwill toward others. Or consider another example. Most people agree that the question, "Why do you eat brown bread?" can be properly answered with, "Because I like it." I should like to convince you, however, that the question, "Why do you like brown bread?" frequently ought to be answered with, "Because I eat it."

Changing Attitudes Over Time

19   Attitudes can also be expected to change over time. In part, this results from having new experiences and developing new understanding and perceptions. As Mark Twain put it: "When I was a boy of fourteen, my father was so ignorant, I could hardly stand to have the old man around. But when I got to be twenty-one, I was astonished at how much he had learned in seven years!"

old man: slang for father
astonished: surprised

20   One parent recalls a conflict of attitudes between herself and her parents when she was a teenager. Evidently they disagreed about how much independence the girl should have at the age of 16. She recalls thinking, "When I get to be a parent and have a 16-year-old daughter, I will allow her as much independence as she wishes." Now, as a parent, she can remember her earlier attitude, but she no longer thinks and feels that way. Because of her age and new point of view, her attitude has changed.

21   The attitudes of most older adults are relatively stable. They may not change much for the rest of the person's life. There are several reasons for this. Some older people may simply be stubborn. Others, who may have more knowledge than younger people, are not continuing to learn at the same pace as younger people, so their attitudes may not be challenged as much. They may also have become satisfied with their ideas and feelings on many subjects, and thus have fixed views on politics, religion, economics, and so on. In such a case, they are not likely to change.

stubborn: unwilling to change their view

22   In addition, older people may not have as much contact with as many different people as they did when they were younger. Since they have settled down socially, there are fewer people influencing their attitudes. Finally, the attitudes of older people may become so much a part of what they are that to change their ideas and feelings would be damaging to their sense of security.

tìm biết

determine: get to know; find out

23   On what basis do you determine the attitudes of others? Some people openly express their beliefs and ideas in discussion groups and in conversation, while others who may have similar attitudes do not share them readily. In any case, for most people, sharing ideas is easier than sharing feelings. Relatively few are willing to express their feelings and when they do, it is only to a limited number of people.

24   In many instances, attitudes are revealed by indirect clues, such as facial expressions and body language. Our thoughts and feelings are revealed in these ways even when we do not realize it. Paying attention or lack of it is also an expression of attitude. If you have a negative attitude about an experience you are having, it probably shows in some way. It is important to realize, however, that facial expressions and body language can be misinterpreted. Thus, someone who is simply not very expressive may be considered apathetic. We are not always accurate in determining the attitudes of others, yet we often react toward them as though we knew what they believe and feel. In sum, attitudes are difficult to determine or change. A little tolerance of others can help us a lot on the job and in every aspect of living.

misinterpreted: did not understand meaning correctly
expressive: full of feeling and meaning

READING CHECK

A. Recall of General Ideas

What do you recall about the general ideas in the reading? Try to answer the questions below. If you can't recall the ideas, scan the reading to find the information.

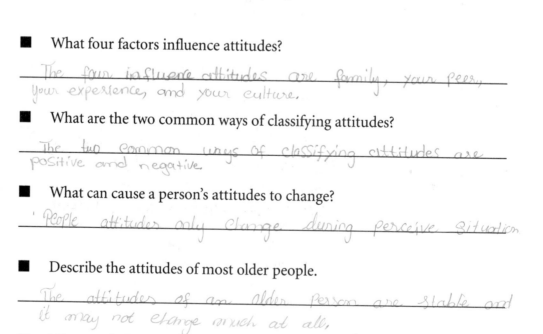

■ What four factors influence attitudes?

The four influence attitudes are family, your peers, your experiences, and your culture.

■ What are the two common ways of classifying attitudes?

The two common ways of classifying attitudes are positive and negative.

■ What can cause a person's attitudes to change?

People attitudes only change during perceive situation

■ Describe the attitudes of most older people.

The attitudes of an older person are stable and it may not change much at all.

■ What can help you determine a person's attitudes?

Openly express their belief and their ideas

B. Guessing the Meaning from Context

Look carefully at the context of the underlined words below. Try to guess their meaning. Use the context clue(s) suggested to help you and be prepared to explain your answer.

1. Even if a person does not care about something, this lack of interest is still an attitude and it is called apathy. (P1)

   — moody-sad

   APATHY *interest is still an attitude*
   context clue: similar words; SEED
   lack of concern or motion.

2. Even though attitudes usually precede behavior, they can also result from behavior. (P11)

   PRECEDE *behavior*
   context clues: contrasting relationship; word parts
   to come before

3. Attitudes and behavior do not always agree. What you say and do may contradict what you think and feel. (P12)

   CONTRADICT *to be inconsistent with*
   context clues: similar words; SEED

4. One parent recalls a conflict of attitudes between herself and her parents when she was a teenager. Evidently they disagreed about how much independence the girl should have at the age of 16. (P20)

   CONFLICT *disagreement between people*
   context clue: similar words; SEED

5. The attitudes of most older adults are relatively stable. They may not change much for the rest of a person's life. (P21)

   STABLE *consistently dependable, remain the same does*
   context clue: similar words; SEED *not change*

   (Reread Paragraph 21 and find the phrase "fixed views." Does it have the same meaning as "stable attitudes"?)

READ THE SELECTION: SECOND TIME

Read more carefully to get a better understanding of each section. Use the dictionary, only if necessary.

A. True or False

Write true or false and the number of the paragraph(s) that supports your answer. Be prepared to explain your answer.

True / _1_   **1.** An attitude is the same as an action.

False / _2_   **2.** It is sometimes difficult to distinguish between what we think and what we feel because these two elements are so closely related.

True / _6_   **3.** Attitudes are learned by watching others and imitating them.

False / _8_   **4.** Because of the strong influence of family, the influence of peers will not affect attitudes.

True / _11_   **5.** Most often attitudes come first and behavior follows from attitudes.

False / _12_   **6.** What you say and do always agrees with what you think and feel.

True / _13_   **7.** Two people can look at the same situation and perceive it differently.

True / _14_   **8.** Although people can see things in either an optimistic or pessimistic way, most believe that they see things in a realistic way.

False / _17_   **9.** To change attitudes, some people say that you should start with a change in attitudes, which can lead to a change in behavior. But there are other people who say the opposite.

True / _20_   **10.** As children grow, their attitudes can become more like those of their parents.

True / _21_   **11.** Although attitudes can change over time, the attitudes of older people remain more fixed.

True / _23_   **12.** Observing the facial expressions and body language of others always gives us an accurate way of determining the attitudes of others.

B. Chart

Complete the chart that lists common factors that influence attitudes. For each factor, give another example of an attitude from the text. Also give your own example of each. Then answer the questions that follow.

COMMON FACTORS THAT INFLUENCE ATTITUDES		
Factors That Influence Attitudes	**Examples of Attitudes from Text**	**Your Own Examples of Attitudes**
1. Family	a. A person's attitude toward spending or saving money b. _Watching TV_ _religion and indial_	_treat_ _animal_ _honestly_
2. Peers	None given in text	_friendship_ _clothes_
3. Personal Experience	a. Roger's attitude toward fishing on Perch Lake b. _attitude to louse_ _toward her friend in_ _Dever_	_age_ _education_
4. Culture	a. A person's attitude toward death b. _Work Leisure time_ _family relationships_ _public transportation_	_preferens clothes_ _marriage, religion_ _language_

■ From the chart, choose one example from the text and one from your own experience and explain each more fully.

■ In addition to these four common factors that influence a person's attitudes, who or what else could influence one's attitudes?

C. Diagrams

In Paragraph 18, Daryl J. Bem discusses two ways to change attitudes and behavior. Bem accepts the conventional wisdom "that attitudes (should) be changed first, since they tend to result in certain kinds of behavior." However, he also believes that in certain situations, behavior should be changed first and this can lead to a change in attitudes.

These two ways of making a change are illustrated by Diagram 1. A diagram is a drawing that shows the relationship between the parts of something. In Diagram 1, what relationship between attitudes and behavior do the arrows show?

DIAGRAM 1: CHANGING ATTITUDES AND BEHAVIOR

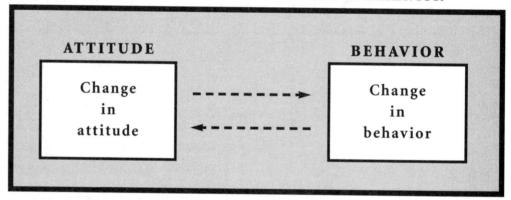

DIAGRAM 2: CHANGING ATTITUDES AND BEHAVIOR TOWARD MINORITIES

To complete Diagram 2, reread Bem's quotation in Paragraph 18. Then add an arrow to the diagram to show the direction in which Bem believes the change should be made. Explain the relationship shown in this diagram. Then answer the question that follows.

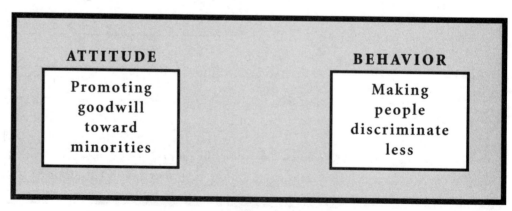

■ What do you think "goodwill" means? Give an example of discrimination against minorities that can happen in the workplace.

_____

_____

DIAGRAM 3: CHANGING ATTITUDES AND BEHAVIOR TOWARD BROWN BREAD

Complete Diagram 3 by using information about brown bread given in Bem's quotation. Write his attitude and behavior toward brown bread. Then add an arrow to show the direction in which he suggests the change be made. Explain the relationship shown in this diagram. Then answer the question below.

ATTITUDE

I like it

BEHAVIOR

I eat brown bread

■ Can you give an example of a food that you eventually liked after you had eaten it for some time? What age were you when this change took place?

_____

_____

D. Analysis of Attitudes and Behavior

Attitudes involve the way we think and feel about something and can result in our behaving in a certain manner. In this exercise, choose one of the topics on the following page or decide on your own topic and analyze your attitude toward the topic and your resulting behavior.

First, state your beliefs (cognitive element) on the topic. Then, state your feelings (emotional element). You can express your feelings by saying that you like, dislike, or have no strong feeling toward the topic. Finally, explain the behavior that results from this attitude. After this, answer the questions that follow.

Example: Topic—Chocolate

Cognitive Element (my belief):
Chocolate is full of calories and is fattening. Chocolate tastes good.

Emotional Element (my feeling):
I love chocolate. It is hard for me to resist chocolate.

My Behavior:
I only eat chocolate when someone gives me some as a treat.
However, sometimes I cheat.

Possible Topics:

smoking	rock music
flying in an airplane	American food
drinking coffee	shopping for clothes
ice cream	physical exercise
drinking alcohol	AIDS

Your Topic: _____

Cognitive Element (your belief): _____

_____

_____

Emotional Element (your feeling): _____

_____

_____

Your Behavior: _____

_____

_____

■ Is there any conflict among the belief, feeling, and be[...]
late" example? Explain.

■ Is there any conflict among the belief, feeling, and beh[...]
example? Explain.

TOPICS FOR DISCUSSION AND WRITING

1. Mark Twain's story illustrates how people's attitudes can change over time. Whose point of view is given in the story? Whose attitude do you think changed in this story? Explain.

    Then perhaps give your own example of an attitude you used to have that may have changed over time. Tell what has caused the change.

2. The reading mentions the following as positive attitudes:

    optimistic   enthusiastic
    tolerant   conscientious

    Explain the meaning of each word; use your dictionary, if necessary. Then tell which student in your class best fits each description and give your reasons.

3. In some cases, facial expressions and body language such as hand gestures or head movements can help you determine a person's attitude. First you must understand the meaning of the facial expression, hand gesture, or head movement because there can be cross-cultural differences.

    Consider, for example, looking a person directly in the eye. What does it mean in the United States if a person does not look another person directly in the eye? What about in your culture?

    What about ways of showing friendship and affection in public? Are these the same in your culture as they are in the United States?

    Have you observed any other facial expressions or body language in the United States that are different from those in your country? Do they show a particular attitude or not?

VOCABULARY EXERCISES

A. Word Forms

Choose the correct word form that completes each sentence. The base form of the word is in **bold.** For nouns, use singular or plural forms. For verbs, use appropriate verb tenses and passive voice where necessary.

(P1)   **1.**   response *n*   **to respond to** *v*

     a. Her _____ *response* _____ to the invitation was negative.

     b. The infant usually _____ *respond to* _____ his mother's voice by smiling.

        ✓

(P2)   **2.**   belief *n*   **to believe** (that) *v*   (un)believable *adj*

     a. Before coming to the United States, he _____ *believed* _____ that it would take only about six months to learn English well.

     b. Her political _____ *belief* _____ are very different from the rest of her family.

     c. It is _____ *unbelievable* _____ how fast John can read; he can read a 100-page book in about one hour.

        ? ✓ an huong

(P2)   **3.**   **effect** *n*   to affect *v*   effective *adj*
                              to have an effect on *v*

     a. What are some _____ *effects* _____ of homesickness on a person?

     b. Feeling homesick can _____ *effect* _____ a student's performance in class.

     c. Which do you think is a more _____ way of improving your listening skills, watching television or watching video tapes? What's the difference?

     d. Being an only child can _____ *effective* _____ the child's attitudes and behavior.

(P10)   **4.**   behavior *n*   **to behave** *v*   behavioral *adj*

     a. The child psychologist studied the effects of mothers starting to work outside the home on the _____ *behavior* _____ of children ages 3 to 5.

attitude – a person's
personality
or behavior

     b. Most of the children showed some type of _____ *behavioral* _____ change.

     c. In one experiment, the psychologist watched how the children _____ *behaved* _____ when their mothers came home from work.

chui dương

(P11)   5.   tolerance *n*   to tolerate *v*   (in)tolerant, (in)tolerable *adj*

   a. Instructors who are easy-going are more ___tolerant___ of their students' behavior.

   b. However, all instructors generally have certain things that they will not ___tolerate___ from their students.

   c. For most instructors, coming late to class every day is ___intolerable___.

   d. Remember that a little ___tolerate___ of people who are different from you can make your daily life easier.

B. Other Useful Words

Complete the sentences with an appropriate word from the list. For nouns, use singular or plural forms. For verbs, use appropriate verb tenses.

behavior toward something
something that oppose
to not be distracted
to have effect on

attitude (toward something) (P1)
to contradict (P12)
to focus on (P14)
to influence (P4)

precise (right) on the target
side

accurate (P3)
favorable (P1) — *supportive to one's*
lasting (P7) — *exist for a long time*
optimistic (P15) — *think of good things.*
pessimistic (P15) — *think of negative things*

   1. One description of a ___pessimistic___ person is someone who "sees a glass as half empty rather than half full."

   2. ___attituded___ toward different cultures can be changed by traveling and living in foreign countries.

   3. Jenny said that she'd be happy to help, but her facial expression ___contradicted___ her words.

   4. Anna was so excited about the arrival of her family that she could not ___focus___ her school work.

   5. Her description of the thief was so ___accurate___ that the police were able to identify him.

   6. His grandfather probably ___influenced___ him more than anyone else as he was growing up.

7. The instructor received a _____ response from the students because she didn't assign any homework over the weekend.

8. Although George tried to be _____, he knew that the chances of getting over 600 on the TOEFL were not good.

9. A divorce can have _____ effects on a child.

C. Vocabulary Oral Practice

Practice using the underlined words by answering the questions below.

1. Capital punishment is a <u>controversial issue</u> in the United States. Is it a <u>controversial issue</u> in your country? If not, explain why. Tell about a <u>controversial issue</u> in your country today. **(P3)**

2. Attitudes are learned and are not <u>inherited</u> from your parents. What can you <u>inherit</u> from your parents? **(P5)**

3. In addition to <u>imitating</u> the behavior of their families, children and young people will <u>imitate</u> the behavior of others. What persons in society provide good role models of behavior for children and young people to <u>imitate</u>? Do children <u>imitate</u> behaviors they see on television? Are these behaviors good or bad? **(P6)**

4. One way of <u>classifying</u> attitudes is as either positive or negative. One way of <u>classifying</u> people is as either friends or acquaintances. What is the difference between a friend and an acquaintance? Can you give another way of <u>classifying</u> people? **(P13)**

5. Students from other countries sometimes observe that American young people are overweight. What kind of food do you think these young Americans should <u>eliminate</u> from their diet in order to lose weight? **(P15)**

6. What situations, places, people, etc., give you <u>a sense of security</u>? When you first arrived in the United States, did you feel you had lost some of your <u>sense of security</u>? Why? **(P22)**

D. Dictation

Study the spelling of the words in the previous exercises. You will have a dictation of sentences that contain these words.

Topic 1

Attitudes are influenced by the culture in which you grow up. Choose an attitude that is common in your country but is not common in the United States. For example, there could be a difference in attitude toward the handicapped, nature, premarital sex, being on time, being independent, or showing respect for old people. Describe the attitude found in your country and how people behave because of this atttitude.

Topic 2

People's attitudes can change over time. Perhaps you have changed your attitude toward something. Discuss the attitude and explain how it has changed. Tell what influenced your change in attitude.

COMMUNICATIVE ACTIVITY **Opinion Poll**

In this activity, you will take an opinion poll to find out the attitudes of Americans and/or people from other countries toward a controversial issue. You will choose an issue being discussed at the present time. After you take the poll, you will report your results to the class.

Procedure:

1. With your classmates, think of a controversial issue(s).

   It could be a local issue (important for your city, town, or school), a state issue, a national issue, or an international issue.

   Examples of a controversial issue:
   - Capital Punishment
     Do you agree or disagree with the use of capital punishment?

   - Grading System
     Should a grading system such as A, B, C, D, F be used to evaluate students, or should a simple grading system of Pass/Fail be used?

2. Together, discuss what you know about the issue(s) and decide which issue the class will study.

3. Together, write a few questions on the issue for the poll. Also, decide what background information to get on the persons being polled, for example, sex, age group, nationality, profession.

4. Divide into pairs (or small groups). With your partner(s), ask five people the questions. After completing each interview, take notes on the person's responses.

5. On poster paper, make a chart of the background information on the five persons polled. Choose a classmate from each pair (or small group) to report to the class on the persons polled and the results of the poll. Write the results on the board. (Each group adds its results to the other results on the board.)

6. Combine the results on the board to get the overall results of the opinion poll. With your classmates, discuss the overall results and your reaction to the poll.

READING FOR PLEASURE

A FOLKTALE

Folktales are stories that were originally passed down from one generation to the next generation orally. They were often told to children and contained important lessons about attitudes and behaviors.

Today, people of all ages enjoy reading folktales. Many are amazed that the lessons contained in folktales are so relevant to their adult lives.

The folktale that you will read originated in Korea several hundred years ago. As you read it, think about what the storyteller wants you to learn about attitudes and behaviors and how you can apply this knowledge to your own life.

READING

The Tiger's Whisker

whisker: long hair that grows near a tiger's mouth

hermit: person who lives alone away from society
sage: wise man
charms and magic potions: objects and drinks with special powers
cure: make a problem or illness disappear

Line
1

A young woman by the name of Yun Ok came one day to the house of a mountain hermit to seek his help. The hermit was a sage of great renown and a maker of charms and magic potions.

When Yun Ok entered his house, the hermit said, without raising his eyes from the fireplace into which he was looking: "Why are you here?"

5 Yun Ok said: "Oh, Famous Sage, I am in distress! Make me a potion!"

"Yes, yes, make a potion! Everyone needs potions! Can we cure a sick world with a potion?"

"Master," Yun Ok replied, "if you do not help me, I am truly lost!"

10 "Well, what is your story?" the hermit said, resigned at last to listen.

"It is my husband," Yun Ok said. "He is very dear to me. For the past three years he has been away fighting in the wars. Now that he has returned, he hardly speaks to me, or to anyone else. If I speak, he doesn't seem to hear. When he talks at all, it is roughly. If I serve him food not to his liking, he pushes it aside

15 and angrily leaves the room. Sometimes when he should be working in the rice field, I see him sitting idly on top of the hill looking toward the sea."

"Yes, so it is sometimes when young men come back from the war," the hermit said. "Go on."

"There is no more to tell, Learned One. I want a potion to give my hus-

20 band so that he will be loving and gentle, as he used to be."

"Ha, so simple is it?" the hermit said. "A potion! Very well; come back in three days and I will tell you what we shall need for such a potion."

Three days later Yun Ok returned to the home of the mountain sage. "I have looked into it," he told her. "Your potion can be made. But the most essen-

25 tial ingredient is the whisker of a living tiger. Bring me this whisker and I will give you what you need."

"The whisker of a living tiger!" Yun Ok said. "How could I possibly get it?"

"If the potion is important enough, you will succeed," the hermit said. He turned his head away, not wishing to talk anymore.

30 Yun Ok went home. She thought a great deal about how she would get the tiger's whisker. Then one night when her husband was asleep, she crept from her house with a bowl of rice and meat sauce in her hand. She went to the place on the mountainside where the tiger was known to live. Standing far off from the tiger's cave, she held out the bowl of food, calling the tiger to come and eat.

35 The tiger did not come.

The next night Yun Ok went again, this time a little bit closer. Again she offered a bowl of food. Every night Yun Ok went to the mountain, each time a few steps nearer the tiger's cave than the night before. Little by little the tiger became accustomed to seeing her there.

accustomed: in the habit of

40 One night Yun Ok approached to within a stone's throw of the tiger's cave. This time the tiger came a few steps toward her and stopped. The two of them stood looking at one another in the moonlight. It happened again the following night, and this time they were so close that Yun Ok could talk to the tiger in a soft, soothing voice. The next night, after looking carefully into Yun Ok's eyes,

45 the tiger ate the food that she held out for him. After that when Yun Ok came in the night, she found the tiger waiting for her on the trail. When the tiger had eaten, Yun Ok could gently rub his head with her hand. Nearly six months had passed since the night of her first visit. At last one night, after caressing the animal's head, Yun Ok said:

trail: dirt pathway

50 "Oh, Tiger, generous animal, I must have one of your whiskers. Do not be angry with me!"

Line

And she snipped off one of the whiskers.

The tiger did not become angry, as she had feared he might. Yun Ok went down the trail, not walking but running, with the whisker clutched tightly in
55　her hand.

The next morning she was at the mountain hermit's house just as the sun was rising from the sea. "Oh Famous One!" she cried, "I have it! I have the tiger's whisker! Now you can make me the potion you promised so that my husband will be loving and gentle again!"

60　The hermit took the whisker and examined it. Satisfied that it had really come from a tiger, he leaned forward and dropped it into the fire that burned in his fireplace.

"Oh, sir!" the young woman called in anguish. "What have you done with it!"

obtained: got

"Tell me how you obtained it," the hermit said.

65　"Why, I went to the mountain each night with a little bowl of food. At first, I stood afar, and I came a little closer each time, gaining the tiger's confidence. I spoke gently and soothingly to him, to make him understand I wished him only good. I was patient. Each night I brought him food, knowing that he would not eat. But I did not give up. I came again and again. I never spoke

reproached: criticized

70　harshly. I never reproached him. And at last one night he took a few steps toward me. A time came when he would meet me on the trail and eat out of the bowl that I held in my hands. I rubbed his head, and he made happy sounds in his throat. Only after that did I take the whisker."

tamed: trained to be gentle

"Yes, yes," the hermit said, "you tamed the tiger and won his confidence
75 and love."

"But you have thrown the whisker in the fire!" Yun Ok cried. "It is all for nothing!"

vicious: mean

"No, I do not think it is all for nothing," the hermit said. "The whisker is no longer needed. Yun Ok, let me ask you, is a man more vicious than a tiger?
80 Is he less responsive to kindness and understanding? If you can win the love and confidence of a wild and bloodthirsty animal by gentleness and patience, surely you can do the same with your husband?"

Hearing this, Yun Ok stood speechless for a moment. Then she went down the trail, turning over in her mind the truth she had learned in the house of the
85 mountain hermit.

COMPREHENSION QUESTIONS

1. Describe Yun Ok's problem.

2. Why did she go to see the mountain hermit?

3. What did the mountain hermit tell Yun Ok the most important ingredient for the magic potion was? How did she respond when she heard this and why? What did the hermit tell her?

4. Describe in detail how Yun Ok tamed the tiger. How long did it take her?

5. Explain why the mountain hermit threw the tiger's whisker into the fire.

6. The folktale ends with the following words: "Then she went down the trail, turning over in her mind the truth she had learned in the house of the mountain hermit." What lesson did she learn about how to solve her problem? Do you think this lesson required a change in attitude or behavior? Explain.

LANGUAGE-LEARNER TRAITS

Learning in the classroom.

Learning in the real world.

In this reading, you will learn about traits that appear to contribute to being a successful language learner. One of these traits is attitude.

READING SELECTION

PRE-READING DISCUSSION

Getting into the Topic

■ What does the word "traits" mean in the title? If you don't know, look it up in the dictionary.

■ Why do you think "attitude" can be a trait of a successful language learner?

■ What is your attitude toward learning English? Has your attitude toward English changed over time?

■ How is learning a language in the classroom different from learning a language in the real world?

Getting an Overview of the Reading Selection

Scan the reading to complete the headings in the outline.

LANGUAGE-LEARNER TRAITS

1.

2.

3.

4.

■ How do you think age influences language learning?

■ How do you think past experiences influence language learning?

READ THE SELECTION: FIRST TIME

Read to get a general understanding of each section. Do not stop to look up words in the dictionary.

READING   **Language-Learner Traits**

1   You, the language learner, are the most important factor in the language-learning process. Success or failure will, in the end, be determined by what you yourself contribute. Many learners tend to blame teachers, circumstances, and teaching materials for their lack of success, when the most important reasons for their success or failure can ultimately be found in themselves. There are several learner traits that are relevant to learning a foreign language, and they usually appear in combination. A combination of these traits is probably more important than any one alone. In this reading, we will examine several of these traits.

relevant: related to what is being discussed

triple

2   Some people think that the best time to begin studying a foreign language is in childhood, and that the younger you are, the easier it is to learn another language. There is little evidence, however, that children in language classrooms learn foreign languages any better than adults (people over age 15) in similar classroom situations. In fact, adults have many advantages over children: better memories, more efficient ways of organizing information, greater concentration, better study habits, and greater ability to handle complex mental tasks. Adults are better motivated than children: they see learning a foreign language as necessary for their education or career. In addition, adults are particularly concerned about using correct grammar and appropriate vocabulary—two factors that receive much attention in most language classrooms.

3   Age does have some disadvantages, however. For instance, adults usually want to learn a foreign language in a hurry, unlike children, who can spend more time on mastering the language. Also, adults have complex communication needs that go beyond the need to carry on a simple conversation. Adults need to be able to argue, persuade, express concern, explain, and present information about complex matters that relate to their work or education. Next, because most adults do not like to appear foolish, they often do not take advantage of opportunities to practice for fear of making mistakes or not explaining their ideas clearly. Also adults have more trouble than children in making new friends who speak the foreign language.

4   One example usually given to support the idea of children's superiority as language learners is their ability to pick up a native-like accent. It is usually found that children of immigrants learn to speak the language of their adopted country without an accent, whereas their parents rarely do. It is also found that even adults with high need and motivation, such as diplomats, rarely learn a foreign language without retaining some of their native accent. There are, however, some adults who do acquire native-like accents, but they are the exception, not the rule.

5   If you consider both the advantages and the disadvantages, however, the advantages of age clearly outnumber the disadvantages. Therefore, the best time to learn a foreign language is when your need is clearest and you have sufficient time. If you are strongly motivated to study a foreign language and if you have the time to do it, it is the best time to begin.

INTELLECTUAL FACTORS

capability: power to do something

6   A person's intellectual capability to learn a foreign language is commonly referred to as language aptitude. In a classroom situation, a person with high language aptitude can usually master foreign-language material faster and better than someone with lower aptitude. In fact, several studies have shown a strong relationship between grades and aptitude.

7   There are several standardized tests that measure language-learning aptitude. They predict how fast and how well an individual can learn foreign languages under formal classroom conditions, when the emphasis is on grammar and memorization. However, these tests may not be such good predictors of

how well a person can learn to communicate in a foreign language, especially if he or she has the opportunity to practice in real-life situations. In other words, language-aptitude tests may predict ability to learn formally and analytically in the classroom, but they may not be as reliable in predicting ability to learn intuitively or naturally in real life.

reliable: dependable

8   Remember that language success may ultimately depend not only on intellectual capability but also on persistence. You may have the potential to be a brilliant language learner, but if you do not put effort into it, chances are you will not learn much. A good combination of language aptitude and persistence is ideal.

persistence: continuing to do something, although difficult
potential: possibility
ideal: perfect

PSYCHOLOGICAL FACTORS

9   A number of psychological factors also appear to have a significant effect on language mastery. Probably the most important one is motivation. Most people need strong motivation to complete the complex task of mastering a foreign language. However, there are many different reasons for learning a foreign language. For example, sometimes the motivation is professional; a person needs to learn a foreign language for his or her job. Other times, the motivation is for educational purposes; a person needs to learn a foreign language in order to satisfy a school requirement or to use academic materials published in another language.

10   Another motivation could be social. Travelers and those living in culturally diverse urban areas often want to learn a foreign language in order to communicate socially with speakers of the language. A different motivation could be that a person simply wants to learn a foreign language for his or her own personal enrichment. He or she may want to satisfy a personal curiosity about a country and its culture.

11   In addition to motivation, attitude is another psychological factor related to language learning. If aptitude is an intellectual trait, attitude is an emotional one. Attitude involves the way learners feel about the foreign culture and its people. They may admire them and want to learn more about them by becoming fluent in their language. They may like the people who speak the foreign language and wish to be accepted by them. Research has shown a definite relationship between attitudes and success when foreign-language learners have an opportunity to know people who speak the language they are studying. Such positive attitudes usually help learners to maintain their interest in language study long enough to master it.

12   It should not be surprising that personality also influences the way a person tries to learn a foreign language. Although we cannot, at present, describe the ideal language-learning personality, several personality types appear to be related to success. Of these, extroversion is often mentioned as a positive trait. An extroverted, sociable person who uses every opportunity to talk with other people may be more successful because, by establishing and maintaining more contacts, he or she has more opportunities to hear and use the new language. An introverted personality, on the other hand, will probably not take advantage of as many opportunities to meet people and speak the language.

13   People who are painfully aware of their limitations and worry about their ability to use the language are usually less willing to participate in either classroom practice or in real-world communication. These people suffer from inhibition, another psychological trait that can influence language learning. Inhibition can block a person from making progress in speaking (perhaps less in the way of reading) a foreign language. It can also prevent a person from taking risks or taking advantage of opportunities to practice and learn. Fear of making a mistake or being misunderstood can prevent a person from trying a more open-minded and active approach to language learning. Such an approach can help to make the language-learning experience more enjoyable and successful.

approach: method of doing something

14   Tolerance of ambiguity is yet another psychological factor related to learning. A person who can tolerate ambiguity is willing to accept ideas or information that may be contradictory. A person who is tolerant of ambiguity does not see everything in terms of black and white, but is willing to accept the fact that there are many shades of gray. Tolerance of ambiguity is viewed as a benefit in learning a foreign language because there are so many exceptions to language rules that even native speakers cannot always agree on correct usage. Also, something may be correct to say in one situation, but not in another. Having an open, flexible approach to language learning can contribute to success in mastering a language.

flexible: able to change easily to new conditions

15   Learning a foreign language is one kind of learning situation. So, whatever learning approach a person applies to other kinds of learning situations, he or she usually applies to a language-learning situation. Thus, learning style is yet another psychological factor that affects language learning. When it comes to foreign language, one type of learner prefers a highly-structured approach with much explanation, many exercises, and constant correction. This type of learner is very analytical and is unwilling to say anything in the foreign language that is not grammatically perfect. This person is a rule learner.

intuition: immediate understanding of something without study

16   Another person depends more on intuition, the gathering of examples, and imitation. This second type of learner is willing to take risks. There is no evidence that one type of learner is more successful than the other. Perhaps what is important is that the learner's style be appropriate to the particular language task he or she is doing. For example, if the task is to communicate, then risk taking is important. If the task is to say or write something correctly, then rules become important.

17   Finally, there is the eye-ear learning factor. When learning a foreign language, some students depend on their eyes, and others depend on their ears. Some learners feel that they learn better if they can see the language written out, while others prefer to listen to tapes and spoken language. However, the relationship between using one's eyes or ears and mastering a foreign language is not clear. For social or travel reasons, using the ears to understand the spoken language may be more important. For professional or educational reasons, however, a person needs to develop all the language skills, both the active skills of speaking and writing and the passive skills of listening and reading.

PAST EXPERIENCES

18   Past experiences with foreign-language study may influence future attempts. If, on the one hand, a person has had a favorable experience studying one language and believes that he or she learned something valuable, that person will be more likely to study another language and will also expect to achieve success.

19   On the other hand, if an individual's first experiences with a foreign language were not particularly pleasant or successful, he or she will tend to expect the next language-learning experience to be just as stressful and unfruitful as the first. Such a person should examine the reasons for the earlier lack of success. Perhaps it was due to a teacher that the learner did not like, a textbook that was not particularly helpful, a teaching method that did not match the learner's learning style, or perhaps it was due to the learner's own inexperience, lack of motivation, or lack of good reasons for studying the particular language. Chances are that the conditions will not be repeated or can be avoided the second time. The best approach in this case is simply to begin the study of the next language as a completely new experience.

20   Keep in mind that people get better at whatever they do over a long period of time. In other words, based on past experiences, they learn how to learn. People who have learned several languages usually report that each became easier to master, particularly if the languages were related. So don't be surprised when the star performer in your class tells you that it is his or her third or even fourth foreign language.

READING CHECK

A. Recall of General Ideas

What do you recall about the general ideas in the reading? Try to answer the questions below. If you can't recall the ideas, scan the reading to find the information.

■ How does age affect the language learner in the classroom?

Children under age 15th learn better than people
over the age of 15th

■ What does language aptitude mean?

A person intellectual capability to learn a
foreign language.

■ Name some of the psychological factors mentioned in the reading.

motivation, academic, diverse

■ How does past experience influence language learning?

The past experience with foreign-langue study my influence future attempts.

B. Guessing the Meaning from Context

Look carefully at the context of the underlined words below. Try to guess their meaning. Use the context clue(s) suggested to help you and be prepared to explain your answer.

1. There is little evidence, however, that children in language classrooms learn foreign languages any better than <u>adults</u> (people over age 15) in similar classroom situations. **(P2)**

    ADULTS *grown up*
    context clue: definition provided by writer

2. Adults usually want to learn a foreign language in a hurry, unlike children, who can spend more time on <u>mastering</u> the language. **(P3)**

    MASTERING *overcoming*
    context clues: similar words

3. Adults have many advantages over children: better memories, more efficient ways of organizing information, greater concentration, better study habits, and greater ability to handle complex mental tasks. So, if you consider both the advantages and the disadvantages of age in language learning, the advantages of age clearly <u>outnumber</u> the disadvantages. **(P5)**

    OUTNUMBER *disavantages,*
    context clue: SEED *to be larger number than*

4. People who worry about their ability to use the language are usually less willing to participate in either classroom practice or in real-world communication. These people suffer from inhibition. Inhibition can <u>block</u> a person from making progress in speaking a foreign language. **(P13)**

    BLOCK *a* ^stop *person from making progress in speaking*
    context clue: SEED; cause and effect relationship

5. If an individual's first experiences with a foreign language were not particularly pleasant or successful, he or she will tend to expect the next language-learning experience to be just as stressful and <u>unfruitful</u> as the first. **(P19)**

    UNFRUITFUL *the first uncusseful*
    context clues: descriptive words; SEED; word parts

94

UNIT TWO   Psychology in Everyday Life

READ THE SELECTION: SECOND TIME

Read more carefully to get a better understanding of each section. Use the dictionary, only if necessary.

COMPREHENSION EXERCISES

A. True or False

Write true or false and the number of the paragraph(s) that supports your answer. Be prepared to explain your answer.

True / _1_   1. The successful language learner usually possesses a ~~have~~ combination of learner traits, rather than just one major trait.

_F_ _True_ / _2_   2. Many studies of language learning in the classroom have proven that children are better language learners than adults.

False / _7_   3. Language-learning aptitude tests are better predictors of success in learning a foreign language in the real world than in the classroom.

True / _8_   4. People who have the intellectual capability to learn a foreign language may not succeed if they do not have persistence.

True / _12_   5. Extroversion refers to being sociable and enjoying the chance to make new friends.

False / _13_   6. Inhibition is a positive trait that contributes to language learning.

_T_ _False_ / _14_   7. Tolerance of ambiguity helps a person deal with ideas that do not agree.

False / _16_   8. Research has proven that the risk taker learns a foreign language faster than the rule learner.

inside classroom adult
out children

B. Chart

Complete the chart with appropriate information. Then answer the questions that follow.

FACTORS THAT INFLUENCE LANGUAGE LEARNING

General Factors	Specific Factors or Types
1. Age	**a.** Children
	b. Adults
2. ~~intellectual~~	~~language aptitude~~
3. ~~Psychological~~	**a.** ~~motivation~~
	b. attitude
	c. ~~personality~~
	d. ~~inhibition~~
	e. ~~tolerace of ambiguity~~
	f. ~~learning style~~
	g. ~~easure ye learning~~
4. ~~past experice~~	**a.** ~~stressful~~
	b. ~~not successful~~

---

attitude how you feel about something you think negative and positive,

■ Explain the meaning of each of the specific psychological factors in your own words or by using the words of the writer.

~~motovation~~ _____

_____

_____

_____

_____

_____

_____

■   Some of the specific psychological factors appear to be closely related to each other. For example, how are motivation and attitude closely related? Can you find any other specific psychological factors that are closely related?

_____

_____

_____

TOPICS FOR DISCUSSION AND WRITING

1. When adults speak a foreign language, their native language affects their accent in the other language. One reason for this is the difference in stress and intonation between the two languages. Explain the meaning of stress and intonation and give an example of each in English. What about the sounds in English? Are there any that are difficult for you? What are they and why are they difficult?

2. In Paragraph 8, the writer states that "a good combination of language aptitude and persistence is ideal" in learning a language. Tell what persistence means in your own words and why it is important in learning a language.

    Decide whether you agree or disagree with the two statements below. Explain the reasons for your position.

    a. Learning to read English requires more persistence than learning to speak English.

    b. Learning to pronounce English words requires more persistence than learning to spell English words.

3. Learning English grammar, spelling, and pronunciation can require tolerance of ambiguity. Take, for example, the two sentences, "They read the newspaper everyday." "They read the book last year." Why do these sentences require tolerance of ambiguity? Give your own examples of English grammar, spelling, and pronunciation that require tolerance of ambiguity.

4. In addition to the language-learning traits, one type of behavior that can be helpful in learning a language is to take risks (safe risks). For example, you might go to the weekly coffee hour sponsored by the International Student Organization to meet people and practice English. Give an example of risk taking that you could try in the language classroom and outside in the real world.

5. Past experiences can have an influence on successful language learning. Describe your past language-learning experiences. How have these experiences influenced your language study now? In a learning situation, how much responsibility do you think the teacher has and how much responsibility do you think the student has in making learning successful?

6. The following statements from the reading are based on research studies that were done by educational psychologists and language researchers. Do these statements express possibility or certainty? Explain how you know.

   a. A combination of language-learner traits is probably more important than any one alone. (**P1**) *posibility*

   b. In a classroom situation, a person with high language aptitude can usually master foreign-language material faster and better than someone with lower aptitude. (**P6**) *Certainty*

   c. Language-aptitude tests may predict ability to learn formally and analytically in the classroom, but they may not be as reliable in predicting ability to learn intuitively or naturally in real life. (**P7**) *possibility*

   d. A number of psychological factors appear to have a significant effect on language mastery. (**P9**) *Certainty*

   Why do you think psychologists cannot be completely certain in their research on the human mind and behavior? Are there other fields of study in which researchers can make statements that express certainty? What are these fields of study and why do you think these researchers can make statements with greater certainty?

VOCABULARY EXERCISES

A. Word Forms

Choose the correct word form that completes each sentence. The base form of the word is in **bold.** For nouns, use singular or plural forms. For verbs, use appropriate verb tenses and passive voice where necessary.

(P1) 1. **success** *n* to succeed *v* successful *adj*
successfully *adv*

a. To be a more ___successful___ language learner, Takis
decided to share an apartment with an American student.

b. After one year, his language skills improved greatly and he
___successfully___ passed all of his courses with good grades.

c. He believes his ___success___ was due primarily to his
persistence and risk taking.

d. He tells new students that if they want to ___succeed___,
they should not be afraid to take risks, safe ones, that is.

(P1) 2. combination *n* **to combine** *v*

a. Lucy has trouble reading in English because of a ___combination___
of factors. Two of these factors are her limited knowledge of vocabulary
and her great difficulty in recognizing many words on the page.

b. So, if you ___combine___ just these two factors, you can
understand why she cannot read well.

(P2) 3. motivation *n* **to motivate** *v* motivated *adj*

a. Choi was not successful in learning English back home because he did
not have much ___motivation___.

b. After he arrived in the United States, he was strongly
___motivated___ by his desire to learn English as fast as
possible.

c. Now he is the most ___motivated___ EFL student in the class.

(P7) 4. prediction *n* **to predict** *v* (un)predictable *adj*

a. Mike's behavior is so ___unpredictable___. One day he might
be very attentive in class and the next day he might be daydreaming.

b. The instructor ___predicted___ that if Mike did not pay
regular attention in class, his grades would suffer.

c. The instructor's ___prediction___ was accurate.

(P9)   5. significance *n*   **significant** *adj*   significantly *adv*

    a. Studying regularly in the library has improved Patrick's class performance _____Signifi Cantly_____.

    b. He has made _____significant_____ progress in his writing ability since he began reading in English for at least 30 minutes each day.

    c. Does a college degree from a foreign university have greater _____significanted_____ than one from a university in your country?

B. Other Useful Words

Complete the sentences with an appropriate word from the list. For nouns, use singular or plural forms. For verbs, use appropriate verb tenses.

concentration (**P2**)   to prevent (**P13**)   flexible (**P14**)
(dis)advantage (**P2**)   to take risks (**P13**)   reliable (**P7**)
lack (of something) (**P1**)   rarely (**P4**)
persistence (**P8**)   ultimately (**P1**)
trait (**P1**)

1. The results of the listening test were not very _____reliable_____ because the tape recorder didn't work well.

2. Her _____concentration_____ during the exam was so great that she did not hear the fire alarm.

3. A language student who is not afraid to _____take risks_____ will probably learn to speak the language faster.

4. The instructor said that tolerance of ambiguity is a _____trait_____ that she finds more often in children than adults.

5. Aziz is a very capable student, but he always points out that getting good grades also requires a lot of _____Presistence_____.

6. Inhibition and a _____lack of_____ of self-confidence can _____prevent_____ a person from participating actively in class discussion.

7. Try to be more _____flexible_____ and open-minded in your thinking; listen to the ideas of other people and don't hold on to just your own idea.

8. Having friends only from your own country is a _di'savantage_ because you will _rarely_ have the chance to speak English outside of class.

9. _ultimately_, each person is responsible for his or her own success or failure.

C. Vocabulary Oral Practice

Practice using the underlined words by answering the questions below.

1. Instructors make rules for their classes. One rule, for example, may be that, when a student misses a major test, the student will not be allowed to take a make-up test. The instructors say that they will make no <u>exceptions</u> to this rule. Under what circumstances do you think an <u>exception</u> to this rule might be made? **(P4)**

2. Reports indicate that American high school students' scores on math and science tests today are not as high as they were 20 years ago. Whom or what can we <u>blame</u> for this drop in scores? **(P1)**

3. Some people believe that women have better <u>intuition</u> than men. For example, when a mother first sees her child entering the house, she may <u>intuitively</u> know that something is wrong. She doesn't need to ask the child. Do you agree with this idea of <u>female intuition</u>? Explain or give another example of <u>female intuition</u>. Do you think there is such a thing as <u>male intuition</u>? If so, can you give an example? **(P16)**

4. Are you satisfied with your present language-learning situation? What would you change if you could? What do you think the <u>ideal</u> language-learning situation would be? **(P8)**

5. A person who is <u>curious</u> about other countries and cultures will probably learn a foreign language faster, especially if he or she visits the other country. How do you think <u>curiosity</u> can help a person learn a language faster when visiting another country? **(P10)**

6. Some people are opposed to the abbreviation "Ms." as in "Ms. Jones" because of its <u>ambiguity</u>. Why do people think this abbreviation is <u>ambiguous</u>? Is the abbreviation "Mr." less <u>ambiguous</u>? Why do you think people are not equally opposed to "Mr."? **(P14)**

D. Dictation

Study the spelling of the words in the previous exercises. You will have a dictation of sentences that contain these words.

JOURNAL WRITING

You have read that certain learner traits can help you master a foreign language. However, in addition to your own learner traits, you can also learn a subject better (whether it is math, history, English, or whatever subject) because of the traits or characteristics of your teacher. What are the characteristics of a good teacher?

To get some ideas on this, think about a good teacher that you had in your home country. Undoubtedly in your past learning experiences, you had a good teacher from whom you learned much. This could be any teacher, not just your English teacher. Think about the particular characteristics of this teacher who helped you learn so well. Then write in your journal about the characteristics of a good teacher.

LECTURE | Traits That Facilitate Cross-Cultural Adaptation

Some foreign students have an easier time adapting to life in the United States than other students. What factors may explain this difference?

This lecture is about cross-cultural adaptation. Everyone who leaves his or her native culture and goes to live in another culture goes through a process called cross-cultural adaptation. During this process, a person begins to understand and feel comfortable in the new culture. This lecture focuses on three psychological traits that facilitate cross-cultural adaptation.

LISTENING STRATEGY

In the introduction to the lecture, the speaker explains what cross-cultural adaptation is and why she is somewhat of an expert on this topic. She explains that she has both studied and worked in other cultures, so she has personally gone through the process of leaving her own culture and adapting to a new culture. She also explains that as a teacher of English as a foreign language, she interacts closely with students who are now going through the process of adapting to American culture.

In the lecture, she discusses three psychological traits that facilitate cross-cultural adaptation and gives advice on what foreign students can do to make their adjustment to the United States more successful.

NOTETAKING SHEET

1. Listen to the lecture. Follow the outline below as you listen. Do not write anything at this time.

2. Listen again and complete the outline. Write only key words or phrases. After the lecture, compare your notes with a classmate's. You may want to listen to the lecture again to confirm any points that you missed.

3. After completing your notes, discuss them with the class.

Outline on Traits That Facilitate

Cross-Cultural Adaptation

1. Personal curiosity

   a. Definition: _____

   _____

Language - Learning Traits

1) *Age < outside the classroom children are more successful*
   inside " " " adults

2) *Intellectual Factors - aptitude for learning language*

3) *Psychological Factors - motivation, attitude, personality, inhibition, tolerance of ambiguity, learning style, ear-eye learning factor*

4) *Past Experience -*

b. Relationship between curiosity and success in cultural adaptation

The more curious you are
about the new culture

The more you explore and learn
about the culture

_____

_____

_____   _____

_____   _____

c. How speaker and family have learned about Senegalese culture

■   Read books—history, religion, ethnic groups, customs and holidays

■   _____

_____

■   Talked with Americans who have lived there and made a list
of "Do's and Don'ts"

■   _____

_____

d. Advice on how to learn about American culture

■   _____

_____

■   _____

_____

■   _____

_____

2. _____

    a. Why adaption process is so difficult

        _____

        _____

    b. Advice on what to do when feeling overwhelmed by cultural differences

        ■ Don't worry if you feel overwhelmed; it's a normal part of adaptation process

        ■ _____

            _____

3. A cross-cultural perspective

    a. Definition: _____

        _____

    b. Two important points about every culture to keep in mind

        ■ _____

            _____

            _____

        ■ Every culture is ethnocentric—believes its own norms are the most logical and correct; this attitude can be a problem if you judge new culture according to norms of own culture

    c. Advice on how to develop a cross-cultural perspective

        ■ _____

            _____

        ■ _____

            _____

1. The speaker and her family have learned about Senegalese culture in a variety of ways. Describe what you did to learn about the American culture and Americans before you came to the United States. In what ways are you now exploring and learning about the American culture?

2. To whom do you turn to for emotional support in the United States? Why do you think the speaker believes it is important to have people from both your culture and the American culture to support you as you adapt to life in the United States?

3. Do you agree that all cultural groups are ethnocentric? Can you give an example of an ethnocentric attitude?

4. Give an example of an American cultural norm that is different from the norm of your culture. Talk with an American to try to understand why Americans think or act this way. Then report back to the class what you have learned.

FRUSTRATION

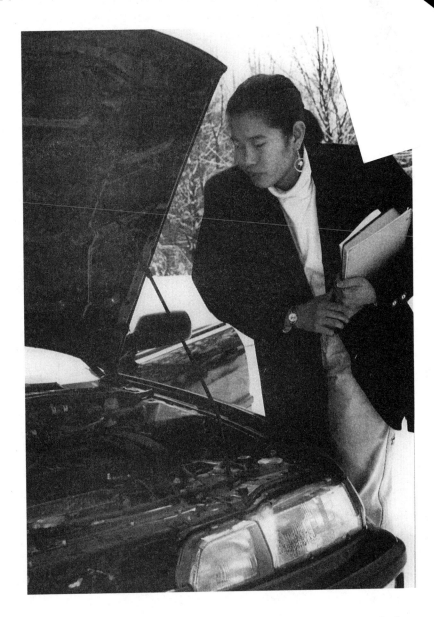

This reading is also taken from an introductory psychology textbook. It is about an unpleasant feeling that all of us experience from time to time. This feeling is called "frustration."

PRE-READING DISCUSSION

Getting into the Topic

■ Look at the photo. Describe the situation. How does the person feel? Describe a frustrating experience you had recently.

■ How did you react to the situation?

Scan the reading to complete the headings in the outline.

FRUSTRATION

1.

2.

3.

4.

■ Look at the cartoon in the reading. What is the source of the man's frustration? How does he react? What is this cartoon saying about this kind of reaction?

■ People have a different tolerance of pain. Some can tolerate a lot of pain, while others complain when they have a simple headache. Do you have a high tolerance of pain? How about your tolerance of frustration? Do you have a higher tolerance of frustration than the other members of your family?

READ THE SELECTION: FIRST TIME

Read to get a general understanding of each section. Do not stop to look up words in the dictionary.

READING **Frustration**

athlete: person who is trained or skilled in sports
satisfy: reach

obstacle: something that blocks a desire

1   "The trouble with Ellen is that she's a frustrated actress." "The trouble with Bill is that he's a frustrated athlete." How often do we hear such statements? Time and time again. When women and men cannot satisfy a goal—such as the desire to be an actress or an athlete—they are said to be frustrated. Frustration, it is generally agreed, can often lead to trouble.

2   To psychologists, the word "frustration," which is so important in the study of the human personality, refers to the blocking of goals and desires by some kind of obstacle. On a very simple level, our goal to get somewhere on time may be blocked or frustrated by a flat tire. On a more complex level, our goal to be an actress or athlete may be blocked or frustrated by a number of possible obstacles.

3   In everyday language, however, the term "frustration" also refers to the unpleasant feelings that result from the blocking of our goals. That is, it refers to the feelings we experience when something interferes with our wishes, hopes, plans, and desires.

SOURCES OF FRUSTRATION

4   Frustration is a universal experience; nobody can possibly go through life without experiencing it many times for many reasons. Our environment is full of events that prevent us from satisfying our goals. Even our own bodies and personalities make frustration inevitable. The possible sources of frustration are usually broken down into four categories:

inevitable: unavoidable

drought: period of no rain

Physical obstacles—such as a drought that frustrates a farmer's attempts to produce a good crop. Or a broken alarm clock, traffic jam, or flat tire that prevents us from getting to class on time. How many such obstacles there are in the world!

Social circumstances—such as when a person does not return our feelings or affection. Or problems in our society such as discrimination, crime, and unemployment that frustrate our desire for equality, physical security, and economic security.

Personal shortcomings. We may have a desire to dance as well as our friends but have "two left feet." Or we may have a desire to speak a foreign language fluently but lack the necessary persistence.

Conflicts. A conflict occurs when we have two or more goals that cannot be satisfied at the same time. For example, a woman wants to leave college for a year to try painting—but she also wants to please her family by remaining in school. The person in conflict experiences uncertainty, hesitation, and the feeling of being "torn." These feelings are an essential part of conflicts and are what make conflicts such an unpleasant part of life.

torn: divided between two things

THE RELATIVE NATURE OF FRUSTRATION

5   What kinds of physical obstacles, social circumstances, personal shortcomings, and conflicts are likely to be the most frustrating? This is an interesting question to which psychologists have found an interesting answer—which is that frustration is entirely relative.

6   A classic experiment which illustrates the relative nature of frustration was performed by observing the behavior of children aged two to five in a playroom that contained only "half toys," such as a telephone without a receiver. Despite the missing parts, the children played quite happily until they saw much better toys in another room. When the children were not allowed to play with the "whole toys," most of them showed signs of extreme frustration. As this experiment shows, what causes frustration is a relative matter. "Half toys" are fun to play with if there is nothing better. When better toys are just beyond reach, the "half toys" are no longer good enough.

7   Adult frustrations are equally relative. A man may be perfectly happy with his old used car until his neighbor buys a new sports model. A woman may be perfectly content with her job until her friend in the next office gets a promotion. Many people who are quite successful and well liked suffer frustration because a brother or sister is even more successful and popular.

TOLERANCE OF FRUSTRATION

8   Let us suppose that two individuals find a certain situation equally frustrating. How well will they be able to tolerate this situation? The answer to this question is that it depends on the individuals. Some people can tolerate a great deal of frustration; others find it difficult to tolerate even a little.

9   Under wartime conditions, while some soldiers break down due to the frustrations of the battlefield, others, in the same situation, seem to find strength they never knew they had. Under more ordinary circumstances, all of us know people who have managed to carry on normal lives despite serious physical handicaps or tragic disappointments, and others who are unable to accept the same frustrations.

REACTIONS TO FRUSTRATION

10   Frustrations are among life's most unpleasant experiences; they result in anxiety and other disagreeable emotions. To escape from this anxiety, we behave in various ways to relieve our frustrations. Unfortunately, however, some of these behaviors can result in even greater anxiety or stress.

11   As mentioned earlier, frustration is a universal experience. Reactions to frustration also appear to be universal. That is, we can observe similar reactions in many different kinds of societies. However, certain reactions may not be as socially acceptable in one culture as in another culture. For instance, all people, when frustrated, may respond with anger. However, in some cultures, such as in the Asian culture, anger should not be displayed publicly, while in other cultures displaying anger in front of others is more acceptable. The most common reactions to frustration are the following.

12   **Assertive coping.** Any discussion of possible reactions to frustration should begin on a positive note, with what might be called assertive coping. One of our desires has been blocked; we feel bad about this—yet, if we can stay calm, perhaps we can somehow find some way to overcome the obstacle. We can look at the situation as an exercise in problem solving.

13   Thus, the motorist with a flat tire can get busy changing it or try to find a phone and seek help. The student who wants to be an accountant but is weak in some areas of mathematics can try hard to master these subjects. People frustrated by a bad marriage can try to cope with their problem by seeing a professional counselor or, if necessary, by ending the marriage.

counselor: person who gives professional advice

14   In all these cases, the emotions produced by the frustration may be extremely unpleasant. However, assertive coping is an attempt to get rid of this frustration in a positive and constructive way. Even though the actions taken to overcome the obstacles may fail, assertive coping is constructive behavior, and therefore quite different from the others that will now be discussed.

15 **Anger and aggression.** Sometimes the reaction to frustration takes the form of aggression. Children frustrated by other children who take their toys often get angry and hit the other children, attacking them with their fists. Adults are more likely to get into verbal fights, screaming and shouting loudly. These are examples of direct aggression.

16 However, if the source of frustration cannot be dealt with directly, aggression is still likely to result, but on an innocent bystander instead. For example, a man angry at his demanding and powerful boss goes home and behaves aggressively toward his wife and children. A little girl angry at her parents takes out her aggression on a smaller child or on a pet. These are examples of displaced aggression. However, aggression, whatever form it takes, is essentially an attempt to get rid of the frustration in a negative and destructive way and often leads to even further trouble.

17 **Depression and apathy.** Another important reaction to frustration, found in different degrees among different people, is depression. Some psychologists believe that depression results when we become angry with ourselves. We may believe that we are the source of our problems and blame ourselves for being stupid or unlovable. Other psychologists believe that depression usually results from an inability to meet unrealistically high goals. Of course, depression may also result from the loss of a loved one—either because someone has died or no longer returns our love. Whatever its cause, extreme depression may lead to such serious apathy that people live their days in what is commonly called a "blue funk"—so sad and disinterested that they seem to lose all interest in what happens to them and have a difficult time finding energy for the ordinary chores of life.

18 **Withdrawal.** Some individuals, when suffering from frustrations, display the kind of behavior called withdrawal. They try to avoid close contact with other people and any kind of goal-seeking behavior. We say that such people, like a turtle, have "retreated into a shell" or that they have "quit trying." Rather than making an attempt to face their frustrations and cope with them, these people prefer to escape from them.

resolution: solution to a conflict

19 **Vacillation.** Often, when faced with frustration resulting from conflict, we display the kind of behavior called vacillation—the tendency to be drawn first toward one possible resolution of the conflict, then toward another. Torn between studying or working and going out with friends, we may change our minds several times. At one moment, we may decide to study, at the next moment, to go out. In an extreme case of vacillation, we may take so long making up our minds that we have very little time left for either of the possibilities.

READING CHECK

A. Recall of General Ideas

What do you recall about the general ideas in the reading? Try to answer the questions below. If you can't recall the ideas, scan the reading to find the information.

■ Identify four major sources of frustration.

_____

_____

■ Describe a person in conflict.

_____

_____

■ Identify a positive reaction to frustration.

_____

■ Identify four negative reactions.

_____

_____

B. Guessing the Meaning from Context

Look carefully at the context of the underlined words below. Try to guess their meaning. Use the context clues(s) suggested to help you and be prepared to explain your answer.

1. Frustration is a <u>universal</u> experience; nobody can possibly go through life without experiencing it many times for many reasons. **(P4)**

   → **UNIVERSAL** _____*same everywhere*_____

   context clue: SEED   *effecting everybody*

2. Frustrations are among life's most unpleasant experiences; they result in <u>anxiety</u> and other disagreeable emotions. **(P10)**

   ANXIETY _____*worried*_____

   context clue: reference words

3. One of our desires has been blocked; we feel bad about this—yet, if we can stay calm, perhaps we can somehow try to find some way to <u>overcome the obstacle</u>. We can look at the situation as an exercise in problem solving. **(P12)**

   OVERCOME THE OBSTACLE ___*to surpass a problem*___

   context clue: similar words   *to solve problem*

4. If the source of frustration cannot be dealt with directly, aggression is still likely to result, but on an <u>innocent bystander</u> instead. For example, a man angry at his demanding and powerful boss goes home and behaves aggressively toward his wife and children. **(P16)**

   INNOCENT BYSTANDER ___*not in purpose*_____

   context clue: SEED; word part   *guiltless on looker*

5. Extreme depression may lead to such serious apathy that people live their days in what is commonly called a "<u>blue funk</u>"—so sad and disinterested that they seem to lose all interest in what happens to them and have a difficult time finding energy for the ordinary chores of life. **(P17)**

   BLUE FUNK ___*sad, depression, gloomy,*___

   _____*disinterested*_____

   context clue: definition provided by writer

READ THE SELECTION: SECOND TIME

Read more carefully to get a better understanding of each section. Use the dictionary, only if necessary.

COMPREHENSION EXERCISES

A. True or False

Write true or false and the number of the paragraph(s) that supports your answer. Be prepared to explain your answer.

_T_ / _~~2~~_   1. Frustration refers to two things: to the blocking of our desires by an obstacle and to the unpleasant feelings that result.

_F_ / _#4_   2. Some people never experience frustration.

_F_ / _4_   3. A conflict involves a single desire.

_~~T~~ #F_ / _6_   4. When the children in the experiment were first given "half toys," they cried and showed other signs of frustration.

_F_ / _7_   5. Adult frustrations are not as relative as the frustrations of children.

_F_ / _8_   6. People have almost the same ability to tolerate frustration.

_F_ / _11_   7. The various reactions to frustration are equally acceptable in every culture.

_T_ / _12_   8. Assertive coping is a positive reaction to frustration, even though the person's efforts to cope with the problem may not always succeed.

_F_ / _15_   9. People who behave aggressively always direct their attack at the source of their frustration.

_T #_ / _14_   10. Except for assertive coping, the other four behaviors can often lead to trouble.

B. Chart

Complete the chart that lists the major sources of frustration. Fill in the major sources and give an example of each from the text. Also give a personal example of each source and be prepared to explain it to the class. Then answer the questions that follow.

SOURCES OF FRUSTRATION

Major Sources	Example from Text	Your Own Example
1. Physical obstacles	A flat tire that blocks our need to get to school on time	*try to get work on time*
2. *social circumstances*	Crime that blocks our desire to feel physically secure	*can make it*
3. Personal shortcomings	*have desire to dance but don't have spoke the language*	*but don't have necessary persistance*
4. *conflict, woman*	*blocking of goals and desires by some kind of obstancle*	*unpleasant feeling that results from the blocking of our goals* *blocking → unpleasant*

■ From the reading, you learned that the word "frustration" refers to two things. List them.

_____

_____

Now complete the diagram.

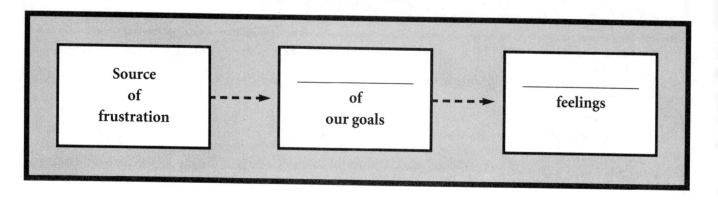

| Source of frustration | _____ of our goals | _____ feelings |

C. Reactions to Frustration

The reading describes five reactions to frustration. What are they? The situations below illustrate these reactions. Read each situation and write the reaction it illustrates on the blank line. Then answer the questions that follow.

vacillation   **1.** Has difficulty making up her mind whether to take courses during the summer or get a job

anger and aggression   **2.** Drives fast and recklessly after having an argument with girlfriend

assertive coping   **3.** Makes an appointment with the teacher to learn how to improve vocabulary skills; follows teacher's suggestions

withdrawal   **4.** Does not go out with friends anymore and is thinking of dropping out of school

depression and apathy   **5.** Has been feeling blue ever since breaking up with boyfriend

Anger and aggression   **6.** Tears up boyfriend's photo and letters after seeing him with another woman

assertive coping   **7.** Works out in the gym three times a week to improve his physical appearance

■ Do any of these five reactions seem closely related?

_____

■ Psychologists classify these reactions into two groups. What are they?

_____Anger_____

_____

■ From the situations that illustrate assertive coping, explain what "to cope with frustration" means. How do psychologists classify this kind of reaction?

_____passive_____

_____

D. Problem-Solving Activity

In psychology, assertive coping is viewed as an exercise in problem solving. One type of problem-solving technique is called *brainstorming*. It is called brainstorming because in this technique, a person can suggest any possible solution that comes into his or her mind, no matter how crazy. Any idea that your brain thinks of is acceptable.

For this exercise, work in groups of three or four. Decide who will be the group leader and the group secretary. Together think of a problem that students often face. Perhaps one of the group members is facing a particular problem at this time.

Here are two examples of student problems, but try to think of your own. Try to choose a problem that can have many solutions.

■ You feel frustrated because a friend in your class is always asking to copy your homework and language lab assignments. Your instructor has said that copied assignments will not be accepted.

■ You feel frustrated because you are having trouble getting along with your new roommate in some way. Maybe she or he likes to play rock music while studying late at night, and you can't sleep.

Procedure:

1. Identify the problem.

2. Explain the problem as fully as possible.

3. Brainstorm to find as many solutions as possible. The leader makes sure that everyone gets a chance to contribute ideas and that there is no evaluation of ideas at this time. The secretary writes down all the possible solutions.

4. Evaluate each solution.

5. Decide which one would be the best or which ones would be good and list them starting with the best.

6. Report on your brainstorming exercise to the class.

TOPICS FOR DISCUSSION AND WRITING

1. "We cannot direct the wind, but we can adjust the sails." assertive coping

   This quotation has two parts. Which part expresses the idea of frustration? Explain. Which part expresses the idea of assertive coping? Explain.
   1st part

2. "If the storm does not break the branch of a tree, it will strengthen it."

   In this quotation, the branch of a tree symbolizes man. What does the storm symbolize? Explain how the storm can actually strengthen man.

3. The expression "blue funk" Sad comes from a kind of music called the "blues." The earliest form of the "blues" was slave work songs. For slaves, singing was a way of relieving their frustrations.

   Gradually, musicians began to accompany blues singers. Around the early 1900s, modern blues appeared with songs like "The St. Louis Blues." Try to find this song at your school or neighborhood library and listen to it. What words would you use to describe this music? Do you like the music?

   Contemporary blues sometimes reflects a somewhat humorous reaction to life's troubles. Do you think humor is a positive reaction to frustration? Explain. A popular contemporary blues singer is B. B. King. Listen to one of his songs. What is the song about? Does B. B. King look at life's trouble in a humorous way at all?

VOCABULARY EXERCISES

A. Word Forms

Choose the correct word form that completes each sentence. The base form of the word is in **bold**. For nouns, use singular or plural forms. For verbs, use appropriate verb tenses and passive voice where necessary.

(P1) 1. frustration *n*   **to frustrate** *v*   frustrating, frustrated *adj*

   a. Registering for courses can be a very ___frustrating___ experience.

   b. When David learned that the class he wanted had been canceled, he felt extremely ___frustrated___.

   c. What ___frustrated___ him even more was standing in line for an hour at the bookstore.

   d. To relieve his ___frustration___, he went over to his friend's house and listened to music.

(P10) 2. anxiety *n*   **anxious** *adj*   anxiously *adv*

   a. When the pilot announced that the plane would be landing late, some passengers became ___anxious___ because they had to catch connecting flights.

   b. They began to look at their watches ___anxiously___.

   c. The flight attendant relieved their ___anxiety___ *anxiety* when she announced that all passengers would be able to make connecting flights.

(P11) 3. reaction *n*   **to react** *v*

   a. How did Maria's parents ___react___ when she told them she wanted to study abroad?

   b. They had mixed ___reaction___; they thought it would be a good experience for her, but they said they would miss her terribly.

(P15)   4. aggression *n*   **aggressive** *adj*   aggressively *adv*

    a. The young student was sent to see a counselor because of his
    _____aggressively_____ behavior toward other students.

    b. After some counseling, the student began to behave less
    _____aggressively_____.

    c. The counselor believed that the student's _____aggression_____
    was a reaction to his parents' divorce.

(P15)   5. **anger** *n*   to anger *v*   angry *adj*   angrily *adv*

    a. Why is it healthier to express your _____anger n_____ than to
    keep it bottled up inside?

    b. Cathy gets _____angry_____ very easily.

    c. It doesn't take much to _____angry v_____ her.

    d. The demonstrators in front of the White House were protesting
    _____angrily_____ against the president's economic policies.

B. Other Useful Words

    Complete the sentences with an appropriate word from the list. For nouns, use singular or plural forms. For verbs, use appropriate verb tenses.

conflict (**P4**)   to cope with (**P13**)   constructive (**P14**)
                              to relieve (**P10**)   destructive (**P16**)
                              to vacillate (**P19**)
                              to withdraw (**P18**)

1. When frustrated, people react in both _____constructive_____ and
   _____distructive_____ ways.

2. People will do almost anything to try to _____relieve_____
   their frustration and other negative feelings.

3. Why do you keep on _____vacillating_____? Make up your mind
   one way or the other.

4. Sometimes people try to escape from frustration by
   _____withdrawing_____.

5. The more frustrations you face, the more you learn how to
_____withdraw to cope with_____ them.

6. When making career decisions, young people often experience
_____conflict_____. They might want the money and prestige
of a lawyer or doctor but not the responsibilities.

C. Vocabulary Oral Practice

Practice using the underlined words by answering the questions below.

1. What do you consider your strengths in English? What are your
   shortcomings? **(P4)**

2. When students leave their own culture to live and study in a different
   culture, certain things are inevitable. For example, it is inevitable that they
   will become homesick at some point. What else is inevitable? **(P4)**

3. Everything is relative. For example, the price of food is relative. To a
   Japanese, food in the United States is relatively cheap, but to a Chinese, it
   is relatively expensive. Explain why. Can you give another example of
   something that is relative? **(P5)**

4. What should college students consider when making up their minds about
   a major? **(P19)**

5. The young couple had planned to get married this year but then changed
   their minds. Give some possible reasons for this. **(P19)**

6. Fear can be an obstacle that prevents us from doing things we would like
   to do. For example, fear of water can prevent us from learning how to
   swim or sail. Think of another fear and describe why it can be an obstacle.
   (P2)

7. Helen Keller was blind, yet she overcame this physical handicap and
   became a teacher of the blind. Describe a person who has overcome a
   physical handicap or another kind of obstacle to lead a successful life. **(P12)**

8. Some women want to have a career and stay home and raise a family. How
   can they resolve this conflict? Does this resolution have any disadvantages?
   (P19)

D. Dictation

Study the spelling of the words in the previous vocabulary exercises. You will have a dictation of sentences that contain these words.

JOURNAL WRITING

Ann Landers is a popular newspaper advice columnist. She receives hundreds of letters a day asking for advice on how to cope with personal problems. She and her staff often discuss the most difficult problems with each other before writing a response.

Below is a letter that was actually written to Ann Landers. Imagine you and your classmates work for Ann Landers. In groups, read the letter from Alice, and discuss the conflict she is facing. Next, share ideas on what advice to give her and why.

Then, in your journal, personally write a letter advising Alice. Make sure you explain the reasons for your advice. After you write your letter, ask your instructor to read Ann Landers' actual response to Alice.

Dear Ann Landers: John and I have been married six years. We have three children. John's parents live two blocks from us. They are good people, not the interfering type, and we all get along fine. The problem is they have few friends and no interests other than our family. Their lives are centered around us and our children. John's company wants him to go to another state as district manager. It would mean a big promotion and a substantial salary increase. My father-in-law says if John will pass it up and remain here, he will make up the financial difference. He says money isn't everything and their lives will be empty without us.
Comment please.—**Alice**

READING FOR PLEASURE

A FOLKTALE

This folktale is from Japan. Like Yun Ok in *The Tiger's Whisker*, the main character of this story experiences a change in attitude and behavior.

READING

The Stonecutter

gravestone: stone with the name, date of birth, and death of a person

1   Once upon a time, there lived a stonecutter, who went every day to a great rock in the side of a big mountain. There he cut out blocks of stone for gravestones or for houses. He understood very well the kinds of stones needed for the different purposes, and because he was a careful workman, he had plenty of

customers. For a long time he was quite happy and contented and asked for nothing better than what he had.

2   In the mountain lived a spirit which now and then appeared to men, and helped them in many ways to become rich and prosperous. The stonecutter, however, had never seen this spirit, and only shook his head with disbelief when anyone spoke of it. But a time came when he learned to changed his opinion.

3   One day the stonecutter carried a gravestone to the house of a rich man, and saw there all sorts of beautiful things, which he had never even dreamed of. Suddenly his daily work seemed to grow harder and heavier, and he said to himself: "Oh, if only I were a rich man, and could sleep in a bed with silken curtains and golden tassels, how happy I should be!"

4   And a voice answered him: "Your wish is heard: a rich man you shall be!"

5   At the sound of the voice, the stonecutter looked around, but could see nobody. He thought he was imagining the voice, and picked up his tools and went home, for he did not feel like doing any more work that day. But when he reached the little house where he lived, he stood still with amazement, for instead of his wooden hut was a palace filled with splendid furniture. And most splendid of all was the bed, which was like the one he had envied. He was full of joy and in his new life the old one was soon forgotten.

6   It was now the beginning of summer, and each day the sun blazed more and more fiercely. One morning the heat was so great that the stonecutter could hardly breathe, and he decided to stay at home until the evening. He was rather bored because he had never learned how to amuse himself. He was looking through the closed curtains to see what was going on in the street, when a little carriage passed by, led by servants dressed in blue and silver. In the carriage sat a prince. His servants held a golden umbrella over his head to protect him from the sun's rays.

7   "Oh, if I were only a prince!" said the stonecutter to himself, as the carriage passed by. "Oh, if I were only a prince, and could ride in such a carriage and have a golden umbrella held over me, how happy I should be!"

8   And the voice of the mountain spirit answered: "Your wish is heard; a prince you shall be."

amazement: surprise

palace: a large and splendid house

envied: desired what others have

amuse: spend time doing pleasant things

carriage: a horse-drawn vehicle, especially for kings

9   And a prince he was. Servants dressed in scarlet and gold carried him along and a golden umbrella was held over his head. Everything his heart desired was his. But yet it was not enough. He looked around still for something to wish for. When he saw that in spite of the water he poured on his grass, the rays of the sun scorched it, and that in spite of the umbrella held over his head each day, his face grew browner and browner, he cried in anger: "The sun is mightier than I; oh, if I were only the sun!"

mightier: more powerful

10   And the mountain spirit answered: "Your wish is heard; the sun you shall be."

11   And the sun he was. He felt mighty and powerful. He shot his rays above and below, on earth and in heaven. He burned up the grass in the fields and scorched the faces of princes as well as poorer folk. But in a short time, he began to grow tired of his might, for there seemed nothing left for him to do. Once more he grew discontent. And when a cloud covered his face and hid the earth from him, he cried in anger: "Does the cloud hold my rays captive, and is it mightier than I? Oh, that I were a cloud and mightier than any!"

12   And the mountain spirit answered: "Your wish is heard; a cloud you shall be!"

13   And a cloud he was, and lay between the sun and the earth. He caught the sun's rays and held them, and to his joy the earth grew green again and flowers blossomed. But that was not enough for him. For days and weeks he poured forth rain until the rivers overflowed, and the crops of rice stood in water. Towns and villages were destroyed by the power of the rain. Only the great rock

untouched: not harmed or destroyed

on the mountainside remained untouched. The cloud was amazed at this sight, and cried in wonder: "Is the rock, then, mightier than I? Oh, if I were only the rock!"

14   And the mountain spirit answered: "Your wish is heard; the rock you shall be!"

15   And the rock he was. Proudly he stood, and neither the heat of the sun nor the force of the rain could affect him. "This is better than all" he said to himself. But one day he heard a strange noise at his feet. And when he looked down to see what it could be, he saw a stonecutter driving tools into his side. Even while he looked, a trembling feeling ran all through him, and a great block of stone broke off and fell upon the ground. Then he cried in anger: "Is a mere child of the earth mightier than a rock? Oh, if I were only a man!"

And the mountain spirit answered: "Your wish is heard. A man once more you shall be!"

And a man he was. He labored again at his trade of stonecutting. His bed was hard and his food scanty. But

he had learned to be satisfied with it, and did not long to be something or somebody else. And because he never asked for things he did not have, or desired to be greater and mightier than other people, he was happy at last, and heard the voice of the mountain spirit no longer.

COMPREHENSION QUESTIONS

1. In the beginning, the stonecutter was a happy man who was content with who he was and what he had. When did he first become discontent with his work and what he had?

2. Retell all the people and things the stonecutter wished to become. Explain the reason for each wish.

3. In the end, the stonecutter wished to be himself again. What is this story's message about the source of frustration? What is its message about the real source of happiness?

4. At last, the stonecutter no longer heard the voice of the mountain spirit. What human characteristic does this spirit represent?

5. Do you think the stonecutter needed to experience what he did before he could learn again to appreciate himself and what he had?

6. Have you had a similar lesson?

LECTURE   Learning to Manage Time Better

Have you ever stayed up really late at night studying for an exam or writing a paper? If so, then you have experienced the stress and frustration caused by poor time management. If this describes you, this lecture on time management is for you.

LISTENING STRATEGY

This lecture describes two time management techniques. The first technique—to keep a diary—can help you to get a clearer picture of how you are presently using your time and to identify problems you may have managing time. The second technique—to make a weekly time schedule—can help you begin to solve these problems.

TERMS USED IN THE LECTURE*

a diary	to become a routine
patterns	to switch
currently	to maintain good
study sessions	health habits

* These terms are defined or made clear from context in the lecture.

NOTETAKING SHEET

1. Listen to the lecture. Follow the outline below as you listen. Do not write anything at this time.

2. Listen again and complete the outline. Write only key words or phrases. After the lecture, compare your notes with a classmate's. You may want to listen to the lecture again to confirm any points that you missed.

3. After completing your notes, discuss them with the class.

Outline on Learning to Manage Time Better

TECHNIQUE #1: KEEP A DIARY

1. Record 3 kinds of information

   a. _____

   b. _____

   c. _____

2. Review diary to look for patterns of poor time management

   Example: Michele's patterns

   a. Morning: not enough time for good breakfast; too much time with friends

   b. Afternoon: _____

   _____

   c. Evening: _____

   _____

TECHNIQUE #2: _____

1. Schedule fixed activities = _____

   _____

   _____

2. _____

   a. How much time

      ■ _____

      _____

   b. When to study

      ■ _____

      _____

      ■ As regularly as possible ⟶ studying becomes routine and easier

   c. What to do during longer study sessions

      ■ _____

      _____

      ■ _____

      _____

      ■ _____

      _____

3. Schedule time for maintaining good health habits

   a. Time to prepare and enjoy meals

   b. _____

   c. _____

   d. Time for breaks

DISCUSSION QUESTIONS

1. Keep a diary of all your activities for a few days. Then review your diary to look for patterns of poor time management. Do you recognize any patterns? If so, describe them to the class.

2. Make a weekly time schedule following the steps given in the lecture. Compare your schedule with a classmate's. Then try to follow your schedule for a week and report to the class on the successes and/or failures you had keeping to the schedule.

3. Do you have any personal techniques to help you manage your time better? If so, share them with the class.

COMMUNICATIVE ACTIVITY

Taking a Break

Taking a break: sharing a funny photo with a friend.

People should leave time in their busy day to take short breaks. Taking a break allows you to take time off from whatever you are doing in order to do something that you really enjoy—listening to music, reading a short story, calling a good friend on the phone, or taking a walk. Taking a break is good for you, physically and psychologically.

In this activity, the class will take a special kind of break—a laughter break. Bring a smile or laughter to your classmates by sharing one of the following:

■ a funny photo

■ an amusing personal experience

■ a joke

■ a magic trick

■ a riddle

■ a cartoon

Remember, a smile or laughter is good medicine.

A typical American family in the 1950s.

UNIT THREE
The American Family at Work

Read these statements. Look for something they have in common.

1. Traditionally, the vast majority of American women who worked were single women. Today, an increasing number of married women and mothers with young children are in the workforce.

2. In the past, most American teenagers who worked did so only during the summer. Today, a growing number are working year-round.

3. Until recently, many people who did volunteer work in the community were stay-at-home moms or retired people, and they mainly helped out at hospitals and schools. Today, other groups are volunteering as well, and they are giving their time to a wide variety of new causes.

What idea do these statements have in common? In this unit, "The American Family at Work," you will learn about several important changes that have been taking place in American society. What change(s) does each statement above focus on?

This unit discusses the reasons for these changes in American society and their effect on the lives of Americans. Here are the titles of the three chapters in this unit.

Chapter 7   Mothers at Work: The New American Family
Chapter 8   When Teenagers Work
Chapter 9   The New Volunteers

Before beginning the unit, write down all the reasons you can think of that motivate people to work. Compare your reasons with others in the class.

_____

_____

_____

MOTHERS AT WORK: THE NEW AMERICAN FAMILY

The author with her two children.

This reading selection is written by Marguerite Connerton, a single mother with two young children, David age 2 and Daniel age 6. The writer is also a labor economist with a Ph.D. from Harvard. As director of Public Policy for the Service Employees International Union, she tries to encourage employers and the government to adopt policies that help women, like herself, balance work and family life.

READING SELECTION

PRE-READING DISCUSSION

Getting into the Topic

■ In your country, do mothers work outside the home? Why or why not?

■ Do you think a woman can be a good mother and good worker at the same time? Why do you feel this way?

Getting an Overview of the Reading Selection

A graph is a way of showing trends or patterns over a period of time. To get an overview of some important points in the reading selection, let's look closely at the two graphs in the reading.

GRAPH 1:
WOMEN'S LABOR FORCE PARTICIPATION RATE
DURING THE 20TH CENTURY

1. In general, what labor trend does the graph illustrate?

2. By what percent did women's labor force participation grow during the following time periods:

   a. the 20 years from 1900 to 1920 ___93 %___
   b. the 20 years from 1920 to 1940 ___28 %___
   c. the 5 years from 1940 to 1945 ___38%___
   d. the 20 years from 1950 to 1970 ___43%___
   e. the 20 years from 1970 to 1990 ___58%___
   f. the 2 years from 1990 to 1992 ___-8%___

3. As you can see from these statistics, women's labor force participation grew at the fastest (record) rate from 1940 to 1945: 8% within only a five-year period. World War II was the reason why such a large number of women left the home to participate in the labor force. Why were they needed?

4. During what time period was there another record growth in women's labor force participation? The reasons for this record growth are different from the reason for the earlier record growth. What do you think these reasons are?

5. From 1990 to 1992, women's labor force participation *leveled off*. Explain what this means.

GRAPH 2:
AMERICAN FAMILIES' INCOME DURING 1970s AND 1980s

1. By how much did American families' income (wages) increase during the following time periods:

   a. the six years from 1967 to 1973 ___30,000___
   b. the six years from 1973 to 1979 ___31,000___
   c. the eight years from 1979 to 1987 _____

2. These statistics show that American families' income has remained *stagnant* during much of the 1970s and 1980s. Explain what this means.

3. There is a relationship between the trend shown in the first graph and the trend shown in the second graph. What do you think this relationship is?

READ THE SELECTION: FIRST TIME

Read to get a general understanding of each section. Do not stop to look up words in the dictionary.

WOMEN IN THE WORKFORCE

1   A revolution in American society is taking place—the workplace is no longer a man's world. Today, 58 percent of the women of working age are in the workforce, compared to just 20 percent at the beginning of the twentieth century.

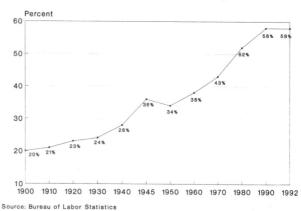

Women's Labor Force Participation Rate During the 20th Century

Source: Bureau of Labor Statistics

2   This revolution didn't happen overnight; in the United States, women's participation in the labor force has increased gradually in almost every decade since the beginning of the twentieth century. At that time, only 20 percent of all women age 14 and older worked. The large majority of these working women did not have husbands or children. Married women were not expected to work outside the home—and in fact only 4.5 percent of married women worked.

3   While women's participation in the labor force has been rising gradually throughout most of this century, there have been two periods when women joined the workforce in record numbers. The first period was during the 1940s when women were needed in America's wartime factories to replace the men who were off fighting World War II. Most of these new women workers were married and the expectation was that they would return home when the war ended. However, that didn't happen.

4   After this sudden wartime growth, the next two decades of the 1950s and 1960s saw a gradual growth in the percentage of women working outside the home. During the 1970s and 1980s, another record number of women joined the workforce. It is this more recent dramatic increase in women's labor force participation which has significantly altered the American workplace and the American family forever.

altered: changed

5   The American workplace and American family life have been altered because of the tremendous rise in the number of married women who work, and especially mothers with young children. In fact, between 1970 and 1988, the percentage of working women with children under the age of six rose from 30 to 56 percent. Today, more than one-half of all mothers with infants are working. Working mothers include both single-parent mothers who must work to support their children and mothers in two-parent families. Since 1970, the

number of mothers in two-parent families working or looking for work has jumped from 39 percent to 61 percent.

6   In earlier times, many women would have left the labor force when they married or had children. The fact that so many have continued to work after marriage and with young children has dramatically altered not only the role of American women, but also everyday family life. The experience of growing up in the United States is different for most children today as they spend more time in the care of adults other than their parents.

7   Women's increasing role in the paid workforce has resulted in conflicts between work and family life. These conflicts have appeared because most working mothers still have primary responsibility for taking care of the family, but few receive much financial support or emotional support to do so. Women who have entered high-paying professional fields, like law and medicine, can afford to pay for quality child care for their children. However, the vast majority of women are still stuck in lower-paying jobs in the service sector of the economy. For many of these women, finding quality child care at an affordable price is often a real struggle.

primary: the most important

quality: very good
service sector: part of the economy that provides services as compared to the manufacturing sector that produces goods

demographic: related to population patterns

WHY MORE WOMEN WORK

8   Undoubtedly, these changes in American families are the result of a complex combination of economic, demographic, and cultural factors.

9   For most of the twentieth century, American families' income has risen. However, wages began to stagnate during much

American Families' Income During 1970s and 1980s

Source: Economic Policy Institute

of the 1970s and 1980s. To make matters worse, inflation began to increase at a faster rate. Economists believe that the stagnation in wages combined with inflation have forced more women into the labor force in an effort to maintain their families' standard of living. They believe that if women had not entered the workforce in large numbers, family incomes would have declined. Even with more two-income families, family income for the 1980s grew at only one-fifth the rate of the 1960s and 1970s.

inflation: economic condition whereby the price of goods increases faster than wages
maintain: keep the same as before

10   The growth of the service economy has also most certainly played a role in the recent dramatic rise in women's participation in the labor force. Growth in the service sector of the economy has resulted in the creation of new jobs and a need for new workers. Since the job requirements of many new service jobs depend less on physical strength, women have been able to meet this need. Today, three-fourths of all new jobs are in service industries like retail sales, food services, and health care. In many of these industries, the labor force is predominately female.

11   Another strong economic factor that is pushing women into the labor force is rising educational levels. Further education enables women to have careers with higher pay and opportunities for promotion, not dead-end jobs. More women than men in this country have completed some college. Women make up half of the graduates of law and medical schools.

12   Demographic factors, like later marriages and declining birthrates, can also partly explain the dramatic increase in women's participation rates in the 1970s and 1980s. That's because unmarried women and married women with no children have higher labor force participation rates than do married women with children. So, changes in marriage patterns and birth patterns will result in higher percentages of women in the workforce. However, the most important demographic factor in recent years has been the rapid growth of single-parent families caused by rising divorce rates—a factor that has forced more women into the workforce as an economic necessity.

13   In addition to economic and demographic factors, cultural factors have also played a powerful role. The 1970s saw the formation of the women's movement. Women collectively demanded an end to sexual discrimination in the workplace. Largely as a result of this movement, the Civil Rights Act of 1964, which had originally been passed to protect the equal rights of blacks, was extended in the 1970s to include the rights of women in the workplace. The law protected women's rights to equal employment opportunities and equal pay, encouraging employers to hire and promote qualified women, including mothers.

qualified: having the knowledge and ability to do a job

14   Another equally important cultural factor was the change in social attitudes, making it more acceptable for women to work, including mothers. In fact, it became socially fashionable for women to work outside the home. This new attitude of the 1970s was clearly reflected in a magazine advertisement of a woman in a business suit holding a child in one arm and a briefcase in the other. The message was that women could do it all.

15   Husbands accepted their new role because women, despite their lower earnings, added significantly to family incomes. Wives working full-time contributed 40 percent of family income on average in 1986.

WORKING WOMEN IN THE 1990s

16   What does the picture look like for the 1990s? Labor economists predict that women will continue to enter the workforce at about the same rate and that 61 percent of all women of working age will be in the workforce by the year 2000. However, in the first two years of the 1990s, the percentage of the nation's working-age women in the labor force has leveled off at about 58 percent.

recession: period of reduced business activity; a slow down in the economy

17   Most labor experts believe this leveling off is due to the recession in the economy. They expect that women's labor force participation rates will begin to climb again after the recession ends. However, others believe that women's participation in the labor force has leveled off because this society gives women primary responsibility for child care but does not provide them with support in the form of child-care assistance.

assistance: help

re-examine: think carefully about something again

18   It is clear that women in the 1990s are beginning to re-examine their roles as mother and worker. Women no longer believe they can do it all. Although

women feel the need to balance work and family responsibilities, many believe that employers and husbands are being only superficially supportive as they try to achieve this balance—causing high levels of stress. Recent books on child development suggest that home-rearing may be more important for infants—causing mothers to reconsider returning to work early. Moreover, the failure to develop an adequate supply of affordable, quality child-care centers in this country, despite the growing demand, is a serious obstacle for many mothers who want to work.

home-rearing: caring for a child at home by the mother

19   However, most mothers must work out of economic necessity, and persistent economic pressures will probably draw women back into the labor force when the economy recovers from the recession. Besides, women's continued strong participation in the labor force in the 1990s and in the twenty-first century is critical. The nation needs to retain a highly skilled, productive workforce in order to rebuild its economic strength.

recovers: gets better; improves

retain: keep; avoid losing

20   In contrast to other industrialized countries, family and work responsibilities are not tightly linked in the United States. A mother is a worker at work and a mother at home. Employers need to help women to better balance the needs of work and the family—providing flexible work schedules and on-site child care.

on-site: provided by the company in the workplace
adopting policies: establishing programs or laws

21   Government must take a major responsibility in adopting policies that invest in our nation's workforce and its children. Child care is considered a public responsibility in many European countries, Canada, and Israel. In this country, the Child-Care Assistance Act was passed in 1990, providing states with funds for child-care assistance. Although very modest, these funds are used to help low-income families pay for child care, to increase the supply of community child-care centers, and to improve the quality of child care by providing training for care-givers. However, this is just a starting point. Much more needs to be done and we can look to other industrialized countries for models of effective family policies.

modest: not very large
funds: money for a special purpose

22   Working mothers need the peace of mind to work away from home.

READING CHECK

A. Marginal Notes

Marginal notes are brief notes that tell what the topics or important points are in the reading. You write these notes in the margin of the reading selection to help you recall what information is found in the reading. Marginal notes help you to study. They are especially helpful when the reading does not have headings.

Look over the ten marginal notes on the next page. Write them in the margin of the reading next to the paragraph that relates to the marginal note. If the marginal note relates to more than one paragraph, draw an arrow down (↓) to indicate this. Not all paragraphs will have notes. The notes are listed in random order.

MARGINAL NOTES

two periods of record participation	who new women workers are
three economic factors	2 cultural factors
women's participation in 1990s and future	3 demographic factors
2 reasons for leveling off	role of employers and government in assisting working mothers
3 reasons why re-examining roles as mother and worker	mothers and economy: need each other

B. Guessing the Meaning from Context

Look carefully at the context of the underlined words below. Try to guess their meaning. Identify the context clue(s) and be prepared to explain your answer. If necessary, refer to **Appendix 2: Vocabulary Strategies for Unfamiliar Words.**

1. Economists believe that the stagnation in wages combined with inflation have forced more women into the labor force in an effort to maintain their families' standard of living. They believe that if women had not entered the workforce in large numbers, family incomes would have <u>declined</u>. **(P9)**

   DECLINED _____Turn or slope downward_____
   context clue(s):

2. Further education enables women to consider careers with higher pay and opportunities for promotion, not <u>dead-end</u> jobs. **(P11)**

   DEAD-END _____No Exit_____
   context clue(s):

3. Although women feel the need to balance work and family responsibilities, many believe that employers and husbands are being only <u>superficially</u> supportive as they try to achieve this balance—causing high levels of stress. **(P18)**

   SUPERFICIALLY _____relating to what is only apparent_____
   context clue(s):

4. Women's continued strong participation in the labor force in the 1990s is <u>critical</u>. The nation needs to retain a highly skilled, productive workforce in order to rebuild its economic strength. **(P19)**

   CRITICAL _____inclined to critticize_____
   context clue(s):

5. Although very modest, these funds are used to help low-income families pay for child care, to increase the supply of community child-care centers, and to improve the quality of child care by providing training for care-givers. **(P21)**

CARE-GIVERS_____

context clue(s):

READ THE SELECTION: SECOND TIME

Read more carefully to get a better understanding of each section. Use the dictionary, only if necessary.

COMPREHENSION EXERCISES

A. True or False

Write true or false and the number of the paragraph(s) that supports your answer. Be prepared to explain your answer.

___True_/_1___ 1. There is a revolution taking place in the American workplace.

T ___Fals_/_~~8~~ 4___ 2. During the 1970s and 1980s, there was a large increase in the number of working mothers with pre-school children.

___False_/_~~8~~ 5___ 3. Mothers who work are mostly single-parent mothers.

False ~~True~~_/_~~7~~ 4. Finding affordable, quality child care is not a problem.

~~False~~ ~~True~~_/_False 10 5. Economic factors alone are responsible for the recent rise in women's labor force participation.

False ~~~~True~~~~_/_14 6. Society has changed its attitude toward wives working, *xã hội* *thần tình* but it still disapproves of mothers who work. *không thích*

___True_/_15___ 7. Husbands approve of their wives' new role.

___False_/_16___ 8. Today, women are reconsidering their ability to cope *deal with* with their two jobs: mother and worker.

F ~~True~~_/_20 9. The writer believes that companies are providing adequate child-care assistance.

T ~~False~~_/_21 10. The U.S. government is the leader in terms of providing child-care assistance for its citizens.

B. Chart

In recent decades, a record number of women have entered the workforce because of a combination of factors. Complete the chart by listing the general factors. Also list the specific factors that relate to each of the general factors. Then answer the questions below.

WHY MORE WOMEN WORK

General Factors

1. Economic

2. _____

3. _____

Specific Factors

a. Stagnation in wages during the 1970s and 1980s combined with inflation

b. _____

c. _____

a. Later marriages

b. _____

c. _____

a. The women's movement of the 1970s

b. _____

_____

■ Select one of the general factors and discuss the specific factors that relate to it.

■ Can you think of other reasons for the dramatic rise in the number of working women?

_____

_____

C. Listing

Make two lists to show how these important points in the reading are developed or explained. Be as brief as possible. Include a heading with each list.

1. Women used to think they could be mothers and also work outside the home. They are now beginning to think differently. List three reasons for the change in women's attitudes. Then circle the reason the writer believes is most responsible for this change.

(Heading) _____

_____

_____

_____

_____

_____

2. The Child-Care Assistance Act addresses three general child-care concerns. They are the supply of child-care centers, the quality of care provided at such centers, and their cost. List the specific way that the act addresses each of these concerns.

(Heading) _____

_____

_____

_____

_____

TOPICS FOR DISCUSSION AND WRITING

1. Working mothers admit that they spend less time with their children than mothers did in the past. However, they believe that they spend more "quality time" with their children. Explain this expression and give an example. Which do you think is more important: the quantity or the quality of time parents spend with their children? Explain.

2. In this country, motherhood is changing, and so is fatherhood. Give examples of how fatherhood is changing. What do you think are the reasons for this change? In your country, is fatherhood much the same today as a few decades ago? Explain.

3. The writer views employer child-care assistance and government child-care assistance as "an investment in today's workers and tomorrow's." Explain why you think she feels this way.

4. You can learn a lot about American culture and American family life from cartoons in the newspaper. *Sally Forth* is about the life of a typical working wife and mother. Look at the cartoon below. What is its message? Do you also see a more subtle (not-so-obvious) message? Check the newspaper for *Sally Forth* and other cartoons about the American family and share them with the class.

SALLY FORTH GREG HOWARD

VOCABULARY EXERCISES

A. Word Forms

Choose the correct word form that completes each sentence. The base form of the word is in **bold.** For nouns, use singular or plural forms. For verbs, use appropriate verb tenses and passive voice where necessary.

(P2)   1. participation, participant *n*   **to participate** *v*

     a. In the past, most women who _____participate_____ in the labor force were single women.

     b. Women's _____participation_____ in the workforce rose dramatically during World War II.

     c. Those two women were active _____participants_____ in the women's movement of the 1970s.

(P4)   2. **dramatic** *adj*   dramatically *adv*

   a. The number of working mothers with children under the age of six has increased ___dramatically___ .

   b. As a result, ___dramatic___ changes have taken place in everyday family life.

(P7)   3. **to afford** *v*   affordable *adj*

   a. Only large companies can ___afford___ to establish on-site child-care centers for their employees' children.

   b. As the supply of child-care centers increases, child care should become more ___affordable___ .

(P12)   4. necessity *n*   **necessary** *adj*

   a. Two incomes are increasingly becoming an economic ___necessity___ for most American families.

   b. The writer believes it is ___necessary___ to retain a highly skilled and productive workforce in order to rebuild the economic strength of this country.

(P17)   5. assistance, assistant *n*   **to assist** *v*

   a. As the ___assistance___ to the director of a highly respected child-care center, the woman develops educational and recreational programs.

   b. In Sweden, the government provides child-care ___to assistant___ , giving mothers the peace of mind to work away from home.

   c. The writer believes that more must be done in this country to ___assist___ working parents.

B. Other Useful Words

Complete the sentences with an appropriate word chosen from the list. For nouns, use singular or plural forms. For verbs, use appropriate verb tenses.

inflation **(P9)**
recession **(P17)**
single-parent family **(P12)**
standard of living **(P9)**
two-income family **(P9)**

to adopt policies **(P21)**
to alter **(P4)**
to level off **(P16)**
to recover **(P19)**
to retain **(P19)**
to stagnate **(P9)**

modest **(P21)**

1. The rise in the divorce rate has led to the rise in the number of _____two-income family_____.

2. In recent decades, wages _____to stagnate_____, causing more married women to seek employment to help maintain the family's _____standard of living_____.

3. The traditional American family was a one-income family, but the new American family is increasingly a _____modest_____.

4. For many American workers, salaries have not kept up with _____single-parent family_____

5. During a period of economic growth, labor force participation increases, but during a _____inflation_____, participation _____recession_____ and may even drop.

6. When is the economy expected to _____recover_____?

7. Why has the government provided only _____to adopt policies_____ funds for child-care assistance?

8. The tremendous rise in the number of working mothers _____to alter_____ American family life and the American workplace.

9. The writer believes companies should _____level off_____ to help working parents, like providing flexible work schedules.

10. By supporting working mothers, companies will be able to _____retain_____ these highly skilled and productive workers.

C. Vocabulary Oral Practice

Practice using the underlined words by answering the questions below.

1. Taking a vacation can be quite expensive. What are some ways to make a vacation more <u>affordable</u>? (**P7**)

2. In your culture, does the husband or wife have the <u>primary responsibility</u> for the following tasks: earning money to support the family, managing the family budget, disciplining the children, doing the shopping, maintaining the yard and the car? Give an example of a shared responsibility. (**P7**)

3. When someone sets a world <u>record</u>, for example, climbs the highest mountain or eats the largest ice-cream cone, this person's name is published in <u>The Guinness Book of Records</u>. Imagine that the name of the classmate who sits next to you is in this book. Tell the class what world <u>record</u> he or she has set. (**P3**)

4. You have just won $50,000 and have decided to <u>invest</u> this money. What would be a good, yet safe <u>investment</u>? (**P21**)

5. As a mayor, it is your responsibility to decide how city <u>funds</u> will be used to improve your city. Because the <u>funds</u> are modest, you can only make two improvements. Decide what they will be. (**P21**)

6. To provide students with a <u>quality</u> education, what must a college have? List the essential characteristics. (**P7**)

7. <u>Divorce</u> is on the rise in many cultures. What is your attitude toward <u>divorce</u>? Is your attitude today the same as it has always been? What factors have influenced your attitude? (**P12**)

8. You must make a decision about which employee to promote: Mr. X, who has been with the company for two years, is very <u>productive</u>, and will probably be a top employee in the future, or Mr. Y, who has been with the company for ten years, has steadily performed well, but is not quite as <u>productive</u>. Decide which employee you will promote and explain why. (**P19**)

D. Dictation

Study the spelling of the words in the previous vocabulary exercises. You will have a dictation of sentences that contain these words.

Topic 1

Do you think educated mothers with young children should remain in the workplace or leave the workforce until their children grow up? Explain the reasons for your opinion.

Topic 2

When couples decide to raise their children themselves, it is most often the wives that stay at home. Although it is not common, there are some fathers today who decide to stay at home and raise the children. Their wives take on the primary responsibility of earning the money. Write your opinion of this switch in roles. Give reasons why you think it is a good or a bad idea, including its effects on the children.

COMMUNICATIVE ACTIVITY   Opinion Poll

In this activity, you will take an opinion poll to find out Americans' opinions about family and work issues. You may choose one of the issues below or one of your own. After you take the poll, you will report your results to the class.

Issues:

■ A mother with pre-school children should stay at home rather than work outside the home.

■ It's not good for a wife to earn more money than her husband.

■ When both the husband and wife work full-time, they should divide the family responsibilities fifty-fifty.

■ Working mothers have the same commitment to their jobs as women without children.

■ Fathers can take as good care of their children as mothers can.

■ Staying at home to care for the children is an acceptable social role for fathers.

Procedure:

1. Divide into pairs (or small groups). With your partner(s), express your opinion on the issues. Then decide which issue your group will study or select one of your own.

2. Together write a few questions on the issue for the poll. Also decide what background information to get on the persons being polled, for example, their sex, age group, marital status, with or without children.

3. With your partner(s), ask five people the questions. After completing each interview, take notes on the person's responses.

4. On poster paper, make a chart of the background information on the persons polled. Choose a classmate from each pair (or small group) to report the results to the class. Write the results on the board. Also discuss the group's reaction to the poll.

LECTURE   **Companies Respond to Child-Care Needs**

In the previous reading on "Mothers at Work: The New American Family," the author points out that today's working women face conflicts in trying to balance work and family responsibilities. Because of these difficulties, she urges employers "to help women to better balance the needs of work and the family." As the title of the lecture indicates, companies are responding to the child-care needs of their employees. The central focus of this lecture is to examine various ways in which companies are helping working mothers.

LISTENING STRATEGY

In this lecture, three major points are discussed. They are various reasons why companies are responding to child-care needs, various ways in which companies are helping, and the estimated number of companies that are responding. Listen for these points in the introduction.

In explaining the second major point, the speaker lists specific ways in which companies can help working mothers. These specific ways or types of help are grouped under two general categories. Listen for these two categories and the specific types of help listed under each category.

TERMS USED IN THE LECTURE*

employee performance   *not be the same*   information and referral service

social responsibility   flexible work policies

child-care benefits   flexible time schedules

child-care assistance   flexible workplace policy   *another day you want to go off site or at home*

day-care programs   *pre-school*   flexible work hours   *work*

on-site day-care center   *the same place*   flexible leave policy   *time of from work*

near-site day-care center   *not in the same place*   cost sharing   *leave the accept*

private day-care center   *same place*   job sharing   *the job*

community day-care center   telecommuting   *telephone*

by government

* These terms are defined or made clear from context in the lecture.

NOTETAKING SHEET

1. Listen to the lecture. Follow the outline below as you listen. Do not write anything at this time.

2. Listen again and complete the outline by adding the important points from the lecture and some explanation. Write only key words or phrases. After the lecture, compare your notes with a classmate's. You may want to listen to the lecture again to confirm any points that you missed.

3. After completing your notes, discuss them with the class.

Outline of Lecture on

Companies Respond to Child-Care Needs

1. First Major Point: Companies' Reasons

    a. Primary reason:_____

        ■ Recently companies hiring many _____

        ■ Women play double role: _____ and

           _____ = conflict

- If working mothers don't have help with child care, this can result in a drop in employee _____ which can affect company _____

- If companies help, employees can _____ _____ and in the long run companies can _____

b. _____

- Both qualified women and _____

- Young, educated people interested in _____

c. _____

- If companies are concerned about workers and _____, companies are more respected and more _____

- By offering child care, companies carry out a _____

2. Second Major Point: Ways in Which Companies Are Helping

a. General Category 1: _____

- Age of child: _____

- Not a babysitting service because _____ _____

Three Types:

(1) On-site day-care centers

Location of center: _____

Desirable because _____ _____

Type of company: _____

(2) _____

Type of company: _____

Location of center: _____

(3) _____

    Type of company: _____

    Not a day-care program

    Service provides:

    ■ List of names of either _____

       _____

    ■ _____

    ■ Qualifications of staff members

    ■ _____

    Who pays for on- and near-site centers:

    _____

    _____

b. General Category 2: Flexible work policies

    ■ Age of child: _____

    ■ Example: _____

    Two Types:

    (1) _____

    ■ Flexible work hours

       tries to match _____

    ■ Flexible _____

       _____

    ■ _____

    ■ _____

    Advantages of job sharing and part-time work:

    _____

    _____

    (2) Flexible Workplace Policy (Telecommuting)

    ■ Place of work: _____

    ■ Communicates by: _____

    ■ Type of work: _____

    Advantage of telecommuting: _____

    _____

3. Third Major Point: Estimated Number of Companies Responding

About 8 % on- or near-site day-care centers

_____ % information and referral service

_____ % cost sharing (for on- and near-site)

_____ % flexible hours (including flexible leave)

_____ % job sharing

_____ % part-time work

_____ % telecommuting

To improve this response: _____

_____

DISCUSSION QUESTIONS

1. A working mother with young children sometimes decides on working part-time or job-sharing rather than stopping work completely. What are the benefits of her decision to stay in the workforce, especially if she is a career or professional woman?

2. Offering child-care programs costs money for a company, but it also saves money for a company. Explain how child-care programs can save money for a company.

3. What are the benefits of an on-site day-care center for the working mother and the company?

4. Is a flexible workplace policy possible for all working mothers? Explain your answer.

5. When a mother works in your country, who takes care of her children? Does the government or do companies provide child-care assistance?

6. Discuss the idea of the social responsibility of a company. Do companies have a responsibility to society? Or can companies carry on their business without responsibility for the social, educational, or health concerns of the community and world outside their doors? Explain.

BIOGRAPHICAL SKETCH:
BILL COSBY (1937–   )

Bill Cosby is America's favorite TV dad. He has also written a best-selling book called *Fatherhood* about his own children, namely his four daughters and one son. In his book, which was published in 1986, he shares with readers the warm and funny experiences of being a father. His book is often given as a present on Father's Day.

Before you read about one of his experiences as a father, it's important to learn more about Bill Cosby himself. Cosby rose from a childhood of poverty to become one of America's favorite humorists. Born in Philadelphia in 1937, Cosby developed his well-known sense of humor as a way of coping with life's hardships. As a young boy, he would shine shoes while his mother worked 12 hours a day to keep the family together after his father abandoned them.

In school, however, Cosby preferred being the class clown rather than a serious student. He had little motivation to study. Eventually, he dropped out of school in the 11th grade to join the Navy. Cosby finally completed high school during his four years in the Navy and then won an athletic scholarship to Temple University in 1961. A year later, however, he left college to make it in the world of comedy.

In 1963, he released his first comedy record, and in 1965, he became the first African-American to star in a dramatic television series for which he won an Emmy Award. Cosby has since dominated the television industry with hit films, comedy specials, cartoons, and children's programs. With *The Cosby Show*, he became the "king of comedy."

To top off these accomplishments, Cosby returned to school and earned a doctorate in education from the University of Massachusetts in 1976. He has been a longtime supporter of education, and in particular, of reading. In 1988, he made the largest financial contribution ever to a black college. Indeed, Bill Cosby is respected not only for his talent as a comedian but also for his dedication to educating himself and others.

Line

sect: religious group

1   Buying a stereo is merely a father's practice for the Big Buy: a car. When his child requests a car, a father will wish that he were a member of some sect that hasn't gone beyond the horse.

      "Dad, all my friends say I should have my own car," the boy says earnestly
5   one day.

      "Wonderful. When are they going to buy it?"

      "No, Dad. They think that you and Mom should buy me the car."

      "Is there any particular reason why we should?"

      "Well, that's what parents *do*."

10   "Not *all* parents. Did Adam and Eve get Abel a car? And he was the *good* one. Tell me this: why do you *need* a car?"

      "To go places by myself."

      "Well, you'd be surprised how many people manage to do that on public transportation. Elderly *ladies* do it every day. It's called a bus and I'd be happy to

token: coin, used
instead of money, to
travel on buses

15   buy you a token. I won't even wait for your birthday."

      "Dad, *you* know a bus isn't cool. My friends say I shouldn't have to ride on a bus now that I'm sixteen."

      "They say that? Well, they couldn't be *good* friends because buses are so much fun. They expand your social circle. You meet new people every three

20   blocks."

      "That's cute, Dad."

      "I know you don't go particularly deep in math, but do you happen to know what a car costs?"

      "I'll get a *used* one."

lottery: contest

25   "Terrific. And then we'll have a family lottery to try to guess the day it will break down."

      "Okay, *slightly* used."

      "Which is slightly more or less than five thousand dollars, not counting insurance."

30   "Insurance?"

      "You getting some used insurance too?"

      "I'll drive it real carefully."

      "And there's a chance you will," you say, suddenly picturing people all over town bouncing off your son's fenders.

35   "Dad, I just *have* to have a car. Say, what about *yours*? Then you could buy yourself a *new* one. Dad, you *deserve* a new car."

ploy: trick

      "That's very thoughtful, son," you say, now having heard the ploy you've been expecting.

      "Think nothing of it, Dad."

40   And so, the moment has come for you to gently remind your son precisely

worthless: without
money
bruising his ego: hurt-
ing his sense of pride

how worthless he currently is—without bruising his ego, of course.

"You see," you tell him, "the thing is that unless a wonderful offer came in last night, you have no job. You are sixteen years old, you have no job, and you have an excellent chance of failing the eleventh grade."

creaming: doing very well

45 "Not *Driver's Ed!* I'm *creaming* that!"

"I'm happy to hear it. You'll go on to college—if we can find one in Baja California—and you'll major in Driver's Ed. Maybe you'll get your M.A. in Toll Booths and even your Ph.D. in Grease and Lube."

toll booths: places where drivers stop to pay a fee to use a road or bridge

grease and lube: putting oil on engine parts so they move better

"Dad, I wish you wouldn't keep bringing up school. I'm just not motivated."

50 "To improve your mind, that is. But you *are* motivated to get a car. The bus may not go to the unemployment office."

"Come on, Dad; *you* know what a car means. I need it to *go* places."

"Like a fast-food joint, where your career will be. Because with the grades you have right now, if you somehow *do* happen to be graduated from high school, which the Vatican will declare a miracle, you'll be competing with only ten million others for the job of wrapping cheeseburgers."

Vatican: symbol of the leader of the Catholic church

55

"Dad, I'd love to talk more about my career, but I gotta tell you something really exciting that's gonna change your mind: I just saw an ad for a sensational sixty-nine Mustang."

60 "Really? How much?"

"Just two thousand dollars."

"Just two thousand dollars. Did you happen to ask if it had an engine? And are brakes optional?"

optional: free to decide to have or not to have

"Dad, I can't understand why you're being so unreasonable."

65 "That's what fathers are. It's one of the qualifications."

"But my friends keep saying I should *have* a car."

"And they certainly have the right to buy you one. I'll tell you what: how's *this* for reasonable? Bring your friends over here and we'll have a collection, a matching funds collection. Whatever you get from them, I'll match it."

winds up: ends up

70 The boy winds up with ninety-six cents.

COMPREHENSION QUESTIONS

1. For teens, like Cosby's son, a car is a symbol. What does a car symbolize for teens? What else symbolizes this for teens?

2. What does Cosby's son say to try to change his dad's mind about letting him have a car?

3. When does Cosby think it is appropriate for teens (his son included) to have their own car?

4. In the end, Cosby agreed to help his son buy a car by having a "matching funds collection." Explain what this is. How much did his son collect from his friends? How much did Cosby contribute to the fund? What lesson was Cosby hoping to teach his son?

1. Based on what you have learned about Cosby's life, do you think Cosby sees a little bit of himself in his son? Explain.

2. When Cosby asked his son why he should buy him a car, his son responded: "That is what parents do." How much responsibility do you think parents have to provide for the *needs* of their children?

3. Because independence is highly valued in American culture, parents try to develop a sense of independence in their children, starting at an early age. In your culture, is independence valued as much? At what age are young people expected to begin to be independent? How do they develop a sense of independence?

Cartoon

"Of course I know the value of a dollar, Dad—that's why I'm asking for twenty."

The expression *the value of a dollar* has two meanings: how much you can buy for a dollar or how much you must work to earn a dollar. When the father asks his son if he knows "the value of a dollar," what does the son think his father means? What is the father really asking his son? How can young people learn the value of a dollar?

CHAPTER 8

WHEN TEENAGERS WORK

Not only have mothers joined the workforce in record numbers, but so have their teenage sons and daughters. In the past, many American teens worked only during the summer months. However, today a growing number are working year-round.

This reading is taken from a book entitled *When Teenagers Work*. Its authors, Dr. Ellen Greenberger and Dr. Laurence Steinberg, are adolescent psychologists who have conducted research on student workers. They have studied the reasons why teens work, the kind of work they do, and the effects working has on their growth and development. This study, which was conducted at four high schools in Orange County, California, included teens of diverse ethnic and socio-economic backgrounds.

PRE-READING DISCUSSION

Getting into the Topic

■ In your country, do some teens work during the summer? As a teenager, did you ever have a summer job or think about getting one?

■ Do teens in your country work during the school year? If not, why not?

Getting an Overview of the Reading Selection

Scan the reading to complete the headings in the outline.

WHEN TEENAGERS WORK

1.

2.

3.

■ Why do you think American teenagers want to work?

■ Do you think working has positive and/or negative effects on their development? Explain.

READ THE SELECTION: FIRST TIME

Read to get a general understanding of each section. Do not stop to look up words in the dictionary.

READING

When Teenagers Work

1   Adolescence in American society has changed dramatically over the past forty years. In increasing numbers, adolescents have entered the workplace, holding part-time jobs after school that consume a substantial part of their afternoons, school nights, and weekends. The large teenage, part-time labor force that works at fast-food restaurants and waits on customers in retail stores has become a familiar scene. By graduation time, 80 percent of the teens between the ages of fourteen and eighteen will have held a job during the school year at some point during their high-school career. A large proportion of them work 20 hours per week, and most are not from economically disadvantaged families, but are middle-class.

2   In most industrialized countries of Europe and Asia, the worlds of school and work are still quite separate. Many high-school students from these countries work during the summer months, but relatively few work during the school year. The more modest teenage labor force participation in these parts of the world is the result of several factors: social priorities, the educational system, and economic conditions.

social priorities: what a society feels is most important

3   In some European and Asian countries, the government contributes to the cost of a student's education. In these countries, education is the top social priority and students may be actually restricted or even prohibited from working. Moreover, social norms concerning the responsibilities of parents dictate that parents provide for the total needs of their children while they are in school.

curriculum: program of study

4   Because of these social priorities, the educational system in Europe and Asia is more demanding. Students have longer school days, more homework, and a more difficult curriculum. The average Japanese student knows more mathematics than ninety-nine out of one hundred comparable American high-school students. Not only is the educational system in these parts of the world more demanding, but also Europeans and Asians place a far greater emphasis than we do on early educational achievement. There are fewer openings in higher levels of the educational system, and these openings go to the top students—often identified by examination scores of students as young as twelve or fourteen. Early school performance has serious consequences for later life possibilities. In such a case, even if opportunities existed for these teens to work, one imagines that youngsters and their parents would consider very carefully becoming involved in an activity that might affect their school performance.

educational achievement: success in school

5   In contrast, the educational system in the United States is less demanding, more "spacious," and more forgiving. Opportunities for higher education are numerous in this country and are not limited to superior students. Mediocre or even poor early school performance does not close the door on the possibility of obtaining a university education. There are even open-enrollment universities that require only that students have a high-school diploma and where students are not turned down because of the quality of their earlier educational achievement. Under such conditions, youngsters who for any reason are late bloomers still may hope to become accountants, lawyers, and doctors.

6   In addition to social and educational factors, economic conditions may also not allow for the development of an adolescent labor force. The most essential economic condition for an adolescent workforce is the opportunity for part-time work. Such opportunities are typically more abundant in the service and retail sectors of the economy. Countries with the most developed service and retail sectors, namely the United States and Canada, now have the largest proportion of student workers. To give the issue a more concrete example, there are more McDonalds in the state of Illinois than in all of Italy.

abundant: in large supply

BAD JOBS FOR ADULTS—GOOD JOBS FOR ADOLESCENTS

7   Although new service and retail jobs were added to the U.S. economy in record number, most of these jobs are "bad" jobs for adults. They are characterized by less than full-time hours of employment, nighttime and weekend work, low wages, and poor opportunities for promotion and pay increases. However, these "bad" jobs for adults are, in some important ways, "good" jobs for school-going youngsters—or if not "good," at least acceptable, and even attractive.

8   Obviously, part-time work is unacceptable to adults who must support themselves and often others as well. However, such jobs are almost the only ones that are possible for a school-going youngster. Similarly, night and week-

end employment is likely to interfere with other responsibilities of adults. Yet many of the new service and retail jobs require such "off-hours." Such jobs are mostly located in the suburbs, and people are most likely to utilize these services after they get home from work or on weekends.

9   The effect of low wages on adults' lives is equally obvious. Unlike adults, most school-going teenagers can afford to work at the minimum wage, because they are subsidized by their parents. Most youngsters do not have to pay the rent or food bills. They do not work to support themselves or others but to earn spending money (and spend they do). In fact, research strongly shows that the relatively low wages most teenagers earn are not a major source of discontent. Finally, adults who seek employment typically consider the likelihood of promotion and pay increases. Since most teenagers do not expect to continue in these part-time jobs after they graduate from high school, these future-oriented aspects of a job tend to be far less important. In short, the same jobs which labor economists criticize because they do not offer high-quality employment to adults meet many of the needs of teenagers.

criticize: speak negatively about

WHY TEENAGERS WANT TO WORK

10   But American high-school students are not only working because there are plenty of part-time jobs available. Inflation has also been a major economic incentive. The cost of being an adolescent has risen steadily—even more steadily than the rate of inflation. An article in *The Wall Street Journal* reported that fifteen items frequently purchased by teens cost 38 percent more during a period when the overall rate of inflation rose just 26 percent. Despite this "kidflation," allowances have stayed more or less the same for several years. Parents tend to give their fourteen-year-old daughter the same allowance her older sis-

allowance: money parents give regularly to their children, like a wage

ter received when she was fourteen, three years earlier. Moreover, the money earned from informal jobs typically held by youngsters, such as babysitting, have not kept up with inflation. Inflation, combined with the thoughts of having a "fixed income," clearly have developed adolescents' interest in entering the labor force.

11   In addition to "kidflation" and the desire to have a "fixed income," young people appear to have developed an inflated interest in luxury goods. We can see designer clothing in the closets not just of adults but also teens. There are fewer old cars in the school parking lot; many are up-to-date models of automobiles that look just like—or better than—our own. The list of other high-priced items advertised on TV and directed at the youth market is a long one: electronic games, twelve-speed racing bicycles, portable tape recorders, and stereophonic equipment for the home or the car are but a few of the more popular objects of teenage consumption. These new and expensive tastes are likely to have motivated youngsters to earn more spending money of their own. There is a limit to what parents will, or can be expected to, provide for their children.

THE EFFECTS OF WORKING ON ADOLESCENT DEVELOPMENT

12   Our study of teens at four high schools in Orange County, California shows that school-year employment can have an effect on schoolwork. Students who work, especially long hours, do not perform as well in class. Teachers complain that they have had to cut back on home assignments. Because students are investing less time in their education, teachers are investing less time in classroom preparation and instruction. Thus, intensive part-time employment during the school year may affect young people's education, which can eventually affect their long-run occupational success and life satisfaction.

13   Our study also revealed that intensive work leads to increased use of alcohol and marijuana, especially when jobs are stressful. Adolescence itself is a difficult period of social and psychological development, but for youngsters who must balance family and school with work, adolescence can be particularly stressful. Thus, kids who work long hours under stressful conditions use alcohol or drugs more frequently, just like an adult who comes home from a hard day at work and makes himself a drink.

14   We observed that the type of work adolescents do does little to prepare them for the adult workforce. The typical adolescent job—food service or retail—is, for the most part, totally different from the type of work youngsters will do in the future. There is little opportunity for decision-making, problem-solving, or self-management. More importantly, because many of these jobs are routine and unchallenging, instead of promoting a respect for work, they may cause teens to develop a negative attitude toward work.

15   In addition, since these part-time service and retail jobs are "bad" jobs for adults, teens are most likely working side by side with other teens rather than with people of a different generation who could serve as teachers, models of adult roles, and helpers in times of stress. Because of this lack of intergenerational contact, teens may become overly attached to their own peer culture, which can slow down their transition to adulthood.

introspection: examination of one's own thoughts and feelings
overcommitted to: spending too much time and effort
profit from: benefit from

16   Our studies also show that adolescent work does not encourage wise spending and saving; instead it encourages luxury spending. Over 80 percent of high school seniors who work, save "none" or only "a little" of their earnings. Money earned and saved during the later years of high school could be used, of course, to help finance further education and to help establish an independent household. The failure of youngsters to save, therefore, also slows down their transition to adulthood.

17   But probably our biggest concern about intensive employment during adolescence is that it may take valuable time away from the unpaid work of growing up. Growing up requires exploration, experimentation, and introspection. When teens are overcommitted to work, this can deprive them of the time needed for such activities.

18   But for adolescents who work, we need to consider what makes for "better" work. We believe most youths can profit from good work experience in suitable amounts, but none will profit from an overdose of low-quality work experience. We must pay attention not only to the type of work teens do, but also to the amount of time they spend working. If we don't their jobs may make them economically rich, but may also make them psychologically poor.

READING CHECK

A. Marginal Notes

Look over the following 12 marginal notes. Write them in the margin of the reading next to the paragraph that relates to the marginal note. If a marginal note relates to more than one paragraph, draw an arrow down (↓) to indicate this. Not all paragraphs will have notes. The notes are listed in random order.

MARGINAL NOTES

dramatic change in adolescence	economic factor
3 factors for modest employment in other industrial countries	poor wages + little promotion and pay increases
social factors	affects schoolwork
4 economic reasons for working	doesn't prepare teens for adult workforce + may cause them to develop negative attitude toward work
part-time + off-hours	
their recommendation	
	encourages luxury spending
educational factors	

B. Guessing the Meaning from Context

Look carefully at the context of the underlined words below. Try to guess their meaning. Identify the context clue(s) and be prepared to explain your answer. If necessary, refer to **Appendix 2: Vocabulary Strategies for Unfamiliar Words.**

1. A large proportion of teens work 20 hours per week, and most are not from economically disadvantaged families, but are middle-class. **(P1)**

    ECONOMICALLY DISADVANTAGED _poor low income_
    context clue(s):

2. Opportunities for higher education are numerous in this country and are not limited to superior students. Mediocre or even poor early school performance does not close the door on the possibility of obtaining a university education. **(P5)**

    MEDIOCRE _just in the midle_
    context clue(s):

3. Night and weekend employment is likely to interfere with other responsibilities of adults. Yet many of the new service and retail jobs require such "off-hours." **(P8)**

    OFF-HOURS _____
    context clue(s):

4. Unlike adults, most school-going teenagers can afford to work at the minimum wage, because they are subsidized by their parents. Most youngsters do not have to pay the rent or food bills. They do not work to support themselves or others but to earn spending money (and spend they do). **(P9)**

    SUBSIDIZED _Supported_
    context clue(s):

5. Since part-time service and retail jobs are "bad" jobs for adults, teens are most likely working side by side with other teens rather than with people of a different generation who could serve as teachers, models of adult roles, and helpers in times of stress. Because of this lack of intergenerational contact, teens may become overly attached to their own peer culture, which can slow down their transition to adulthood. **(P15)**

    INTERGENERATIONAL _Contact between young or old people_
    context clue(s):

READ THE SELECTION: SECOND TIME

Read more carefully to get a better understanding of each section. Use the dictionary, only if necessary.

COMPREHENSION EXERCISES

A. Chart

The chart lists three general factors for the more modest teen employment in most industrialized countries of Europe and Asia. For each factor, a specific explanation(s) is given. Complete the chart. Then answer the questions below.

FACTORS FOR MORE MODEST TEEN EMPLOYMENT IN EUROPE AND ASIA

General Factors	Specific Explanations
1. Social	**a.** Government may restrict or prohibit students from working because education is the top priority
	b. _most important_
2. Educational	**a.** _success in school_
	b. Schools place a far greater emphasis on early educational achievement
3. _fixed income_	**a.** _increase by same speed._

■ In Europe and Asia, schools place a far greater emphasis on *early* educational achievement. What is the reason for this?

So that the children could get a job easily.

■ What do you think are the advantages and disadvantages of such an educational system?

The advantage is that the education gives the children a good life. The disadvantage is that you can't learn enough.

B. Terms with Special Meanings

As you know, words have different meanings in different contexts. Words have their common meaning(s) when used in everyday situations. However, the same words can also have a special, or more narrow, meaning when used in a particular context.

Take, for example, the word "star." The common meaning of *star* is a heavenly body that appears as a bright point in the sky. What does a "star" mean in the context of entertainment? In reading, it is important to understand the special meaning of words when used in a particular context. The five terms below have a special meaning. Analyze these terms.

1. **spacious (P5)**

   a lot a space

   a. What does the descriptive word "spacious" mean in the following context? This apartment is very *spacious*.
   b. The American system of higher education is more *spacious* than the higher education system of other countries. Explain what this means. Is this good or bad for American high-school students?

2. **forgiving (P5)**

   a. When would someone say to you, "I *forgive* you."?
   b. What does the American system of higher education "forgive" high-school students for doing or not doing?
   c. How does it show that it "forgives" them? What allows the American system of higher education to be more "forgiving" than the higher education system of other countries?

3. **late bloomers (P5)**

   the flower open

   a. What does the word "bloom" mean in the following context? Flowers *bloom* in the springtime.
   b. A child who talks several months before most other children begin to talk is an "early bloomer." Describe a student who is an "early bloomer" in high school.
   c. Now describe a student who is a "late bloomer" in high school. In this country, can a "late bloomer" one day be an accountant, lawyer, or doctor? Explain. Is this also common in your country?

4. **kidflation** (P10)

   a. Explain the economic term "inflation."
   b. A more specific kind of inflation is "kidflation." Explain this term, and if possible, give an example. What is the relationship between "kidflation" and the rise in the number of adolescent workers?

5. **overdose** (P18)

   a. An *overdose* is a medical term which refers to an excessive and often deadly amount of a drug. Tell which part of this term indicates an excessive amount.
   b. The writers believe that teens do not profit from an "overdose" of low-quality work experience. Explain what this means. Do you think the writers believe that teens may actually die as a result of working intensively? If not, then explain why the writers use such a strong term as an "overdose."

C. Listing

Make two lists to show how these important points in the reading are developed or explained. Be as brief as possible. Include a heading with each list.

1. Many of the new service and retail jobs are unacceptable to most adults seeking employment. List the reasons for this. Be prepared to discuss why these jobs are more acceptable to teens.

   (Heading) _____

   _____

   _____

   _____

   _____

   _____

2. List the reasons why many teens work year-round.

   (Heading) _____

   _____

   _____

   _____

   _____

D. Chart

The chart lists the two major findings of Drs. Greenberger and Steinberg's research on adolescent work and their effects on adolescent development. Complete the chart. Then answer the questions below.

DRS. GREENBERGER AND STEINBERG'S RESEARCH

**Two Major Findings on
Adolescent Work**

**Their Effects on
Adolescent Development**

1. Amount of time working is often too intensive

  a. _student don't learn enough when they are working._

  b. Causes teens to have more stress and thus to use more alcohol and marijuana

  c. _Students drop out of school to work early._

2. Type of work is often low quality

  a. _makes teens have lots of stress._

  b. Is often routine and unchallenging and thus can lead to a negative attitude toward work

  c. _Teens challeng the unchalleong atthiude._

■ In addition to these effects, Greenberger and Steinberg found that adolescent work encourages luxury spending, not saving. Learning how to save money is an important skill. Do you think you have learned to manage money well? If so, how did you learn this skill?

Yes you would have to learn manage money so that I could have a good life and I would do this by spend money on the stuffs that I need only.

■ In the reading, Greenberger and Steinberg state that they believe "most youths can profit from good work experience in suitable amounts." Based on the chart, what can you infer they think is necessary for high-quality work experience? Do you think these kinds of jobs are available to teens? Explain.

No because teens are not responsible enough.

TOPICS FOR DISCUSSION AND WRITING

1. Drs. Greenberger and Steinberg stress the importance of intergenerational contact. Do you think teens in your country have more intergenerational contact than American teens do? Explain the reason for this. Describe how intergenerational contact can affect adolescent development.

2. American teens are more "materialistic" today than in the past. What does this word mean? If you don't know, look it up in the dictionary. Who or what has caused them to become this way? List as many possible factors as you can.

3. Greenberger and Steinberg believe that school-related extracurricular activities provide a better opportunity for teens to explore and experiment. Give some examples of school-related extracurricular activities. Then select an extracurricular activity you have been involved in and explain how this activity has helped you to develop socially and/or psychologically.

4. Greenberger and Steinberg studied American high-school students. Conduct your own study of American college students to find out about their school-year employment:

   ■ whether they work, and if so

   ■ where they work (on-campus or off-campus)

   ■ what kind of work they do

   ■ how many hours a week they work

   ■ why they work

   ■ whether working has a positive or negative effect on their school performance and why

Take notes and be prepared to tell the class about what you have learned.

VOCABULARY EXERCISES

A. Word Forms

Choose the correct word form that completes each sentence. The base form of the word is in **bold**. For nouns, use singular or plural forms. For verbs, use appropriate verb tenses and passive voice where necessary.

(P1)   1.   adolescence, **adolescent** *n*   adolescent *adj*

    a.   Drs. Greenberger and Steinberg are _____adolescent_____ psychologists.

    b.   Why is _____adolescence_____ often a difficult time for both teens and their parents?

    c.   During this period, an _____adolescent_____ is gradually learning to become an adult.

(P9)   2.   criticism *n*   **to criticize** *v*   critical *adj*

    a.   Why are Greenberger and Steinberg so _____critical_____ of the typical job in the adolescent workforce?

    b.   They _____criticize_____ these jobs because they are often routine and unchallenging.

    c.   Despite this _____criticim_____, they believe teens can profit from a limited dose of high-quality work experience.

(P12)   3.   complaint *n*   **to complain** *v*

    a.   What _____complaint_____ did Greenberger and Steinberg hear most often from teachers whose students work intensively?

    b.   The young boy's boss _____complained_____ that he was talking too much to the young female customers and ignoring the other customers.

(P12)   **4. intensive** *adj*   intensively *adv*

     a. After studying ___intensively___ for his history test until 3 A.M., the student went to bed exhausted.

     b. Regular study during the semester rather than ___intensive___ study the night before a test is a better way of preparing for an important test.

(P17)   **5.** (over)commitment *n*   **to be (over)committed to** *v*

     a. Because the man ___committed to___ his job, his wife and children rarely got to see him.

     b. His ___committment___ to his job led to the breakup of his marriage.

B. Other Useful Words

Complete the sentences with an appropriate word from the list. For nouns, use singular or plural forms. For verbs, use appropriate verb tenses.

allowance **(P10)**   to keep up with **(P10)**   intergenerational **(P15)**
     to place a greater emphasis on **(P4)**   luxury **(P11)**
     to profit from **(P18)**   routine **(P14)**
     to slow down **(P15)**

   1. Some people believe it is more important to have good friends, while others _____ having material things.

   2. Does giving children an _____ encourage wise spending or _____ spending?

   3. Employers can turn a _____ job into an interesting learning experience for teens through job rotations.

   4. If teens do not learn how to save money, this can _____ their transition to adulthood.

   5. What kinds of work experience can teens _____ the most?

6. Even though some teens get an allowance, it has not _____ inflation.

7. Both adolescents and adults can mutually benefit from _____ contact.

C. Vocabulary Oral Practice

Practice using the underlined words by answering the questions below.

1. Who has been your most <u>demanding</u> teacher? Why do you consider this person <u>demanding</u>? Did you like this teacher? Did you learn a lot? **(P4)**

2. A person's life is full of <u>achievements</u>, some small and some major. Describe something important that you have <u>achieved</u> as a result of your own efforts. **(P4)**

3. Some parents encourage their children to improve their grades by offering money as an <u>incentive</u>. For example, for every A, they might give their children $25. Do you approve of offering money to children as an <u>incentive</u>? Why or why not? **(P10)**

4. What are some factors that can facilitate the <u>transition</u> from living in one's own culture to living in a different culture? **(P15)**

5. What is your country's <u>top</u> national <u>priority</u> at this time? Why is this issue so important? **(P3)**

D. Dictation

Study the spelling of the words in the previous vocabulary exercises. You will have a dictation of sentences that contain these words.

JOURNAL WRITING

Drs. Greenberger and Steinberg believe that young people need experiences that provide them with the opportunity to explore, experiment, and reflect upon themselves and their role in society. In your journal, write about an experience you had during your adolescence that provided you with such an opportunity. Also tell how you grew and developed socially and/or psychologically as a result of this experience.

AN AUTOBIOGRAPHY

You have read about the growing number of young people who now work in the United States and about their reasons for getting a job. Now let's look back to an earlier time in this country and consider the situation of a young boy who started working when he was eight. Let's learn the reasons why he worked. The young boy's name was Russell Baker.

This selection is taken from Russell Baker's autobiography, entitled *Growing Up*. Baker was born in 1925 and grew up during the days of the American Depression in the late 1920s and 1930s. His father died when he was young and his mother was responsible for raising the children. With love and determination, she encouraged her children, especially her son, Russell, to "make something" of themselves. She wanted her children to work hard and succeed in life.

One of her favorite words was *gumption,* a word that means you show qualities for success like initiative (starting something on your own) and good sense. In this excerpt from *Growing Up*, Russell's mother sadly realizes that he has "no more gumption than a bump on a log." In other words, he lacks initiative and ambition. However, after a long, unsuccessful effort to develop his gumption, she one day discovers that there is hope for her son, and in fact, Russell is quite "enchanted" with her discovery.

Russell Baker worked for most of his remarkable career as a newspaper columnist for the *New York Times*. In 1982, he won his second Pulitzer Prize for his autobiography, *Growing Up*.

HOW TO READ THE AUTOBIOGRAPHY

This autobiographical selection about an American family and the importance of work is for your reading pleasure. Don't worry if you don't understand all the words and all the details of the story. Try to understand generally what is happening in the lives of the people in the story, what their personalities are like, and what they want.

After the first reading, try to briefly retell the story. Then look over the comprehension and discussion questions after the story, and reread the selection with these questions in mind.

READING   A Mother's Advice: Make Something of Yourself

Line

1   I began working in journalism when I was eight years old. It was my mother's idea. She wanted me to "make something" of myself and, after a levelheaded appraisal of my strengths, decided I had better start young if I was to have any chance of keeping up with the competition.

flaw: weakness

despised: disliked strongly

A&P: grocery store; supermarket

self-pity: feeling sorry for oneself

paupers: very poor people

5   The flaw in my character which she had already spotted was lack of "gumption." My idea of a perfect afternoon was lying in front of the radio rereading my favorite Big Little Book, *Dick Tracy Meets Stooge Viller.* My mother despised inactivity. Seeing me having a good time in repose, she was powerless to hide her disgust. "You've got no more gumption than a bump on a log," she said.
10 "Get out in the kitchen and help Doris do those dirty dishes."

    My sister Doris, though two years younger than I, had enough gumption for a dozen people. She positively enjoyed washing dishes, making beds, and cleaning the house. When she was only seven she could carry a piece of short-weighted cheese back to the A&P, threaten the manager with legal action, and
15 come back triumphantly with the full quarter-pound we'd paid for and a few ounces extra thrown in for forgiveness. Doris could have made something of herself if she hadn't been a girl. Because of this defect, however, the best she could hope for was a career as a nurse or schoolteacher, the only work that capable females were considered up to in those days.

20   This must have saddened my mother, this twist of fate that had allocated all the gumption to the daughter and left her with a son who was content with Dick Tracy and Stooge Viller. If disappointed, though, she wasted no energy on self-pity. She would make me make something of myself whether I wanted to or not. "The Lord helps those who help themselves," she said. That was the way her
25 mind worked.

    She was realistic about the difficulty. Having sized up the material the Lord had given her to mold, she didn't overestimate what she could do with it. She didn't insist that I grow up to be President of the United States.

    Fifty years ago parents still asked boys if they wanted to grow up to be
30 President, and asked it not jokingly but seriously. Many parents who were hardly more than paupers still believed their sons could do it. Abraham Lincoln had done it. We were only sixty-five years from Lincoln. Many a grandfather who walked among us could remember Lincoln's time. Men of grandfatherly age were the worst for asking if you wanted to grow up to be President. A surprising
35 number of little boys said yes and meant it.

    I was asked many times myself. No, I would say, I didn't want to grow up to be President. My mother was present during one of these interrogations. An elderly uncle, having posed the usual question and exposed my lack of interest in the Presidency, asked, "Well, what do you want to be when you grow up?"
40   I loved to pick through trash piles and collect empty bottles, tin cans with pretty labels, and discarded magazines. The most desirable job on earth sprang instantly to mind. "I want to be a garbage man," I said.

    My uncle smiled, but my mother had seen the first distressing evidence of a bump budding on a log. "Have a little gumption, Russell, " she said. Her calling
45 me Russell was a signal of unhappiness. When she approved of me I was always "Buddy."

    When I turned eight years old she decided that the job of starting me on the road toward making something of myself could no longer be safely delayed. "Buddy," she said one day, "I want you to come home right after school this
50 afternoon. Somebody's coming and I want you to meet him."

When I burst in that afternoon she was in conference in the parlor with an executive of the Curtis Publishing Company. She introduced me. He bent low from the waist and shook my hand. Was it true as my mother had told him, he asked, that I longed for the opportunity to conquer the world of business?

55 My mother replied that I was blessed with a rare determination to make something of myself.

"That's right," I whispered.

"But have you got the grit, the character, the never-say-quit spirit it takes to succeed in business?"

60 My mother said I certainly did.

"That's right," I said.

He eyed me silently for a long pause, as though weighing whether I could be trusted to keep his confidence, then spoke man-to-man. Before taking a crucial step, he said he wanted to advise me that working for the Curtis Publishing

65 Company placed enormous responsibility on a young man. It was one of the great companies of America. Perhaps the greatest publishing house in the world. I had heard, no doubt, of the *Saturday Evening Post?*

Heard of it? My mother said that everyone in our house had heard of the *Saturday Post* and that I, in fact, read it with religious devotion.

70 Then doubtless, he said, we were also familiar with those two monthly pillars of the magazine world, the *Ladies Home Journal* and the *Country Gentleman.*

Indeed we were familiar with them, said my mother.

Representing the *Saturday Evening Post* was one of the weightiest honors

75 that could be bestowed in the world of business, he said. He was personally proud of being a part of that great corporation.

My mother said he had every right to be.

knighthood: special title given to a man by the king

Again he studied me as though debating whether I was worthy of a knighthood. Finally: "Are you trustworthy?"

80 My mother said I was the soul of honesty.

"That's right," I said.

The caller smiled for the first time. He told me I was a lucky young man. He admired my spunk. Too many young men thought life was all play. Those young men would not go far in this world. Only a young man willing to work

spunk: spirit; courage

85 and save and keep his face washed and his hair neatly combed could hope to come out on top in a world such as ours. Did I truly and sincerely believe that I was such a young man?

"He certainly does," said my mother.

"That's right," I said.

90 He said he had been so impressed by what he had seen of me that he was going to make me a representative of the Curtis Publishing Company. On the following Tuesday, he said, thirty freshly printed copies of the *Saturday Evening Post* would be delivered at our door. I would place these magazines, still damp with the ink of the presses, in a handsome canvas bag, sling it over my shoulder,

canvas bag: bag made of very strong cloth

95 and set forth through the streets to bring the best in journalism, fiction, and cartoons to the American public.

He had brought the canvas bag with him. He presented it with reverence fit for a chasuble. He showed me how to drape the sling over my left shoulder and across the chest so that the pouch lay easily accessible to my right hand, allow-

100 ing the best in journalism, fiction, and cartoons to be swiftly extracted and sold to a citizenry whose happiness and security depended upon us soldiers of the free press.

The following Tuesday I raced home from school, put the canvas bag over my shoulder, dumped the magazines in, and tilting to the left to balance their

105 weight on my right hip, embarked on the highway of journalism.

commuter town: town from which people travel to work in the city

We lived in Belleville, New Jersey, a commuter town at the northern fringe of Newark. It was 1932, the bleakest year of the Depression. My father had died two years before, leaving us with a few pieces of Sears, Roebuck furniture and not much else, and my mother had taken Doris and me to live with one of her

110 younger brothers. This was my Uncle Allen. Uncle Allen had made something of himself by 1932. As salesman for a soft-drink bottler in Newark, he had an income of $30 a week; wore pearl-gray spats, detachable collars, and a three-

threadbare: poor

piece suit; was happily married, and took in threadbare relatives.

Line

filling stations: gas stations 115

**made myself highly
visible:** could be easily seen

120

125

intervened: broke into the
conversation

135

140

**you've got another think
coming:** think again

145

150

wean: change his attitude 155

legacy: what is passed on to
the next generation

160

With my load of magazines I headed toward Belleville Avenue. That's where the people were. There were two filling stations at the intersection with Union Avenue, as well as an A&P, a fruit stand, a bakery, a barber shop, Zuccarelli's drugstore, and a diner shaped like a railroad car. For several hours I made myself highly visible, shifting position now and then from corner to corner, from shop window to shop window, to make sure everyone could see the heavy black lettering on the canvas bag that said *The Saturday Evening Post*. When the angle of the light indicated it was suppertime, I walked back to the house.

"How many did you sell, Buddy?" my mother asked.

"None."

"Where did you go?"

"The corner of Belleville and Union Avenues."

"What did you do?"

"Stood on the corner waiting for somebody to buy a *Saturday Evening Post*."

"You just stood there?"

"Didn't sell a single one."

"For God's sake, Russell!"

Uncle Allen intervened. "I've been thinking about it for some time," he said, "and I've about decided to take the *Post* regularly. Put me down as a regular customer." I handed him a magazine and he paid me a nickel. It was the first nickel I earned.

Afterwards my mother instructed me in salesmanship. I would have to ring doorbells, address adults with charming self-confidence, and break down resistance with a sales talk pointing out that no one, no matter how poor, could afford to be without the *Saturday Evening Post* in the home.

I told my mother I'd changed my mind about wanting to succeed in the magazine business.

"If you think I'm going to raise a good-for-nothing," she replied, "you've got another think coming." She told me to hit the streets with the canvas bag and start ringing doorbells the instant school was out the next day. When I objected that I didn't feel any aptitude for salesmanship, she asked how I'd like to lend her my leather belt so she could whack some sense into me. I bowed to superior will and entered journalism with a heavy heart.

My mother and I had fought this battle almost as long as I could remember. It probably started even before memory began, when I was a country child in northern Virginia and my mother, dissatisfied with my father's plain workman's life, determined that I would not grow up like him and his people, with calluses on their hands, overalls on their backs, and fourth-grade educations in their heads. She had fancier ideas of life's possibilities. Introducing me to the *Saturday Evening Post*, she was trying to wean me as early as possible from my father's world where men left with their lunch pails at sunup, worked with their hands until the grime ate into the pores, and died with a few sticks of mail-order furniture as their legacy. In my mother's vision of the better life there were desks and white collars, well-pressed suits, evenings of reading and lively talk, and perhaps—if a man were very, very lucky and hit the jackpot, really made something important of himself—perhaps there might be a fantastic salary of

Line

$5,000 a year to support a big house and a Buick with a rumble seat and a vacation in Atlantic City.

And so I set forth with my sack of magazines. I was afraid of the dogs that snarled behind the doors of potential buyers. I was timid about ringing the
165 doorbells of strangers, relieved when no one came to the door, and scared when someone did. Despite my mother's instructions, I could not deliver an engaging sales pitch. When a door opened I simply asked, "Want to buy a *Saturday Evening Post*?" In Belleville few persons did. It was a town of 30,000 people, and most weeks I rang a fair majority of its doorbells. But I rarely sold my thirty
170 copies. Some weeks I canvassed the entire town for six days and still had four or five unsold magazines on Monday evening; then I dreaded the coming of Tuesday morning, when a batch of thirty fresh *Saturday Evening Posts* was due at the front door.

"Better get out there and sell the rest of those magazines tonight," my
175 mother would say.

I usually posted myself then at a busy intersection where a traffic light controlled commuter flow from Newark. When the light turned red I stood on the curb and shouted my sales pitch at the motorists.

"Want to buy a *Saturday Evening Post*?"
180 One rainy night when car windows were sealed against me I came back soaked and with not a single sale to report. My mother beckoned to Doris.

"Go back down there with Buddy and show him how to sell these magazines," she said.

Brimming with zest, Doris, who was then seven years old, returned with
185 me to the corner. She took a magazine from the bag, and when the light turned red she strode to the nearest car and banged her small fist against the closed window. The driver, probably startled at what he took to be a midget assaulting his car, lowered the window to stare, and Doris thrust a *Saturday Evening Post* at him.
190 "You need this magazine," she piped, "and it only costs a nickel."

Her salesmanship was irresistible. Before the light changed half a dozen times she disposed of the entire batch. I didn't feel humiliated. To the contrary. I was so happy I decided to give her a treat. Leading her to the vegetable store on Belleville Avenue, I bought three apples, which cost a nickel, and gave her one.
195 "You shouldn't waste money," she said.

"Eat your apple." I bit in mine.

"You shouldn't eat before supper," she said. "It'll spoil your appetite."

Back at the house that evening, she dutifully reported me for wasting a nickel. Instead of a scolding, I was rewarded with a pat on the back for having
200 the good sense to buy fruit instead of candy. My mother reached into her bottomless supply of maxims and told Doris, "An apple a day keeps the doctor away."

By the time I was ten I had learned all my mother's maxims by heart. Asking to stay up past normal bedtime, I knew that a refusal would be explained
205 with, "Early to bed and early to rise, makes a man healthy, wealthy, and wise." If I whimpered about having to get up early in the morning, I could depend on her to say, "The early bird gets the worm."

timid: shy

sales pitch: how a salesperson speaks to get people to buy

dreaded: feared

soaked: very wet from the rain

fist: hand with fingers closed tightly
assaulting: attacking

humiliated: feel bad from loss of respect

scolding: being blamed for something

The one I most despised was, "If at first you don't succeed, try, try again."
This was the battle cry with which she constantly sent me back into the hopeless
210 struggle whenever I moaned that I had rung every doorbell in town and knew
there wasn't a single potential buyer left in Belleville that week. After listening to
my explanation, she handed me the canvas bag and said, "If at first you don't
succeed..."

Three years in that job, which I would gladly have quit after the first day
215 except for her insistence, produced at least one valuable result. My mother finally concluded that I would never make something of myself by pursuing a life in
business and started considering careers that demanded less competitive zeal.

One evening when I was eleven I brought home a short "composition" on
my summer vacation which the teacher had graded with an A. Reading it with
220 her own schoolteacher's eye, my mother agreed that it was top-drawer seventh
grade prose and complimented me. Nothing more was said about it immediately, but a new idea had taken life in her mind. Halfway through supper she suddenly interrupted the conversation.

"Buddy," she said, "maybe you could be a writer."
225 I clasped the idea to my heart. I had never met a writer, had shown no previous urge to write, and hadn't a notion how to become a writer, but I loved stories and thought that making up stories must surely be almost as much fun as
reading them. Best of all, though, and what really gladdened my heart, was the
ease of the writer's life. Writers did not have to trudge through the town ped-
230 dling from canvas bags, defending themselves against angry dogs, being rejected
by surly strangers. Writers did not have to ring doorbells. So far as I could make
out, what writers did couldn't even be classified as work.

I was enchanted. Writers didn't have to have any gumption at all. I did not
tell anybody for fear of being laughed at in the schoolyard, but secretly I decided
235 that what I'd like to be when I grew up was a writer.

complimented: praised

urge: desire

COMPREHENSION QUESTIONS

1. Identify the five people in the selection and tell something about each.
   When and where does most of the story take place?

2. Why was it unfortunate that Doris was a girl, especially at that time?

3. What was Russell Baker's first idea for a future job? How did his mother
   respond to this?

4. Who was the visitor who came one day to Russell's home? Why did he
   come?

5. Why didn't Russell sell any magazines on the street corner the first
   evening? Who first bought a magazine from him?

6. Reread aloud the paragraph beginning at line 148. Look carefully at the detailed description that the writer gives of his father's life and work. Give some of this description. What was the real reason why Russell's mother wanted her children to make something of themselves?

7. Who had the better sales pitch, Russell or Doris? Explain.

8. After Russell's mother finally realized that he would never make something of himself in business, what did she then discover? How did Russell react to her discovery?

DISCUSSION QUESTIONS

1. Russell's mother often quoted maxims (or proverbs). At the beginning of the reading, she said, "The Lord helps those who help themselves." This suggests that you must have gumption. Later in the reading, she quoted several other maxims. What are these maxims and what do they mean? What common theme do you find in most of these maxims? Do you or does a member of your family have a favorite maxim? What is it?

2. At the end of the selection, Russell says that "what writers did couldn't even be classified as work." He was delighted with the idea of becoming a writer. If you were Russell, which career would you choose? Would you choose to be a writer or a business person? Why? What are some differences between these two careers?

3. Did Russell Baker follow his mother's advice and eventually make something of himself? Did he have gumption after all? How do you know this?

4. Reading an autobiography can lead us to reflect on our own lives. What can you learn from Russell Baker's childhood experience? What did you especially like about this story?

CHAPTER 9

THE NEW VOLUNTEERS

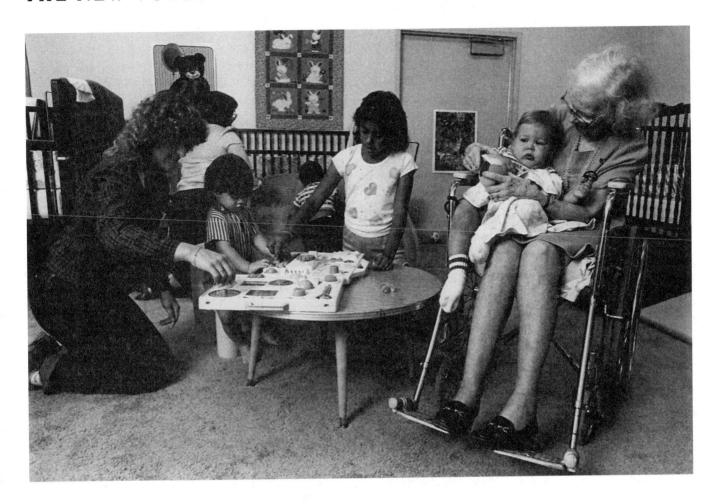

The vast majority of Americans need a paying job in order to support themselves. However, more and more of them are offering their time and energy, without pay, to help others. They are *the new volunteers*. The reading selection gives reasons why more Americans are volunteering and presents a few examples of volunteerism from around the nation.

READING SELECTION

PRE-READING DISCUSSION

Getting into the Topic

■ Give examples of different kinds of volunteer work that people do in your country.

■ Have you ever done any volunteer work? What did you do? What did you learn from this experience?

■ Why do you think people volunteer?

Getting an Overview of the Reading Selection

■   Read the title and the two first sentences below the title. What three points do the sentences make?

■   Read the first paragraph and the first sentence of Paragraphs 2–8. As you read, look for the different groups of people that the writer identifies as volunteers.

■   Read the first sentence of Paragraph 9. What does the rest of the reading selection describe? Is there a concluding paragraph?

READ THE SELECTION: FIRST TIME

Read to get a general understanding of the selection. Do not stop to look up words in the dictionary.

READING

The New Volunteers

More Americans than ever before are giving their time and energy to help others. The people and the issues they help are quite varied—the homeless, the illiterate, the environment, AIDS, gun control, drug abuse, but their purpose is the same—to help those in need, to help make a better society for all of us to live in.

avarice: too great a desire to get and keep wealth for oneself; greed
altruism: concern for others; selflessness

1   If the '80s were the Age of Avarice, then the '90s appear to be the Age of Altruism. The message is clear: Get Involved.

2   After years of little concern for the problems of others in society, Americans are volunteering more than ever. According to a 1987–1988 survey, 45 percent of the adults surveyed said they regularly volunteered—and more than a third of these volunteers reported spending more time on volunteer work in recent years. In all, it is estimated that 80 million adults gave a total of 19.5 billion hours in 1987, at a cost value of about $150 billion.

cuts in funding: reduction in financial support
social programs: programs that help the poor, handicapped, and elderly, for example, food, medical assistance, and recreation centers

3   They certainly were needed. The large cuts in government funding of social programs during the 1980s have had negative effects on the needy. To reduce the consequences of these cuts in funding, volunteer organizations have tried to provide greater help by increasing their number of volunteers. They now seek people from all age groups, including the elderly and the young, and from almost every socio-economic level. These volunteers participate most often through religious organizations, as well as through educational institutions, civic groups, and employers.

growing gap: increasing difference
ignore: not pay attention to
bag ladies: women who are homeless and carry all their possessions in bags

4   Some of this interest in public service or helping others may be a response to the avarice of the '80s. The growing gap between the very rich and the hopelessly poor is obvious; it is impossible to ignore. Bankers on their way to work in the morning have to walk past bag ladies. Often, these professionals will con-

tribute their business skills to solve social problems. Stan Curtis, a 40-year-old stockbroker from Louisville, Kentucky, established Kentucky Harvest, an all-volunteer agency that has distributed 1.6 million pounds of surplus food to the needy.

5   Many of the social problems that are attracting volunteers today were unknown a decade ago—organizations like Mothers Against Drunk Drivers (MADD) and AIDS groups. One of the fastest-growing volunteer groups is the self-help group in which people who have overcome a problem, like drugs, help those who are experiencing the same problem. There are self-help groups for everything from adults with alcoholic parents to couples with infertility problems.

6   Among the volunteers, working women are more likely than housewives to give time to charitable work. Because of the number of working women, many organizations are creating night and weekend programs for the busy schedules of two-income couples. Men, too, are volunteering almost as often as women, although they are more likely to participate in programs such as the Boy Scouts and Little League Baseball.

7   Senior citizens have always given their time. Since they are living longer and staying healthier, many volunteer groups are designing programs specifically to match older people's skills. "There is a genuine feeling that the time has come to make really organized use of older people," says Bill Oriol of the National Council on the Aging. One of the more successful programs his organization has started is called Family Friends. It pairs older volunteers with the families of children with serious disabilities. The volunteers help out for several hours a week, giving the parents a much-needed break. Other organizations recruit senior citizens for tutoring or child care.

compassionate: showing feeling for others' sufferings and wanting to help them

8   Younger people, too, are increasingly attracted to the idea of public service. About 25 percent of American colleges and dozens of high schools have recently made volunteer work part of the school curriculum. One of the most extensive efforts is in California, where students at the state's 29 public universities are encouraged—but not required—to perform 30 hours of community service annually. About a quarter of the system's 400,000 students are participating in the program.

9   Here are some other examples of volunteerism from around the country. These volunteers are compassionate men, women, and children, who earn the quiet satisfaction of helping the needy. They reflect the diversity of the American people and show that anyone, regardless of status, can be an outstanding citizen.

A. FROM NEW MEXICO:
"ROLE MODEL"

Pauline Gomez considers herself among the fortunate few. Although she was born blind, Gomez was raised not to feel pity for herself. "When I said I couldn't do something, my mother would just say 'Have you tried?'" she says. In 1956, she helped to found the National Federation of the Blind of New Mexico. Now 69, self-supporting and a role model for the blind, Gomez is still giving her time to organizations that try to spread her mother's message, teaching the blind self-confidence and self-acceptance.

B. FROM SOUTH CAROLINA:
"DAY AND NIGHT, A CHEERLEADER FOR CANCER KIDS"

As Willie Maxwell lay in bed in 1982, recovering from throat cancer surgery, he promised that if he survived, he would do more to help others. His job as the midnight-shift security supervisor at Columbia's Richland Memorial Hospital introduced him to the special problems and needs of young cancer patients. "I started looking for ways to help," he says.

Maxwell, 59, contributes to the lives of these children in two ways. Five mornings a week, when his shift at the hospital ends, he collects scrap paper and aluminum cans to raise money for Camp Kemo, a local summer camp for kids with cancer. In six years he has collected more than $16,000. "I help as many as I can," Maxwell says, with his voice a whisper from his own cancer. "There are a lot of children who, if they don't go this year to the camp, won't make it next year." Maxwell also finds out which children in the hospital need cheering up, and he talks with them and brings them books, cards, flowers and fruit. "I visit as much as possible," he says, "and if they die, I'll try to make it to the funeral. I follow them to the end."

C. FROM NEVADA:
"MORE LOAVES AND FISHES"

A sign above the fruit counter in the Las Vegas grocery store says it all: "Touch it. Take it. No limit." Gleaners, established in 1982 by Celeste McKinley with the help of her husband David, is a supermarket for the needy. Shocked that stores threw away tons of edible food because the freshness dates had

edible: eatable

expired, Celeste convinced one manager to donate this food to her so she could help the hungry. Soon she had enough to set up a food bank in a garage. Now, with food and supplies also donated by casinos and wholesalers, Gleaners has moved into bigger quarters, serving 20,000 people a month.

Most of Gleaners' customers are not homeless but senior citizens on fixed incomes or mothers who are single or have sick husbands. A strong believer in individual initiative, McKinley, 40, recruits shoppers as volunteers. Funds to support the program can still be limited. However, McKinley, a devout Christian who one time sold her jewelry to pay expenses, is always hopeful: "God has never failed us."

D. FROM UTAH:
"KIDS CLEAN UP TOXIC WASTE"

Democracy and environmental protection are doing well at Jackson Elementary School in Salt Lake City. In 1987, students in Barbara Lewis' advanced class learned that there was a toxic-waste site near the school. They collected people's signatures on a petition letter and the waste was removed. Later they decided to expand their fight for toxic-waste cleanup.

toxic waste: poisonous material that is thrown away

After raising $2,700, they discovered there was no legal way to contribute the money to the state health department and also to request that the money be used for a specific purpose, such as toxic-waste cleanup. Unwilling to give up, 20 fifth and sixth graders went to the state legislature and fought to change the law. Their effort succeeded and the kids made the first contribution marked specifically for toxic-waste cleanup. Now they're trying other actions, winning a money grant to buy and plant trees, working to get sidewalks repaired. "We've learned about the growing of the world," says Kory Hansen, 12. "A kid can make a difference, too."

E. FROM FLORIDA:
"GIVING BACK"

As an intern in Miami, Jose Pedro Greer, Jr., was shocked when a homeless patient died of tuberculosis, a treatable disease. So five years ago he started a free health clinic next to a downtown shelter for the homeless. Today the Camillus Health Concern, with 200 volunteers and a paid staff of 12, treats thousands of poor patients annually. University of Miami medical students even get credit for work at the clinic. "You're supposed to give back," says Dr. Greer, 33, whose father emigrated from Cuba.

READING CHECK

A. Recall of General Ideas

What do you recall about the general ideas in the reading? Try to answer the questions on the following page. If you can't recall the ideas, scan the reading to find the information.

■ What is the message of the '90s? What does the message really mean?

_____

_____

■ What did the government do in the 1980s that resulted in a need for more volunteers in the 1990s?

_____

_____

■ What are some new volunteer programs that have started recently?

_____

_____

■ Identify different groups of volunteers or individual volunteers mentioned in the reading.

_____

_____

READ THE SELECTION: SECOND TIME

Read more carefully to get a better understanding of the selection. Use the dictionary, only if necessary.

COMPREHENSION EXERCISES

A. Listing

Make a list to show how this important point in the reading is developed or explained. Be as brief as possible. Include a heading with the list.

Two factors in the 1980s have caused more people to volunteer in the 1990s. List these two factors. Be prepared to discuss the factors.

(Heading)_____

_____

_____

B. Chart

Complete the chart by giving the type of volunteer work that each group performs. In the selection, the volunteer work is stated in either general or specific terms. Then answer the question below.

VOLUNTEER WORK OF FOUR GROUPS	
Four Groups	**Volunteer Work** (can be general or specific)
1. Women	_____
2. Men	_____
3. Senior Citizens	_____
4. Younger People	_____

■ Explain each type of volunteer work given. If the work is stated in general terms, give a specific example.

_____

_____

_____

_____

C. Chart

Complete the chart by giving appropriate information about each example of volunteerism. Then answer the questions that follow.

EXAMPLES OF VOLUNTEERISM FROM AROUND THE NATION		
Volunteers	**Who Is Helped**	**Type of Volunteer Work**
1. NEW MEXICO Blind Hispanic woman	_____ _____	_____ _____ _____ _____
2. SOUTH CAROLINA Older man who is recovering from cancer and works in a hospital	_____ _____	Raises money to send kids to summer camp; visits kids who need cheering up and brings them little presents
3. NEVADA _____ _____	The hungry: mostly senior citizens on fixed incomes and poor mothers	_____ _____ _____ _____
4. UTAH _____ _____	_____ _____	_____ _____ _____ _____ _____
5. FLORIDA _____ _____	_____ _____	_____ _____ _____ _____

■ The people listed in the chart are volunteers because they believe in helping the less fortunate and they want to make the world a better place for everyone. Also, some probably also have a special, more personal reason for helping a particular group. Which volunteers do you think have a more personal reason and what is it?

_____

_____

■ Was the volunteer work of the school children also an educational experience for them? Explain.

_____

_____

■ Why do you think the writer included these five detailed examples of volunteerism in the article?

_____

_____

TOPICS FOR DISCUSSION AND WRITING

1. In the first paragraph, the writer uses two descriptive words to suggest there is a great difference between the '80s and the '90s in the attitudes and behavior of some Americans. What words does she use to show this contrast? Explain what you think the attitude and behavior would be of a person in an Age of Avarice and of a person in an Age of Altruism. Two sets of contrasting words you might use are "greedy / generous" and "selfish / unselfish."

2. Bill Oriol of the National Council on the Aging says that "the time has come to make really organized use of older people." Why are senior citizens a good source of volunteers today? In your country, do many senior citizens volunteer? Explain.

3. The five examples of volunteerism at the end of the article have special headings. Can you explain the meaning of each heading in relation to its example? Some are quite obvious; others are not.

      A. "Role Model"
      B. "Night and Day, A Cheerleader for Cancer Kids"
      C. "More Loaves and Fishes" (taken from the Bible)
      D. "Kids Clean Up Toxic Waste"
      E. "Giving Back"

VOCABULARY EXERCISES

A. Vocabulary Oral Practice

Practice using the underlined words by answering the questions below.

1. The needy are especially hurt by cuts in government funding of social programs. What groups of people can be included in the needy? **(P3)**

2. What does disabilities mean in the phrase "children with disabilities"? In the United States, efforts have been made to help people with disabilities participate more fully in society. For example, because people in wheelchairs cannot climb stairs, what has been added to the front of buildings to make it easier for them to enter? Have you noticed any other ways in which the disabled have been helped in this country? **(P7)**

3. Large organizations like the Red Cross and small ones like a university tutoring service recruit volunteers. If you were in charge of a school organization that needed more volunteers, in what ways would you try to recruit students? **(P7)**

4. Do you think it is a good idea to require that all high school or college students perform a certain number of hours of public service each year? What are some benefits to society from this required community service? What are some arguments against it? **(P8)**

5. What kind of volunteer work could people with extensive teaching experience do after they have retired? **(P8)**

6. Doctors recommend that people have a medical exam annually. This annual check-up is especially important for the elderly. What other activities do people do annually? **(P8)**

7. The instructor said that the student had given an outstanding oral report. What did the student do that made the oral report outstanding? **(P9)**

8. Students who have scholarships to college are very fortunate. A child who has good health and loving parents is very fortunate. Give two examples of people who are less fortunate. **(P9, A)**

9. Children need role models in order to learn good values and good behavior. Who are good role models in society for children? **(P9, A)**

10. After a natural disaster like an earthquake or hurricane, the Red Cross and other volunteer organizations ask for donations to help the unfortunate victims. What kinds of things can people donate? **(P9, C)**

11. Suppose you were writing a letter of recommendation for a student applying to college. Would it help or hurt the student's admission if you wrote that he/she had <u>initiative</u>? Explain. **(P9, C)**

12. Why is <u>environmental protection</u> necessary today? What can individuals do to help <u>protect the</u> Earth's <u>environment</u>? Is there something you personally do to <u>protect the environment</u>? **(P9, D)**

B. Dictation

Study the spelling of the words in the previous exercise. You will have a dictation of sentences that contain these words.

JOURNAL WRITING

Topic I

Write about a person that you know who gives his/her time, energy, and skills to help others. First, identify who the volunteer is and describe what he/she is like. Then tell what group or organization the volunteer helps and what he/she does to help.

Topic 2

If you had both the time and money to give one year of your life to volunteer work, what would you choose to do? Describe what you would do and tell why this volunteer work is of special interest to you.

COMMUNICATIVE ACTIVITY

Survey on Volunteerism

In this activity, you will take a survey to find out information about some aspect of volunteerism in your community. Before you do the survey, make a prediction about what the results of the survey will be. After taking the survey, you will report your results to the class and tell whether or not your prediction was correct.

Procedure:

1. **Make Survey Questions:** Together suggest survey questions on different aspects of volunteerism in the community.

   Sample Survey Questions:
   - Do most young people do volunteer work?
   - Should high school or college students be required to perform community service in order to graduate?

2. **Make Predictions:** Change each survey question into a prediction about what you think the survey results will show.

   Sample Predictions:
   - Most young people do volunteer work.
   - High school or college students should not be required to peform community service in order to graduate.

3. **Decide on Survey Question:** Divide into pairs (or small groups). Choose one of the survey questions and its prediction.

4. **Write "You" Questions for Survey:** Divide into pairs (or small groups). Choose your survey question and make a prediction. Write at least two "you" questions to get information about your survey question.

   Sample "You" Questions: (for Survey Question above on young people)
   - Do you do volunteer work?
   - (If yes, then) What kind of volunteer work do you do?
     (If no, then) Is there a particular reason why you don't volunteer?

5. **Take the Survey:** Ask five people your questions and record the answers.

6. **Report the Results, including the Prediction:** Report the results to the class and tell whether or not your prediction was correct. If the results show that the prediction was wrong, revise it so that it is correct. Give your reaction to the survey.

LECTURE **An Interview with Today's Senior Citizens**

    In this unit on "The American Family at Work," you have learned about the busy lives of working mothers and fathers and their teenage sons and daughters. Today, you will learn about another segment of the American population: older Americans. In this interview, two senior citizens talk about what they and other older Americans are doing to keep busy.

*Mary Katherine Holden
and Bob Adamson*

This is an interview with two senior citizens who are neighbors in the same apartment complex in Washington, D.C. Mary Catherine Holden, who is 76 years old, worked as a senior consultant in international affairs for 28 years. Bob Adamson, who is 65, held various positions in journalism for 35 years. Both retired from their jobs in 1985.

In this interview, Mary Catherine and Bob talk about four aspects of older Americans: the volunteer work they do, their interest in physical fitness and other leisure activities, their interest in life-long learning, and their role in the workforce.

TERMS USED IN THE LECTURE*

American Hiking Society
national parks and forests
to repair hiking trails
camping out in the woods
linguistics course
crisis intervention hot-line
fitness craze
long-distance bicycling
square dancing / ballroom
    dancing / cowboy dancing
triathlon (a three-sport
    competition)
to swim the length of the pool
to play bridge
purpose travel
United Nations Conference on the
    Environment Development

conference of adult educators
Elder Hostel Program (education
    program and service program
    for senior citizens)
course catalogue
flora and fauna (plant and
    animal life)
the Musk ox (endangered animal
    in Alaska)
watch stations
senior work revolution
to augment one's income
bed-and-breakfast guest house
marketing executive
mortgage banking area

* These terms are defined or made clear from context in the lecture.

1. Listen to the interview. Follow the questions below as you listen. Do not write anything at this time.

2. Listen again and take notes on the responses to the questions. Write only key words or phrases. After the interview, compare your notes with a classmate's. You may want to listen to the interview again to confirm any points that you missed.

3. After completing your notes, discuss them with the class.

An Interview with Today's Senior Citizens

VOLUNTEER ACTIVITIES

1. Bob, you once told me that shortly after you retired you took a vacation, but that this vacation was a *volunteer vacation*. What is a *volunteer vacation*?

   _____

   _____

   _____

2. Why did you choose this kind of work?

   _____

   _____

3. Mary Catherine, what kind of volunteer work have you been involved in?

   _____

   _____

4. What other kinds of volunteer work are seniors involved in?

   _____

   _____

5. Bob, you did a different kind of volunteer work a while back, right?

   _____

   _____

6. Let's talk a little bit about physical fitness. It seems that recently more and more older Americans are becoming involved in physical fitness. Mary Catherine, is this true?

_____

7. How about you personally? How do you keep fit?

_____

8. Bob, you're in pretty good shape, yourself. What do you do to keep in shape?

_____

_____

9. Mary Catherine, wasn't it a few years back that you participated in a triathlon?

_____

_____

10. People who see you two and hear you two might not believe that you are typical senior citizens. Mary Catherine, do you consider yourself a typical older American?

_____

11. Besides keeping fit, what other kinds of leisure activities are senior citizens involved in?

_____

12. Bob, what kind of leisure activities do you think Americans are involved in?

_____

13. We were talking about one leisure activity earlier. We were talking about travel, and you said that you're interested in adventure travel. Is that true?

_____

_____

14. What kind of travel do you and your husband like to do?

_____

_____

INTEREST IN LIFE-LONG LEARNING

15. It seems from what you two have talked about that older Americans have a strong interest in life-long learning. Is that true, Mary Catherine?

_____

_____

16. And there's also this other program—Learning in Retirement Program.

_____

_____

17. Bob, you were talking about that you were interested in possibly taking one of these courses at American University.

_____

_____

Mary Catherine: _____

_____

_____

SENIORS IN THE WORKFORCE

18. So far, we've talked about older Americans and volunteer work, older Americans and their physical and leisure activities, and older Americans and their interest in life-long learning. Now, let's talk about older Americans in the workforce. Bob, are there more senior citizens in the workforce today?

_____

_____

_____

19. Mary Catherine, you were talking about that you had a friend who retired and started a second career.

_____

20. Bob, you were saying that your son has asked you to possibly go into business with him.

_____

_____

1. After retiring, Bob took a volunteer vacation. What kind of volunteer work did he do? In what way(s) was it a vacation?

2. Why does Mary Catherine have an interest in working with people from other cultures? Although she now teaches English as a second language in an adult education center, she taught English *informally* for many years. What does this mean? What initiative did she take to prepare herself to teach English in a more formal classroom situation?

3. Bob was also a volunteer for a crisis intervention hot-line. Explain what hot-line volunteers do. Why do crisis hot-lines need a large number of volunteers? Explain why seniors make good hot-line volunteers. Would you be interested in doing similar volunteer work? Why or why not?

4. In this country, there is a fitness craze, and seniors are joining this craze. What physical fitness activities do Mary Catherine and Bob enjoy? Explain why you think seniors are joining the fitness craze.

5. Why do you think seniors are becoming the largest market group for pleasure travel? Describe the kind of travel they are becoming interested in and why. Have any seniors in your family taken an adventure trip?

6. How are the Elder Hostel Program and the Learning in Retirement Program similar? The Elder Hostel Program is also a service program. For example, through the Elder Hostel Program, seniors volunteer to sit in watch stations in Alaska to observe the behavior of the Musk Ox. Explain why they are doing this. Look up this animal in the encyclopedia to find out more information about it.

7. Bob believes that a *senior work revolution* is taking place. Explain what he means and the reasons for this revolution.

8. Mary Catherine talks about a friend who retired and then started a *second career*. What is his new career? Is it related to his long-time career? Why do you think he chose this new kind of work? Think about the future and your retirement. Describe what you might enjoy doing after you retire.

Early twentieth century inventions by two famous entrepreneurs: Henry Ford and King Gillette.

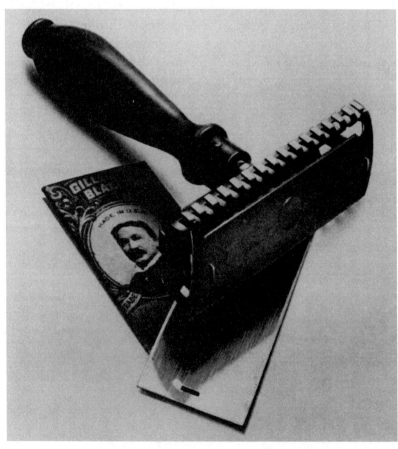

UNIT FOUR
Business and the Entrepreneur

The previous unit looked at work from the point of view of the American family. It dealt with economic and social factors that have brought more family members into the work world, most of them to earn money but some simply to earn personal satisfaction.

In this unit, we will look at work from the point of view of business, and in particular, of business and the individual. Whether from the past or present, there have always been individuals who wanted to "do their own thing" and start their own business. These individuals are called *entrepreneurs*.

Many entrepreneurs have been satisfied with running a rather small business. A special few whose businesses expanded have been responsible in some way for the development of today's large industries and corporations. No matter what the size, these individuals were the innovators who thought up a new business idea and worked very hard to see it grow. We will learn about some of these risk-taking entrepreneurs, their products and services, and their interaction with consumers.

FAMOUS ENTREPRENEURS

Think of some well-known entrepreneurs whose names are the same as the product or service that they created. What are their names and what did they create?

One famous American entrepreneur from the past is Henry Ford. As you know, his name is used for both his product, the Ford car, and his business, the Ford Motor Company.

Now, look at the chapter titles in this unit. What do you think each chapter will discuss?

Chapter 10   The American Entrepreneur: A Historical Perspective
Chapter 11   The Making of Two Entrepreneurs
Chapter 12   Selling to the New America

THE AMERICAN ENTREPRENEUR:
A HISTORICAL PERSPECTIVE

This reading is taken from the introduction to the book, *The Entrepreneurs: An American Adventure* by Robert Sobel and David B. Sicilia. The book describes the lives and achievements of various American entrepreneurs from the past to the present.

In this excerpt from their book, the writers give two definitions of "entrepreneur," discuss characteristics of the entrepreneur, and give some brief examples of entrepreneurs from the past and present.

READING SELECTION

PRE-READING DISCUSSION

Getting into the Topic

■ Do you personally know an entrepreneur? This could be a family member or a person from your hometown who started his/her own business. What kind of business is it? What characteristics does a person who starts his/her own business have?

■ Would you prefer to work for an established company or to start your own business? Why?

Getting an Overview of the Reading Selection

■ Read the first and last paragraphs. From the first paragraph, tell what the American attitude toward entrepreneurs of today is. From the last paragraph, tell what the American attitude toward entrepreneurs of the past is now.

■ Read the first (and perhaps second) sentence of each of the other paragraphs. From these sentences, try to figure out which paragraphs discuss the definition of "entrepreneur," which paragraphs discuss characteristics of the entrepreneur, and which paragraphs give examples of entrepreneurs from the past and present.

Read to get a general understanding of the selection. Do not stop to look up words in the dictionary.

| **READING** | **The American Entrepreneur: A Historical Perspective** |

1   Entrepreneur. Americans have fallen in love with this French noun, which the dictionary tells us means "one who manages, and assumes the risks of, a business or enterprise." In 1985, Lee Iacocca's autobiography was at the top of the best-seller book lists, and since then, guidebooks to starting your own business, self-help books for careers in management, and descriptions of successful companies have filled the bookstore shelves. Numerous seminars on entrepreneurship are now offered at business schools, trying to explain what the main ingredients in entrepreneurship are and how one can apply them to small businesses and modern corporations.

2   Although people have recently become fascinated with the idea of the entrepreneur, it has been a part of the American economy since the beginning of the country. The first European settlements in North America were entrepreneurial ventures (and failures at that). Before Virginia and Massachusetts Bay were colonies, they were settled by companies in which investors risked their incomes, and in some cases their lives, hoping to have a better life later on. Since these early colonial times, entrepreneurs have performed the same basic activities. They have sought opportunities, planned strategies, invented new products and services, taken risks, and found better ways to create industries and thereby make fortunes. Indeed, the American soil proved fertile ground for developing new businesses, and businesses based on minerals from aluminum to zinc, on manufactured goods from corn flakes to computers, and on services from small shops to supermarkets flourished.

ventures: uncertain business attempts

flourished: grew well

3   Most Americans think of their leading citizens as being politicians, social leaders, and entertainers, but not entrepreneurs. Entrepreneurs are the unsung heroes of our past. Their achievements and their influence on our lives have not been recognized or appreciated until just recently. These men and women saw challenges and opportunities for business where others saw nothing at all. Some recognized existing opportunities, while others actively created opportunities. For either type of opportunity, entrepreneurs held on to their new ideas and worked tirelessly to overcome obstacles. They sacrificed savings and sometimes their personal lives in the search for new products and services. They took risks, although they often found creative ways to reduce the risks. These men and women greatly influenced how we live today, from the way in which we earn our income to the ways in which we are likely to spend it.

4   According to the first great theorist of entrepreneurship, Joseph Schumpeter, entrepreneurs perform an important function known as "creative

conventional assumptions:
traditional beliefs accepted
as true without evidence
discard: throw away
pattern of production: way
that something is produced

market: demand for goods

in retrospect: looking back
to the past

profile: description

key variable: important factor in a research study that
may go up or down

obsession: fixed idea in the
mind that does not go away

destruction," that is, they rethink conventional assumptions and discard those that may have been useful in the past but are no longer. In place of these discarded ideas, Schumpeter wrote in 1942, the entrepreneur reforms or revolutionizes the pattern of production. To do this, the entrepreneur introduces an invention, tries new and untried business possibilities, produces a new commodity or produces an old one in a new way, develops a new source of supply of raw materials, opens up a new market for products, or reorganizes an industry.

5   In short, Schumpeter's definition of an entrepreneur emphasizes that the entrepreneur is a person who creates something new, either an innovation or a new combination of existing factors that are available to everyone. In retrospect, the new combinations created by entrepreneurs like King Gillette (inventor of the safety razor in 1901) seem fairly simple. But these new combinations require a special kind of imagination that few people, it seems, possess. So, if an entrepreneur is defined in this way, then not everyone who founds a business or develops a product is an entrepreneur. The Chinese laundry of the late nineteenth century, the tailor shop run by an East European Jew in the 1920s, and the Korean-managed grocery store of today, for example, became successful, not through the creation of any new product or service, but through hard work and long hours.

6   What about the entrepreneurs themselves? Can we identify other characteristics of the typical entrepreneur? Is King Gillette, Frederic Tudor, or Fred Smith the typical entrepreneur? A few students of this subject are now attempting to develop a profile of common characteristics. One study has concluded that entrepreneurs tend to be shorter than average height. Another study identifies birth order as a key variable; it found that innovators tend to be the oldest or youngest child in their families. But characteristics of this sort, however fascinating, will probably be of limited use, because there will always be exceptions.

7   In addition to the special imagination of which Schumpeter spoke and wrote, entrepreneurs show other common characteristics. Their willingness to take risks suggests a higher tolerance for uncertainty and ambiguity than most people have. And entrepreneurs are disciplined and focused on the task at hand, almost to the point where the task becomes an obsession.

8   Money, of course, is important too, and the vast majority of entrepreneurs are profit-seekers. However, it would be a mistake to assume that money is the only, or even primary, motivator for all. Instead it is the contest that motivates them, or what social scientist David McClelland has called the "need for achievement." Entrepreneurs often have little time to spend the money they earn, since for them twenty-hour workdays are not unusual. Most love challenges, even when on vacation or relaxing.

9   This search for achievement or success often has its costs. Entrepreneurs typically suffer serious personal problems; many are brash, self-centered, difficult to live with, impatient with structured organizations, and blind to the effects of their actions on family and friends. Such behavior undoubtedly results from the constant threat of failure, whether potential or actual.

ruthless: very unkind or cruel

10   However, not only individual family members and friends but society itself has suffered at times from the actions and behavior of entrepreneurs. This was the case in the late nineteenth century when some ruthless "robber barons" had power and control over large industries, and thus over many workers' lives. As the name implies, these "robber barons" were not viewed in a very favorable light by working people.[1] In fact, it is only in recent years that business historians have begun to examine seriously the contributions made by these industrial giants to the growth of the American economy and the advancement of modern managerial methods.

11   A more balanced view is now possible, a view that recognizes not only the abuses but also the significant contributions of these industrial giants. Business historians recognize that entrepreneurs played a key role in the economic growth of the United States because they were very concerned with economic challenges and were willing to accept risks to meet these challenges. Schumpeter likewise recognized their contributions in using the factors of production in different ways. He understood that capital became more important when entrepreneurs invested it more productively and that labor could achieve more when entrepreneurs organized it in new ways.

factors of production: capital, labor, natural resources, and entrepreneurship
capital: money
labor: work force

12   At each historical period, entrepreneurs both affected and were affected by the social and economic conditions of the time. Consider how King Gillette affected the daily lives of millions of American men in the early twentieth century by developing the safety razor. Then, on the other hand, consider how Gillette himself was affected by the existing conditions. His innovation was successful because the appropriate social conditions for its acceptance were present and the appropriate technology needed to mass produce it was available.

13   Indeed, the ability to make what appears ordinary into the extraordinary is the achievement of the entrepreneur. For example, in the first half of the 1800s, Frederic Tudor, the Ice King, made a fortune harvesting the common substance, ice. In 1816, he shipped 1,200 tons from Boston harbor; by 1856, he was shipping 146,000 tons of ice to such places as the Philippines, China, and Australia, as well as the West Indies and the southern states. This product influenced the way people lived, what they ate and what they drank, and led to the demand for refrigeration in the home. By the end of the 1800s, the "icebox" was common in the American home.

icebox: large box with ice inside to preserve food

---

[1] Since the end of the nineteenth century, labor laws have been passed to control the abuse of power by such "robber barons."

14   Another example is the present-day entrepreneur Fred Smith, who in the early 1970s entered a very old business, shipping the mail, in a most modern way. Using a fleet of jumbo jets, he began an overnight mail delivery service, known as Federal Express. Much of the demand for his service came from the fast-growing high-technology industry, since for this industry, time is a major priority. Shipping a needed small electronic part to a distant customer, for instance, requires the speed and reliability of air delivery. From a start-up investment of $90 million in 1971, the company had revenues of $590 million by 1980. These examples prove that entrepreneurs have been especially skillful at recognizing the constant development of new opportunities.

15   From this historical perspective, therefore, American entrepreneurship can be seen as an important and complex phenomenon. By examining entrepreneurs in different historical periods, and by focusing on the challenges they faced and the achievements they realized, we can better appreciate these brash, unconventional, original people. Today these entrepreneurs of the past are considered heroes who played an important role in the rise of the American economy.

A. Marginal Notes

Look over the following ten marginal notes. Write them in the margin of the reading next to the paragraph that relates to the marginal note. If a marginal note relates to more than one paragraph, draw an arrow (↓) to indicate this. Not all paragraphs will have notes. The notes are listed in random order.

MARGINAL NOTES

Schumpeter's term "creative destruction"

activities of entrepreneurs since colonial times

"robber barons"

Example: Fred Smith

Schumpeter's definition of entrepreneur + requires special imagination

important common characteristics

Example: Frederic Tudor

unsung heroes of past

contributions of industrial giants

social/economic conditions
Example: King Gillette

B. Guessing the Meaning from Context

Look carefully at the context of the underlined words below. Try to guess their meaning. Identify the context clue(s) that helped you and be prepared to explain your answer. If necessary, refer to **Appendix 2**.

1. Entrepreneurs held on to their new ideas and worked <u>tirelessly</u> to overcome obstacles. **(P3)**

   TIRELESSLY _____
   context clue(s):

2. The entrepreneur produces a new <u>commodity</u> or produces an old one in a new way. **(P4)**

   COMMODITY _____
   context clue(s):

3. Entrepreneurs typically suffer serious personal problems; many are <u>brash</u>, self-centered, difficult to live with, impatient with structured organizations, and blind to the effects of their actions on friends and family. **(P9)**

    BRASH _____

    context clue(s):

4. Some ruthless "robber barons" had power and control over large industries, and thus over many workers' lives. As the name implies, these "robber barons" were <u>not viewed in a very favorable light</u> by working people. **(P10)**

    NOT VIEWED IN A VERY FAVORABLE LIGHT _____

    context clue(s):

5. A more balanced view is now possible, a view that recognizes not only the <u>abuses</u> but also the significant contributions of these industrial giants. **(P11)**

    ABUSES _____

    context clue(s):

READ THE SELECTION: SECOND TIME

Read more carefully to get a better understanding of the selection. Use the dictionary, only if necessary.

COMPREHENSION EXERCISES

A. True or False

Write true or false and the number of the paragraph(s) that supports your answer. Be prepared to explain your answer.

_____ / _____ 1. It can be inferred that Lee Iacocca was an entrepreneur.

_____ / _____ 2. The idea of the entrepreneur is a recent one.

_____ / _____ 3. The contributions of entrepreneurs have only recently been appreciated or recognized.

_____ / _____ 4. If opportunities for business are not available in society, entrepreneurs try to create opportunities themselves.

_____ / _____ 5. Some entrepreneurs have had to make financial and personal sacrifices.

_____ / _____ 6. According to Schumpeter's definition, an entrepreneur is a person who starts a business, whether it is a new business or not.

_____ /_____   **7.** Money is the main goal of all entrepreneurs.

_____ /_____   **8.** Throughout American history, entrepreneurs have worked tirelessly to improve the lives of workers and society in general.

_____ /_____   **9.** Industrial giants contributed to the growth of the American economy by improving the use of the factors of production such as investing capital more productively and organizing labor more effectively.

_____ /_____   **10.** Frederic Tudor's ice business helped to create the demand for refrigeration, while Fred Smith's overnight mail delivery service responded to the existing demand for fast mail delivery from the high-tech industry.

B. Terms with Special Meanings

The three terms below have a special meaning. Analyze these terms in order to understand their meaning.

1. **creative destruction (P4)**
    According to Joseph Schumpeter, one function of an entrepreneur is "creative destruction." Analyze this function of the entrepreneur.

    a. What does he destroy (or discard)?
    b. What does he create (or reform / revolutionize)?
    c. Why do you think Schumpeter used such a strong word as "destruction" instead of a word like "discard" to describe the work of the entrepreneur?

2. **entrepreneur (P1,5)**
    The reading gives two definitions for entrepreneur: the dictionary definition and the definition given by Schumpeter. Compare these two definitions.

    a. What is the dictionary definition for entrepreneur given in the text?
    b. What is Schumpeter's definition? What one word does Schumpeter emphasize in his definition that is not found in the dictionary definition?
    c. Which of these two definitions is more general and which is more specific? Explain why.
    d. The six people below would all be considered entrepreneurs according to the dictionary definition. Would all six be considered entrepreneurs according to Schumpeter's definition? Explain your answers.

        1. King Gillette
        2. Nineteenth-century Chinese laundry shop owner

3. East European Jewish tailor in the 1920s
4. Korean grocery store manager today
5. Frederic Tudor
6. Fred Smith

3. robber baron (P10)

a. What is the common meaning of each word in this special term? Use your dictionary, if necessary.
b. This term was used to describe some entrepreneurs in the late nineteenth century. What particular group of people do you think made up this term at that time?
c. What do you think these entrepreneurs did that caused this particular group of people to call them "robber barons"?

C. Listing

Make three lists to show how these important points in the reading are developed or explained. Be as brief as possible. Include a heading with each list.

1. American entrepreneurs have been involved in the same basic activities since the early history of this country. List these basic activities.

(Heading) _____

_____

_____

_____

_____

_____

2. In creative destruction, the entrepreneur discards old ideas and, in their place, reforms and revolutionizes the pattern of production. List the ways in which the entrepreneur can reform or revolutionize the pattern of production. Then, next to each way, write "IN" if it is "an innovation" or "NC" if it is "a new combination of existing factors."

(Heading) _____

_____

_____

_____

3.   The writers present common characteristics of the typical entrepreneur in Paragraphs 5–8. List the different characteristics given in these paragraphs. Mark the one(s) that seems the most important and the least important. Be prepared to support your choices.

(Heading) _____

_____

_____

_____

_____

_____

_____

_____

_____

D. Diagram

Explain the relationship that this diagram illustrates. Then find the paragraph in the reading that discusses this interaction and reread it.

WHAT RELATIONSHIP DOES THE DIAGRAM ILLUSTRATE?

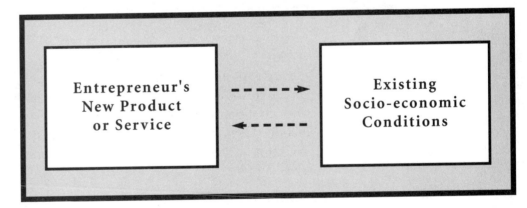

E. Charts

Using the examples of Gillette and his safety razor and Fred Smith and Federal Express, complete the following charts. These charts show how the entrepreneur and the socio-economic conditions of the time affected each other.

CHART 1

HOW GILLETTE'S INVENTION AFFECTED THE SOCIAL AND ECONOMIC CONDITIONS OF HIS TIME

The invention of the safety razor undoubtedly affected the daily lives of millions of American men and the economy in the early twentieth century. In answering the questions, think about the time period.

Gillette's Effect on Social Conditions

How do you think shaving at home with the safety razor, instead of going to the barber, affected the daily lives of American men?

_____

_____

_____

Gillette's Effect on Economic Conditions

How do you think the invention of the safety razor affected the economy? Think about the job of the barber and the need for workers to produce the safety razor.

_____

_____

_____

CHART 2

HOW THE SOCIAL AND ECONOMIC CONDITIONS AFFECTED
FRED SMITH AND FEDERAL EXPRESS

The existing social and economic conditions in the second half of the twentieth century were right for Fred Smith to start his overnight mail delivery service. When Smith recognized that these conditions were right for his new business, he decided to take the risk. In answering the questions, think about the time period.

Effect of Social Conditions on Fred Smith

In recent times, how has American society viewed the importance of time efficiency? Recognizing this viewpoint, what did Fred Smith decide to do?

_____

_____

_____

Effect of Economic Conditions on Fred Smith

Was the technology available for Fred Smith to deliver mail overnight? Explain.

_____

_____

_____

TOPICS FOR DISCUSSION AND WRITING

1. A hero is a person who is remembered for brave and good actions. However, the writers of this selection use the expression "unsung heros" to describe the entrepreneurs of the past. What do you think an "unsung hero" means? Name someone (not an entrepreneur) that you consider an "unsung hero." Why?

2. Studies of the characteristics of entrepreneurs have identified height and birth order as two common traits of entrepreneurs. Although these two are not as important as the other characteristics, they appear to have some effect on the making of an entrepreneur.

    Why do you think that being shorter than average height and being the oldest or youngest child in the family are common characteristics among entrepreneurs? In other words, what effect do you think these two traits can have on a person?

3. In Paragraph 9, the writers state that the entrepreneur's "search for achievement or success often has its costs." Based on information in the selection and your own ideas, explain in your own words what these "costs" are and why many entrepreneurs suffer in this way.

   Now think about other individuals, perhaps members of your own family, who search for some type of success in their work. Do you think that all professions have their costs? Explain. What are the costs of being a teacher, a medical doctor, a chemist, or other type of professional person?

4. We have seen how an entrepreneur's product or service can affect the social and economic conditions of the time. Think of a new product or service from the recent past and explain how it has affected social and/or economic conditions today.

5. John D. Rockefeller (1839–1937) is a well-known American entrepreneur of the past, who at one time was the richest man in the world. His wealth came from the oil business. However, some of the methods he used to expand his business, which were legal at the time, are illegal today.

   After his retirement, Rockefeller began to give large amounts of money to charitable organizations. One of these organizations, The Rockefeller Foundation, received almost $200 million from him. Look up the subject "Rockefeller Foundation" in an encyclopedia and find out when it was founded and what its purpose is. Report back to the class on what you have learned.

VOCABULARY EXERCISES

A. Word Forms

Choose the correct word form that completes each sentence. The base form of the word is in **bold**. For nouns, use singular or plural forms. For verbs, use appropriate verb tenses and passive voice where necessary.

(P1) 1. **entrepreneur**, entrepreneurship,   entrepreneurial *adj*
           enterprise *n*

   a. Thomas Edison showed many of the characteristics of a typical
       _____.

   b. Are there any special _____ skills that are needed
       to be successful in the service industry?

   c. In the past 20 years, business schools have begun to offer courses on
       _____.

   d. Fred Smith began a mail service _____ known as
       Federal Express.

(P1) 2. management, manager *n*   **to manage** *v*   managerial *adj*

    a. What are the five functions of a _____?

    b. After _____ his own lumber company for 35 years, he sold it for a good sum of money and retired with his wife to Hawaii.

    c. The dispute between _____ and labor led to a strike.

    d. Does a college instructor need _____ skills?

(P2) 3. creativity, creation, creator *n*   **to create** *v*   creative *adj*

    a. She is a well-known _____ of children's television programs.

    b. Since he left the rock band, he has not _____ any new music.

    c. A _____ person usually has a different perspective of the world than other people.

    d. What do you think of the architect's most recent _____?

    e. Do you think there is a connection between the traits of imagination and _____?

(P2) 4. invention, inventor *n*   **to invent** *v*

    a. Today when people _____ things, they must obtain a patent from the government.

    b. This patent gives the _____ the sole right to make, use, and sell the _____ for a certain number of years.

(P5) 5. imagination *n*   **to imagine** *v*   imaginative *adj*

    a. Let's _____ that you could get any job you wanted. What job would you want?

    b. Why are children usually more _____ than adults?

    c. You must use your _____ in order to figure out what the abstract painting means.

B. Other Useful Words

Complete the sentences with an appropriate word from the list. For nouns, use singular or plural forms. For verbs, use appropriate verb tenses.

abuse (**P11**)   labor (**P11**)   to make a fortune (in) (**P2**)
capital (**P11**)   profile (**P6**)   to mass produce (**P12**)
characteristic (**P6**) unsung hero (**P3**)   to seek opportunities (**P2**)
innovation (**P5**)

1. Name three _____ of an outstanding salesperson.

2. The start of the _____ movement in the United States was due in part to the poor working conditions of factory workers at the end of the nineteenth century.

3. Before a company begins to _____ a product, it will test the product in the market to see if there is a favorable response by consumers.

4. Because he didn't have enough _____ to start his own business, he had to borrow money from the bank.

5. Can you give a _____ of the typical Korean businessman?

6. Under what circumstances can an ordinary person be considered an _____?

7. The entrepreneur is constantly _____ to try new ventures.

8. What are the latest _____ in the plastics industry?

9. One of the _____ of the "robber barons" was the very low salaries they paid workers. These salaries forced many workers to work long hours each day to earn a living.

10. In the late nineteenth century, John D. Rockefeller, an American entrepreneur, _____ in the oil business. So after his retirement, he contributed large amounts of money to charitable organizations.

C. Vocabulary Oral Practice

Practice using the underlined words by answering the questions below.

1. Does a person have to make <u>sacrifices</u> when studying in a foreign country? If so, what kinds of <u>sacrifices</u> does a person make? Is the educational goal worth the <u>sacrifices</u>? (**P3**)

2. All people do things which <u>in retrospect</u> they wish they had not done or had done differently. Can you give an example of this from your own experience? **(P5)**

3. Who was an important <u>leading citizen</u> of your country? Explain what this person is most remembered for. **(P3)**

4. Which child is usually the most <u>self-centered</u>: the oldest child, the middle child, or the youngest? Why do you think this is true? **(P9)**

5. If a person wants to be accepted by a highly competitive business school, what factors can <u>play a key role</u> in one's acceptance to such a school? **(P11)**

6. Some Americans recycle their aluminum cans and newspapers, and others simply <u>discard</u> them. What is the benefit of recycling? Why do others simply <u>discard</u> these items? **(P4)**

7. Grades are important in college. Some students have an <u>obsession</u> about grades; they tell themselves that they have to get all As. What factors might contribute to this <u>obsession</u>? What might be a negative consequence of this <u>obsessive</u> behavior? **(P7)**

D. Dictation

Study the spelling of the words in the previous exercises. You will have a dictation of sentences that contain these words.

JOURNAL WRITING

Topic 1

The writers of this selection consider the American entrepreneurs of the past as unsung heroes. Think of a person in your country from either the past or today that you think is an unsung hero. This person does not have to be an entrepreneur. Write in your journal about this person (or perhaps a group of people). Tell why you consider him/her an unsung hero. What contribution(s) did this person make to society?

Topic 2

Our lives have been greatly affected by the innumerable inventions and new services of the nineteenth and twentieth centuries. These inventions and services have benefited and changed society in big and little ways, and in some cases, the changes may have also caused a few disadvantages. Consider, for example, the elevator, the air conditioner, and the credit card. Choose one of these (or your own) and describe ways in which it has affected life and/or work in industrialized countries.

READING FOR PLEASURE

POETRY

The American entrepreneurs described in the previous reading show what is called a "can-do attitude." A "can-do attitude" was, and for some people still is, a popular American cultural belief. The following poem by Edgar Guest illustrates this attitude. Read the poem to find out what this attitude means.

BIOGRAPHICAL SKETCH: EDGAR GUEST (1881–1959)

The American poet Edgar Guest was born in England and immigrated to the United States when he was ten. At the age of 14, he began working as an office boy for the *Detroit Free Press* newspaper. A few years later, after Guest became a newspaper staff writer, the paper published his poems from time to time.

Eventually, his poems became so popular that they were published weekly in the paper. Guest wrote over 10,000 poems, which are known for their simple language and content. The principal theme of his poetry is the life and attitudes of common people. He has been called "the poet of the plain people."

POEM

It Couldn't Be Done

chuckle: soft laugh

buckled right in: started working hard
grin: big smile

tackled: started working on

Somebody said that it couldn't be done
    But he with a chuckle replied
That "maybe it couldn't," but he would be one
    Who wouldn't say so til he'd tried.
So he buckled right in with the trace of a grin
    On his face. If he worried he hid it.
He started to sing as he tackled the thing
    That couldn't be done, and he did it.

scoffed: spoke disrespectfully

Somebody scoffed: "Oh, you'll never do that"

At least no one ever has done it";

But he took off his coat and he took off his hat,

and the first thing we knew he'd begun it.

With a lift of his chin and a bit of a grin,

Without any doubting or quitting,

He started to sing as he tackled the thing

That couldn't be done, and he did it.

There are thousands to tell you it cannot be done,

There are thousands to prophesy failure;

There are thousands to point out to you, one by one,

The dangers that wait to assail you.

But just buckle in with a bit of a grin,

Just take off your coat and go to it:

Just start to sing as you tackle the thing

That "cannot be done," and you'll do it.

prophesy: predict

assail: attack

go to it: get started

DISCUSSION QUESTIONS

1. Briefly tell what the American "can-do attitude" means. In which stanza does the poet speak directly to the reader and tell him/her to have a "can-do attitude"?

2. The first and second stanzas of the poem describe the same situation. Briefly retell in your own words what happens in these two stanzas.

3. In the second stanza, what does the expression "he took off his coat and he took off his hat" really mean?

4. What personal traits does the person in the first and second stanzas show by his behavior?

5. Who does "thousands" refer to in the third stanza? Why do you think the poet uses "thousands" instead of "many"?

6. Is a "can-do attitude" popular in your culture? Explain.

7. What is the theme of the poem?

CHAPTER 11

THE MAKING OF TWO ENTREPRENEURS

Leone Ackerly is one of two entrepreneurs you will learn about in this chapter who have made it big in the world of business.

Now that you have a basic understanding of entrepreneurs, you will read about the lives and work of two entrepreneurs.

The first tells about a well-known Frenchman who represents the classic entrepreneur. He introduced the first of his several inventions in the post-World War II period.

The second tells about a relatively unknown American woman who represents one type of modern-day entrepreneur. She was an average housewife who started a service business in the 1970s to meet a common need.

ENTREPRENEUR 1: MARCEL BICH

This is the story of the famous French entrepreneur, Marcel Bich, who, among other things, invented the Bic pen.

READING SELECTION

PRE-READING DISCUSSION

Getting into the Topic

This reading is taken from a book entitled *Entrepreneurs: The Men and Women behind Famous Brand Names and How They Made It* by Joseph J. Fucini and Suzy Fucini. As the title indicates, the book is about men and women who are entrepreneurs and who have developed products that carry their names.

The last part of the title, *and How They Made It*, is an idiom and in this context means "and how they became successful."

■ Think of some *famous brand names*. These names may or may not be the same name as the person who developed the product. For example, think about the names of some famous brand athletic shoes or women's clothing.

Getting an Overview of the Reading Selection

The reading gives a short biographical sketch of Bich's work life. Since it is a biography, it is organized in time order.

■ To check for time order, read the first sentence of each paragraph. Most contain words and dates that indicate time order. Underline these words and dates.

READ THE SELECTION: FIRST TIME

Read to get a general understanding of the selection. Do not stop to look up words in the dictionary.

READING

Marcel Bich

rivals: competitors

consumer trends: new and popular tendencies of buyers

disposable: intended to be thrown away after using
ballpoint pens: pens with a ball at one end that rolls ink onto paper

shed: small building used for storing things

market: buying and selling of goods
"inkwell" models: pens that need an ink bottle
novelties: new and unusual things

1   Even his most bitter business rivals have been forced to admit that Marcel Bich was a genius at predicting consumer trends. An early prophet of the "throwaway culture," the astute Frenchman has built a $700 million company since 1953 by responding to the worldwide demand for inexpensive, but reliable, disposable products, first with ballpoint pens and then with cigarette lighters and razors.

2   Born in Turin, Italy, to French parents (his father was a civil engineer), Bich began his career at eighteen selling flashlights door to door in Paris. A few years later he went to work for a large ink manufacturer and eventually was made production manager, before he was called up by the French air force at the outbreak of World War II.

3   Following the war, Bich and a friend, Edouard Buffard, raised $1,000 and bought an old shed in the run-down Paris suburb of Clichy, where they manufactured ink refills for the ballpoint pens that were just beginning to appear in France.

4   At the time, the French pen market was dominated by the traditional "inkwell" models. Refillable ballpoint pens (mostly American imports) were regarded as novelties, and their popularity was limited by their relatively high price and unreliable performance. Marcel Bich was very familiar with the ballpoint's shortcomings through his ink business, so he came up with the idea of producing a less expensive yet improved pen. With its lower price and better

quality, he was convinced that the new pen would claim a better share of the market.

5   Working in his small factory-shed, the ink maker began to experiment with different ballpoint designs in 1949 and eventually his idea for a new pen took shape. Unlike the ballpoints then on the market, virtually all of which were refillable, the prototypes that Bich developed were intended to be used only until their ink ran out and then thrown away. The farsighted businessman believed that this disposable feature would increase his pen's appeal to the convenience-oriented consumer of the post-World War II era.

6   After four years of research and development, Bich finally came up with a pen that met all his requirements. The simple stick-shaped writing instrument was strong and dependable; and because it consisted of only a thin plastic ink tube, a tiny metal ballpoint, and a rigid plastic outer tube, it could be made and sold very inexpensively. Bich called his new disposable pen by the catchy name "Bic," his own name with the last letter omitted.

7   As its inventor had expected, the Bic pen was an immediate hit with the French public. Three years after introducing the pen in 1953, Marcel Bich was selling a quarter of a million disposable ballpoints a day in his native land and was beginning to market his product in other European countries. The spectacular success of the unpretentious Bic (it sometimes sold for less than 5 cents) surprised the entire pen industry, which had traditionally been controlled by high-priced, high-status products.

8   In December 1958, the stocky, balding pen maker entered the U.S. market by taking over the Waterman Pen Company. Disposable ballpoints were almost unheard of in the United States at the time, but the handy Bic fit comfortably into the American lifestyle, and within a decade of its introduction, the French product was accounting for half of all retail pen sales in the nation. To measure this achievement another way, Bich was selling 330 million ballpoints a year, more than one and a half pens for every American.

9   Encouraged by the success of his pen, Bich test-marketed a disposable cigarette lighter in Sweden in 1972. A year later, he introduced the lighter to America, where it challenged the already established leader, the Cricket Lighter, made by Gillette. The two companies had done battle once before when the surprising Bic ballpoint pen had surpassed Gillette's Papermate pen to become the king of the U.S. retail pen market.

10  This time, however, Gillette was determined to put up a better fight. Both companies invested heavily in television advertising; Gillette hoped that its singing Cricket cartoon character would beat its competitor, Bic's "Flick My Bic" slogan. They also engaged in some fierce price competition, taking 60 cents or more off lighters that originally were supposed to retail for $1.49. When the dust finally settled, Bic emerged the winner once again. Its lighter surpassed Gillette's in 1977 and has remained well ahead in sales ever since.

11   History seemed about to repeat itself in 1976, when Bich brought yet another of his throwaways to America—the Bic razor. This was an attack on the original product that the Gillette Company had developed. Gillette responded by introducing its own disposable razor, Good News. Because of Gillette's reputation and expertise in shavers, Good News outsold its French competitor from the beginning, and Bic sales accounted for less than 20 percent of the U.S. disposable razor market by 1981.

12   Bich's failure to top Gillette in the razor market was one of the rare setbacks that he has experienced in his success-filled career of more than three decades. The competitive Frenchman (who once was described by *Time* magazine as a "stubborn, opinionated entrepreneur") hasn't been as lucky in his favorite pastime, sailing, however. A dedicated sailor, Bich has tried and failed on several occasions to win the America's Yacht Cup race. In 1970 he spent $3 million and worked fourteen hours a day preparing for the event, only to lose when his yacht named "France" got lost in the fog off Newport, Rhode Island.

13   Bich's yachting activities have given the public its few chances to see the pen millionaire. A very private person, he avoids interviews and forbids photographs. When not on his yacht, Bich's leisure time is usually spent with his family, which includes his wife and ten children. This wealthy businessman very seldom seeks or appreciates others' advice. Bich once said that his impressive success was due to his refusal to listen to anyone's advice but his own.

READING CHECK

A. Reaction to Bich

Answer these questions as completely as possible.

1. What did you find most interesting about Marcel Bich?

    _____

    _____

2. In the first paragraph, Bich is referred to as "an early prophet of the 'throwaway culture.'" Explain what this expression means. What entrepreneurial characteristic does this show that Bich has?

    _____

    _____

B. Guessing the Meaning from Context

Look carefully at the context of the underlined words below. Try to guess their meaning. Identify the context clue(s) that helped you and be prepared to explain your answer. If necessary, refer to **Appendix 2**.

1. After four years of research and development, Bich finally <u>came up with</u> a pen that met all of his requirements. **(P6)**

    CAME UP WITH _____
    context clue(s):

2. As its inventor had expected, the Bic pen was an immediate <u>hit</u> with the French public. Three years after introducing the pen in 1953, Marcel Bich was selling a quarter of a million disposable ballpoints a day in his native land. **(P7)**

    HIT _____
    context clue(s):

3. The Gillette and Bic companies also engaged in some fierce price competition, taking 60 cents or more off lighters that originally were supposed to retail for $1.49. When the dust finally settled, Bic emerged the winner once again. Its lighter <u>surpassed</u> Gillette's in 1977 and has remained well ahead in sales ever since. **(P10)**

    SURPASSED _____
    context clue(s):

4. Because of Gillette's reputation and expertise in shavers, its Good News shaver <u>outsold</u> the French competitor Bic from the beginning, and Bic sales accounted for less than 20 percent of the U.S. disposable razor market by 1981. **(P11)**

    OUTSOLD _____
    context clue(s):

5. Bich's failure to top Gillette in the razor market was one of the rare <u>setbacks</u> that he has experienced in his success-filled career of more than three decades. **(P12)**

    SETBACKS _____
    context clue(s):

READ THE SELECTION: SECOND TIME

Read more carefully to get a better understanding of the selection. Use the dictionary, only if necessary.

A. Chart

Complete the chart by giving evidence of how Bich demonstrated each of the general characteristics of entrepreneurs identified in the previous reading on the American entrepreneur. Then answer the question below.

BICH'S ENTREPRENEURIAL CHARACTERISTICS	
General Characteristics of Entrepreneurs	**How Bich Demonstrated Each Characteristic**
1. Imagination	_____ _____
2. Willingness to take risks	_____ _____
3. Disciplined and focused on the task at hand; hardworking	_____ _____
4. Profit-seeker	Built a $700 million company
5. Need for success and achievement	_____ _____ _____
6. Love of challenges and competition	_____ _____

■ Do you find that any of these characteristics overlap with each other? Which may overlap? Explain.

_____

_____

B. Chart

To become a successful pen maker, Marcel Bich went through several stages of entrepreneurial development. In the chart, you find the five typical stages of development for an entrepreneur. Briefly explain how Bich carried out each of these stages. Then answer the question below.

BICH'S STAGES OF ENTREPRENEURIAL DEVELOPMENT

Stages of Entrepreneurial Development	How Bich Accomplished Each Stage
Stage 1 Gain business experience	_____ _____
Stage 2 Start own business	_____ _____
Stage 3 Come up with new idea	_____ _____
Stage 4 Turn idea into developed product or service	_____ _____
Stage 5 Market product widely	_____ _____

■ Could these stages be arranged in a different order? If so, what would the order be?

_____

_____

TOPICS FOR DISCUSSION AND WRITING

1. When disposable products first entered the market in the 1950s, why do you think consumers were eager to buy them? Name other disposable products than the three given in the reading. What disposables do you buy or use regularly? What do you think the U.S. public opinion on disposables is today? How do you know this?

2. Companies that produce the same product compete fiercely with each other in today's market. What are some ways that companies try to attract customers to buy their product? (Some are mentioned in the reading.) Which approach do you think attracts the most buyers? Why?

3. Listen to TV and radio commercials or read magazine and newspaper advertisements and find some interesting slogans used to sell a product or service. Write down the names of one or two products or services and the slogan that each uses.

   In class, tell or perhaps sing the slogan, and then have the class guess the name of the product or service. After everyone has presented his or her slogan, decide which ones are the most appealing and tell why.

VOCABULARY EXERCISES

A. Vocabulary Oral Practice

Practice using the underlined words by answering the questions below. This oral practice focuses on descriptive adjectives.

1. One of Marcel Bich's <u>fierce</u> competitors was Gillette. Name some <u>fierce</u> competitors in business today. (**P10**)

2. A synonym for a fierce competitor is a <u>bitter</u> rival. Bich and Gillette were <u>bitter</u> business rivals. Why were they <u>bitter</u> business rivals? (**P1**)

3. Bich was a <u>farsighted</u> businessman. Why should a businessman or a leader be <u>farsighted</u>? (**P5**)

4. Bich was a <u>dedicated</u> sailor because he worked very hard to do well in sailing. Are you a <u>dedicated</u> student? Name some professions in which you find many <u>dedicated</u> people. (**P12**)

5. Bich is described as a very <u>private</u> person. How does a <u>private</u> person act? (**P13**)

6. Sailing is Bich's <u>favorite</u> pastime. What does pastime mean? What is your <u>favorite</u> pastime? (**P12**)

7. As an entrepreneur, Bich recognized the <u>worldwide</u> demand for inexpensive, but reliable, disposable products. What would a medical doctor or an environmentalist recognize as a <u>worldwide</u> issue? **(P1)**

8. *Time* magazine described Bich as <u>stubborn</u>. Why do you think it described him as stubborn? Describe something that a <u>stubborn</u> child might do. **(P12)**

9. Bich is described as a <u>competitive</u> Frenchman. Perhaps he first learned to be <u>competitive</u> when he was a student. In your country, are students more <u>competitive</u> in high school or in college? Explain why. **(P12)**

10. Gillette's cigarette lighter was the <u>established</u> leader in the U.S. market until Bich challenged it with his own. In this case, the <u>established</u> company lost. What is the opposite of an <u>established</u> company? **(P9)**

ENTREPRENEUR 2: LEONE ACKERLY

Now that you have read about a well-known Frenchman who represents the classic entrepreneur, let's take a look at a relatively unknown American woman who represents the modern-day entrepreneur.

An average housewife, Leone Ackerly started her own one-person housecleaning business called Mini Maid in 1973. Her business soon developed into a team operation.

A couple of years later, Mini Maid expanded in a big way. This time, Ackerly turned her team housecleaning business into a nationwide housecleaning franchise. In the 1970s, fast-food franchises, like McDonald's, were quite popular. However, Mini Maid was the first *housecleaning* franchise.

PRE-READING DISCUSSION

Getting into the Topic

This reading is taken from a book entitled *The Service Edge: 101 Companies That Profit from Customer Care* by Ron Zemke and Dick Schaff.

■ What does "customer care" mean? The service a company provides its customers can make or break a business. Explain what this means.

■ Mini Maid expanded into a franchise business. To understand franchising better, let's take a look at some business terms:

Franchising: A system whereby a business owner expands a business by selling the rights to duplicate the business concept.

Franchisor: The business owner who sells the rights to duplicate the business concept.

Franchisee: The person that buys the rights to duplicate the business concept.

Franchise: A business owned by a franchisee, but still part of the franchisor's system.

Getting an Overview of the Reading Selection

■ Read the first sentence of Paragraphs 4–14. Which paragraphs describe Ackerly's one-person business? Which describe her team business? Which describe her franchise business?

■ Now read Paragraphs 15 and 16. Did Mini Maid's service standards change when it became a franchise business? Explain.

READ THE SELECTION: FIRST TIME

Read to get a general understanding of the selection. Do not stop to look up words in the dictionary.

Leone Ackerly

1   In the good old days, well-to-do people had live-in maids to keep all the things they had worked for clean and shiny. Not-quite-so-well-to-do people had a "cleaning lady" who came in once a week or so to perform some of the

same services. Domestic work wasn't the kind of high-minded profession that people spent years in preparation for. It was, pretty much by definition, the kind of work nobody really wanted to do. Maybe that explains why, until the early 1970s, no one had really looked at cleaning homes and apartments as a real service business.

2   However, that view of domestic work has recently changed. Today, cleaning up after well-to-do professionals and two-career families has made the housecleaning service one of the brightest of franchise opportunities. There are Merry Maids, Dial-a-Maids, Maids for a Day, Maids Easy, and even McMaids. But the pioneer housecleaning franchise is Mini Maid, and its founder, Leone Ackerly, is a self-made maid.

3   Back in 1973, Ackerly, then 28, had a comfortable home in an affluent community in Atlanta, Georgia. She had three daughters, no professional degree or office training, and a husband who had worked his way up to vice president of a security business. She was used to doing her own housework because often she couldn't get a maid. Other people probably had the same problem, she reasoned. It was at this point that she started looking at the old saying "good help is hard to find" from an entrepreneurial perspective.

4   One day she announced to her husband Bill that she was going to clean houses and apartments as a business. The first job took her half a day and wore her out. Her first customers weren't sure what was included in her services. In response, she quickly made a list of minimum tasks that should be done at least weekly. Minimum Maid Service, which is what she called her business, was later shortened to Mini Maid.

5   The key to professional housecleaning services, she discovered first-hand, was management of time and motion. Making the service systematic made it more reliable, consistent, and customer-pleasing. From her husband's training in security work, Ackerly adopted the thorough, top-to-bottom, left-to-right, one-room-at-a-time approach.

6   She also learned to avoid retracing her steps and to make sure she had everything she needed with her when she entered a room. She used a stopwatch to time herself as she made beds, cleaned bathrooms, vacuumed rugs, and scrubbed floors. That continuing, first-hand learning process also taught her the value of using a long extension cord with a vacuum. A long extension cord only had to be plugged in once instead of making many separate bends to plug in and unplug a vacuum.

7   Ackerly listened to everyone, from her mother to people in charge of museums, to pick up cleaning tips. It was her mother who helped Ackerly make the biggest breakthrough in the business: team cleaning. When mom arrived for a visit shortly after the business had started to grow, Ackerly took her along. Her mother, who was her first teammate, lasted two weeks doing bathrooms before going back to Florida.

8   But that was long enough for Ackerly to switch from a do-it-yourself operation to a team operation. Today, a four-person Mini Maid team can clean a house in less than 30 minutes, using the systematic approach she developed through her own experience. (This approach has been copied and used in some form or another by virtually all of the other maid services now cleaning up

pioneer: one who does something first and so prepares the way for others
affluent: wealthy; well-to-do

security business: protects people, places, or things

tasks: jobs

first-hand: based on personal experience
motion: physical movement
systematic: following a fixed plan

tips: suggestions
breakthrough: discovery (often suddenly and after earlier failures) that can lead to other discoveries

around the country.) A typical Mini Maid team can handle 10 houses or as many as 14 apartments in a seven-and-a-half-hour day.

9   In 1976, Ackerly pioneered the housecleaning franchise business, turning her innovative little business into a national business. A number of competitors soon followed. No matter: The annual market for housecleaning services is over $7 billion and growing, so there's plenty of room.

10   New Mini Maid franchisees receive a 300-page operations manual that contains many of her housecleaning ideas and helps new Mini Maid franchisees learn the business side of housework. In addition to the operations manual, new franchisees get two weeks of training in Atlanta and have access to a library of videotapes and other training materials they can use to develop their own professional teams. Mini Maid's franchising agreement includes everything from training in the housecleaning procedures to programs for payroll, tax accounting, personnel management, and advertising. There's also a line of Mini Maid cleaning products, all of them developed on the job.

procedures: steps or rules for doing something properly

11   When Mini Maid franchise teams arrive on the job, they come fully equipped with their own cleaning supplies, vacuums, and other necessary materials; they take their used-up supplies with them. In less than an hour, they can clean the standard house top to bottom, and then be gone without a trace. That's a big change from the days of sometimes troublesome workers who had to be trained, equipped, and checked up on.

12   During the franchising training sessions, Ackerly stresses the importance of quality control, from the team members hired (generally housewives and young mothers) to the follow-up phone calls franchises make the next day to each and every customer. A follow-up call is not typical of most other maid services, but it is a business practice that contributes to the success of Mini Maid franchises in 24 states.

quality control: guaranteeing the quality of service at each franchise is the same

13   A franchisee must pay a franchisor a monthly fee in exchange for permission to use the company's name and to sell its products or services. In most cases, the fee is a percentage of the franchise's sales. This means, the more successful a franchise is, the more money the franchisor gets. However, Ackerly charges her franchises a flat, fixed fee, which allows them to keep more of the results from their labor. There's even no fee at all for the first two months, which helps ease cash-flow problems during the critical start-up period of a new business.

14   "We still have our first franchise from 1976," Ackerly told us. "That's because we look for stability in franchising—we're a family, not a factory." When a franchise encounters an operational problem, the founder herself often lends a hand. Another one of her longstanding business practices is to pair up a new or struggling franchise with a nearby franchise who can provide support and advice. And even when the business is running smoothly, Ackerly still tries to keep in touch with each Mini Maid franchise once or twice a month.

service standards: actions to guarantee good service

15   When Mini Maid first started, Ackerly established two service standards: an opportunity for her customers to inspect her work before she left, and a money-back guarantee if the work wasn't done satisfactorily. Both standards still exist now that Mini Maid has grown into a franchise business, although

many Mini Maid teams are invisible to their customers since they come and go while the adults are at work and the kids are at school.

16   Maybe good help isn't so hard to find.

READING CHECK

Reaction to Ackerly

Answer these questions as completely as possible.

1. What did you find most interesting about Leone Ackerly?

    _____

    _____

2. In the second paragraph, Ackerly is referred to as a "self-made maid." Explain what this expression means. What entrepreneurial characteristic does this show that Ackerly has?

    _____

    _____

READ THE SELECTION: SECOND TIME

Read more carefully to get a better understanding of the reading. Use the dictionary, only if necessary.

COMPREHENSION EXERCISE

True or False

Write true or false and write the number of the paragraph(s) that supports your answer. Be prepared to explain your answer.

_____ /_____   1. Professional housecleaning is a growing business because of the increasing number of affluent professionals and working couples.

_____ /_____   2. Ackerly had previous experience in professional housecleaning and running a business.

_____ /_____   3. Ackerly's idea for a housecleaning business was a response to a problem.

_____ /_____   4. Ackerly learned that management of time and motion was essential in professional housecleaning.

_____ / _____   5. Ackerly's biggest breakthrough in housecleaning was the idea of team cleaning because it allowed her to handle more business.

_____ / _____   6. In a typical workday, a Mini Maid team can clean as many as seven houses.

_____ / _____   7. Ackerly helps others start up and run their own Mini Maid housecleaning service.

_____ / _____   8. When Mini Maid developed into a franchise business, Ackerly became less concerned about quality control.

_____ / _____   9. The more money a Mini Maid franchise makes, the more money Ackerly gets.

_____ / _____   10. Once a franchise is running smoothly, Ackerly's contact with it is over and the franchise is on its own.

TOPICS FOR DISCUSSION AND WRITING

1. Ackerly realized that the key to professional housecleaning is management of time and motion. To do this, she developed a *systematic* approach to housecleaning. Explain what this means. Then give examples of ways in which Mini Maid housecleaners save time and energy.

2. Because customer satisfaction is Ackerly's main goal, she established two service standards. What are these standards? Since customers are not often at home to inspect the work of Mini Maid teams, what does each Mini Maid franchise do to make sure customers are satisfied? Explain how this business practice benefits her franchise business.

3. Ackerly describes her franchise business as "a family, not a factory." As the franchisor, she is like a parent, and individual franchises are like her children. Give examples of the parental support she provides each franchise.

4. Compare the entrepreneurial characteristics of Ackerly and Bich. How are they similar? How are they different? What factors might explain any differences?

5. Ackerly went through some of the same stages of entrepreneurial development as Bich, but *in a different order*. Reread the selection and make a chart of her entrepreneurial stages and how she accomplished each one. Use the chart on page 222 as a model. If Ackerly went through any stages that Bich did not go through, include them in your chart.

VOCABULARY EXERCISES

A. Vocabulary Oral Practice

Practice using the underlined words by answering the questions below.

1. Your classmates are planning to travel to your country. Give them <u>tips</u> on what time of the year to come, what to bring with them, and what to see. (**P7**)

2. What is the <u>key</u> to learning a foreign language? (**P5**)

3. What is your least favorite <u>task</u> to do around the house? (**P4**)

4. People help each other out in both large and small ways. Describe a time when a stranger <u>lent</u> you <u>a</u> helping <u>hand</u> or when you <u>lent a</u> helping <u>hand</u> to a stranger. (**P10**)

5. Do you write letters to <u>keep in touch with</u> your friends? If not, how do you <u>keep in touch with</u> them? (**P14**)

6. Think of something people usually learn <u>first-hand</u>, that is, from personal experience rather than from books. (**P5**)

7. Describe someone you know who is a <u>self-made</u> person. (**P2**)

8. Because of the discovery of penicillin, doctors are able to treat many kinds of infections. Name another important medical <u>breakthrough</u> and its benefits. What medical <u>breakthrough</u> are researchers hoping to make in the near future? (**P7**)

B. Dictation

Study the spelling of the words in the previous vocabulary exercises (Bich and Ackerly). You will have a dictation of sentences that contain these words.

JOURNAL WRITING

You have just read about the lives of two people who made it and became successful. Both had goals and worked hard to achieve them..

A writing assignment that many college students are given is to write their own obituary. To understand what this is, read the obituary on the next page written by Chung, a student from Korea. After reading his obituary, explain what you think an obituary is. Why do you think college students are given this kind of a writing assignment?

Then, in your journal, write your own obituary. You can be totally serious, or like Chung, you can combine seriousness with humor.

The Wall Street Journal
Friday, June 6, 2030
Special Edition

Today early at dawn, the world lost one of its most renowned entrepreneurs, politicians, and philanthropists—Rockefeller-Kissinger-Forbes Chung. Mr. R. K. F. Chung received his doctorate in political science from The George Washington University. At the age of 35, he completed his Ph.D. in international business at Oxford.

A self-made trillionaire, R. K. F. Chung began his career in fashion retail. He was responsible for such famous brand names as Alligator, Eve St. Laurant, and Nora Ricci. With his marketing strategies, he was able to penetrate the markets in all countries from the North Pole to the South Pole. At 45, Chung became a member of the Parliament in Korea. He was one of the prominent figures in the reunification of North and South Korea in 2020. He became the ninth Nobel Peace Prize winner of Korea. From 2021, R. K. F. Chung began donating part of his fortune to the poor and the needy. At midnight on June 6, 2030, he held an exclusive world press conference. In this live television announcement, he revealed his plans to distribute all of his fortune—6.6 trillion dollars—and expressed his desire to return to being a private citizen. After the press conference, he suddenly became ill and died as he was getting into his Abraham Continental.

Although he achieved success in all aspects of life, he most wanted to be remembered as a humanist. He is survived by his only daughter, Dr. Darwin Chung, a famous biologist, who is writing a book, *The Origin of Women.*

LECTURE   The Fundamentals of Franchising

You have read about Leone Ackerly and how she transformed her housecleaning business into a successful franchise business. In this lecture, you will learn more about the fundamentals of franchising.

LISTENING STRATEGY

This lecture presents several important points about franchising as noted in the next paragraph. In many cases, these points in the lecture are explained by listing their various parts. Listen for the important points and the listing of their various parts.

After a brief introduction, you will learn some background information on franchising and some definitions of topic-related words. Then the lecture describes the basic way that franchising works and lists the responsibilities and the advantages and disadvantages of franchising for the people involved.

TERMS USED IN THE LECTURE*

single-owner business
corporation
franchisor
franchisee
franchise
parent company
legal right
to operate a business
the business format
established conditions

established plan of operation
quality control procedure
monthly royalty
monthly percentage of sales
brand-name recognition
standardized quality and service
profit sharing
limited financial risk
limited capital
limited decision making

* These terms are defined or made clear from context in the lecture.

NOTETAKING SHEET

1. Listen to the lecture. Follow the outline below as you listen. Pay attention to the difference between the major points and the listing of their various parts. Do not write anything at this time.

2. Listen again and complete the outline by adding details about the important points or by making lists of the various parts of the important points. Write only key words or phrases. After the lecture, compare your notes with a classmate's. You may want to listen to the lecture again to confirm any points that you missed.

3. After completing your notes, discuss them with the class.

Outline of Lecture on

the Fundamentals of Franchising

1. Background information

_____

_____

_____

_____

_____

2. Definitions

_____

_____

_____

_____

_____

_____

_____

_____

3. How franchising works

_____

_____

_____

4. Responsibilities

For parent company:

_____

_____

_____

_____

_____

For franchisee:

_____

_____

_____

_____

_____

_____

5. Advantages

For parent company:

_____

_____

_____

_____

For franchisee:

_____

_____

_____

_____

_____

_____

6. Disadvantages

For parent company:

_____

_____

For franchisee:

_____

_____

_____

_____

_____

DISCUSSION QUESTIONS

1. As a franchisee, would you prefer to pay a monthly royalty or a monthly percentage of sales? Explain your choice.

2. Leone Ackerly doesn't use national advertising for her franchises, but McDonald's does. Why do you think some franchises use national advertising and others don't?

3. Would you rather operate a franchise or your own independent small business? Explain.

COMMUNICATIVE ACTIVITY

Entrepreneur Project: Creating a New Product

In this activity, you will create your own new product and then present the new product to possible buyers. The presentation could be for the television audience.

Procedure:

1. **Deciding on a New Product**

   Think of a new product that you can sell. To help you decide what your product will be, think about something that you personally would like to have, something that would help you but is not available in stores. Remember, if you need it, other people probably need it too. It can be something crazy and funny, something which uses new technology that is not yet developed or is impossible to develop.

2. **Preparing Your Presentation**

   Make an attractive visual of your product or show the actual product. Include the following information about the product and organize as listed below. Your presentation should be 3–5 minutes.

   a. Give an introduction that catches the audience's attention. Identify the product and briefly tell what it does and who can use it.

   b. Describe how the product works. Give as much detail as possible. This will help to sell your product.

   c. Tell about the sizes, colors, etc., in which the product is available and about the price(s). Tell about any additional features that the product might have and about their cost.

   d. Tell your audience where they can buy the product by giving the names of local stores or how they can place an order by giving the telephone number and/or mailing address of the manufacturer.

   e. Convince your audience that they should buy the product. Give convincing reasons why they need the product.

   f. End with your product's slogan.

Schumpeter's definition of an entrepreneur is one who revolutionizes the pattern of production by developing a new product or service or by discovering a new market. This selection is about three entrepreneurs who discovered a new market for their product or service. This market is "the New America."

READING SELECTION

PRE-READING DISCUSSION

Getting into the Topic

■   Are there businesses in the city where you are now living which meet the needs of people from your country? If so, tell what kinds of businesses there are. Who mostly owns and operates them—immigrants or Anglos?

■   Do these businesses also attract more mainstream consumers, that is, Anglo consumers? If so, which ones?

Getting an Overview of the Reading Selection

■   This selection is quite long. However, it is divided into four sections. The first section introduces the idea of selling to the New America, especially to the growing number of Hispanics and Asians. Look at the headings and photos in the selection. What do you think the reading will discuss?

The two bar graphs below show why the New America is a profitable market. Let's analyze these graphs.

BAR GRAPH 1

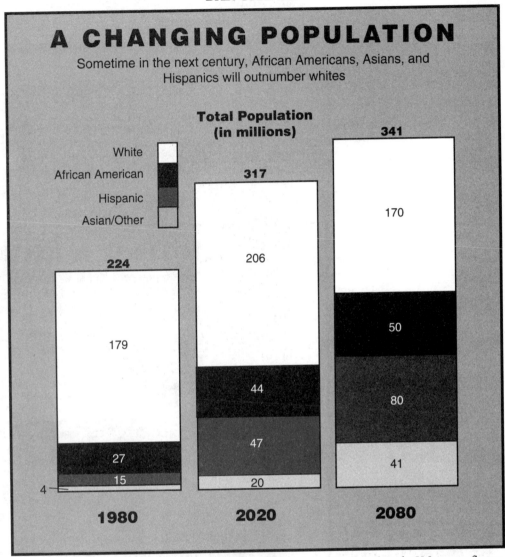

Source: Population Reference Bureau, Washington, D.C. Figures for 1980 based on the U.S. census figures for 2000 and beyond are projections. Projections assume a rate of illegal immigration of 500,000 per year.

BAR GRAPH 1: A CHANGING POPULATION

1. From 1980 to 2020, the number of whites is expected to increase by 27 million, from 179 million to 206 million. By how much is each of the other groups below expected to increase? Which two groups are expected to be the fastest growing?

    a. white   __27 million__
    b. African American   _____
    c. Hispanic   _____
    d. Asian/other   _____

2. From 2020 to 2080, the number of whites is expected to decrease by 36 million, from 206 million to 170 million. By how much is each of the

other groups below expected to increase or decrease? Which two groups are expected to be the fastest growing?

a. white   _____−36 million_____

b. African American   _____

c. Hispanic   _____

d. Asian/other   _____

3. In the year 2020, the number of whites is expected to reach 206 million. The combined number of African Americans, Hispanics, and Asians is expected to reach 111 million. Compare the expected number of whites to the combined number of African Americans, Hispanics, and Asians expected in the year 2080. Who will be in the majority?

BAR GRAPH 2

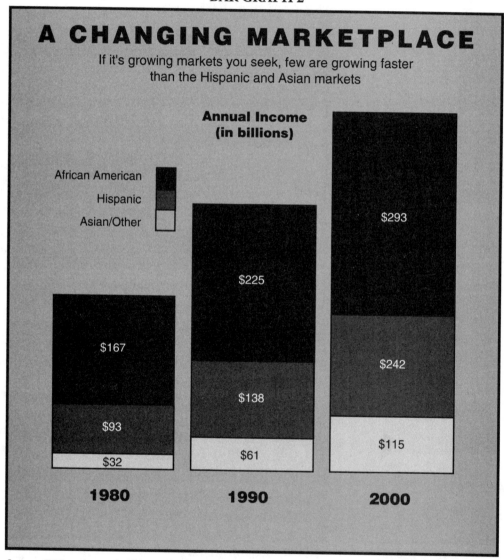

Source: INC. estimates based on population figures from the Population Reference Bureau, Washington, D.C., and per capita income figures from the Bureau of the Census. All figures in 1985 dollars.

BAR GRAPH 2: A CHANGING MARKETPLACE

1. From 1980 to 1990, by how much did the annual income of each group below increase?

    a. Asian/other   _____
    b. Hispanic   _____

2. From 1990 to 2000, by how much is the annual income of each group below expected to increase?

    a. Asian/other   _____
    b. Hispanic   _____

Graphs 1 and 2 illustrate two reasons why entrepreneurs are now beginning to market to Hispanics and Asians. What are these reasons?

READ THE SELECTION: FIRST TIME

Read to get a general understanding of each section. Do not stop to look up words in the dictionary.

READING	Selling to the New America

wholesale: selling goods in large quantities, especially to a retail store

1   Nineteen years ago, Mark Roth left his job as manager of the food division of a chain of discount stores to take over a dying grocery store in a working-class section of Los Angeles. Within a week, he had doubled sales at the grocery store. In addition to his store, he has now become a wholesale supplier of specialty food.

2   In 1981, dentist Ron Greenspan took over the ownership of a dying Volkswagen dealership in San Francisco. With a radical change in marketing strategies, he transformed the auto dealership into the second largest Volkswagen dealership in America.

3   Harriet Nickolaus, a mother of three from Connecticut, had virtually no marketing experience when she started selling her homemade Muscle Medic lotion. Yet with a change in her market focus and a healthy advertising budget, she increased her sales last year tenfold and even opened up important new export markets.

lotion: cream used to make skin feel softer or relieve pain

descent: family origins

4   These three entrepreneurs have two things in common. They are all white, native-born Americans of European descent, and they all have businesses that sell to the New America.

5   In terms of numbers and purchasing power, it is immigrants, most of them now from Asia and Latin America, who represent the fastest-growing domestic consumer markets. While Asians and Hispanics were only a few drops in the national melting pot just 20 years ago, they now account for nearly 10 percent of the American population. At some magic moment in the next

century, they and their children—together with America's black population—will constitute an absolute majority of American consumers.

crystal ball: a clear ball fortune tellers use to see the future

6   You don't need a crystal ball to see what America will be like in the future. In New York City, Hispanics are about to become the largest minority group, surpassing blacks, while in such cities as Miami, San Antonio, and El Paso, they already constitute an absolute majority of the population. San Francisco's Asians, about 15 percent of the population in 1970, already outnumber the local Anglo population by some estimates. Los Angeles, once an ethnically homogenous city, now is a city of diverse ethnic and racial minorities who together easily outnumber its residents of European descent.

ethnic: cultural

7   These new demographic patterns represent just the most recent chapter in what sociologist Nathan Glazer calls the "permanently unfinished story" of America, a nation that continues to take in more immigrants each year than all the rest of the countries in the world combined. Immigration has always been the source of new people, new ideas and products, and new markets.

8   To those who welcome the New America comes a unique and special business opportunity—the opportunity to sell to rapidly growing markets that are largely free from competition. As Mark Roth, Ron Greenspan, and Harriet Nickolaus all happily discovered, the new immigrants are market groups that are eagerly waiting to be served.

MARK ROTH

9   The New America arrived in the Los Angeles suburb of El Monte in the late 1960s. Like many suburban communities of Los Angeles, El Monte was changing rapidly from a predominately white community to one that was predominately Hispanic. To the owner of the local Mars Market, it was a transformation he wanted no part of.

10   "The guy simply wanted no Mexican business," recalls Mark Roth, who purchased the failing business in 1969 for $72,000. "He didn't carry the products they wanted or the cuts of meats they could afford. He just wanted to serve the well-to-do of El Monte. As a result, he was starving to death."

11   However, where the old owner saw an unwanted transformation, new owner Mark Roth saw a unique business opportunity. As a child in Belfield, North Dakota, the young Roth had watched his father build the family grocery store by serving the community of Ukrainians who had settled there in the early 1920s following the Russian Revolution. The majority population in Belfield—German, Dutch, and Scandinavian in origin—generally looked down on the newly arrived Ukrainians and kept them at a distance. Roth's father's grocery store was one of the few places where the Ukrainian immigrants felt welcomed.

12   Roth's father made a special effort to import the foods traditional to eastern European cooking. When products were unavailable he made them himself. If his customers were low on cash, Roth would extend credit to the immigrants as best as he could. He even taught himself the Ukrainian language—and in the process, taught his son a valuable lesson about selling to the New America.

staples: everyday supplies like milk, eggs, etc.

13   "My father always said that the new arrival was the best customer," the son remembers. "They are settling down, so they need pots and pans and staples. And they are people on the way up. Today, the Ukrainians dominate the whole area back there now."

14   Mark Roth sees in today's Mexican immigrants a grocery customer as ideal as the Ukrainians of the 1920s. They represent a growing market, both in terms of numbers and purchasing power. Los Angeles Hispanics spend more on food than Anglos—$20 more per week than other shoppers, according to a recent supermarket study.

15   To attract this market group, Roth started by hiring local Spanish-speaking employees. They serve to facilitate communication with non-English-speaking customers and to tie the store to the community. Today, about two-thirds of the employees at Mars Market are Spanish speaking. The community ties are strong: an employee once had ties to 52 different families in the area.

16   For Hispanics, shopping is a social affair. The entire extended family goes together as a social outing to have a good time. Roth took advantage of this cultural difference by creating a friendly, party-like atmosphere at his store that would appeal to the whole family. On the first weekend after taking over the store, he had a fiesta (Spanish for party) at his grocery store. He brought in the star of a popular TV show to attract customers. A Mexican mariachi band provided music for the adults, and there were balloons and prizes for the kids. When the week was over, Mars Market's sales had doubled.

17   Such fiestas are now regular weekend occurrences at Roth's store. Even on weekdays, Mars Market has more of the feel of a Mexican town plaza than an American supermarket. In his store, the aisles are gaily decorated in bright colors. Customers chat with one another while eating complimentary salsa and corn chips. Although Roth himself never learned to speak Spanish, he is a friendly and familiar face to both employees and customers.

town plaza: center of a Latin town where people meet and socialize
complimentary: given free
salsa: hot, spicy sauce

install: set up ready for use

staple: main dish

exceeds: is more than

18   Product selection, too, is directed toward Hispanics, who now account for nearly three of every four customers. Next to the lettuce and onions in the vegetable section are cactus leaves, hot chilies, and other Mexican vegetables. The meat department has long since stopped pushing high-priced meats in favor of large supplies of lower-priced ones used in many traditional Mexican dishes.

19   Perhaps Roth's most clever and important move was to install a tortilleria—a bakery for making tortilla corn chips. By producing hot, fresh tortilla corn chips, the staple of the Mexican diet, Roth gave every Mexican family in El Monte a reason to shop at his store. Later, he began producing fresh burritos, tamales, and other Mexican baked specialties.

RON GREENSPAN

20   Mark Roth's success in El Monte reflects the more traditional side of marketing to ethnic groups—selling specialized food and everyday low-cost staples to first- and second-generation Americans right in their neighborhoods. However, today's immigrants are not all recent immigrants looking for entry into the middle class. Many immigrants are already there.

21   Asian-Americans are perhaps the largest of such groups. They are two or three times as likely to hold a college degree as the average American adult. They are also more likely to hold positions as managers, executives, or professionals. Among the Japanese, Chinese, and Filipinos, average family income already exceeds that of whites.

22   San Francisco has long been the capital of Asian America. During the past 15 years, Asians have more than replaced the whites who left the city for surrounding suburbs. The San Francisco Chinese are no longer the poor immigrant FOBs (fresh off the boat), washing dishes in a small Chinese restaurant and living in crowded quarters in Chinatown. Today, they constitute an affluent consumer market, with 41 percent owning their own houses.

23   Ron Greenspan was a dentist who opened a small medical practice in a San Francisco neighborhood in 1969. Back then, 70 percent of his patients were white. A decade later, at least 70 percent were Asian, mostly Chinese. "I learned fast that these folks had money when they began paying with cash," recalls Greenspan.

24   Straightening teeth, however, was never Greenspan's great love—cars were. In 1981, he bought one of San Francisco's two Volkswagen dealerships for $250,000. At the time, this was a failing business. The young, white San Franciscans who had bought Volkswagens by the boatload now were buying more expensive German imports or cheaper cars from Japan. Once one of the strongest Volkswagen operations, the San Francisco dealership had dropped near the bottom of the list of the country's 900 dealerships.

25   It was natural that Greenspan would find his Chinese patients among his new car customers. What was not so predictable is that this dentist could build a large business selling German cars to the Chinese. That required a good deal of skill.

flyers: advertisements

26   Greenspan started out by placing ads in the *Asian Yellow Pages*, a popular Chinese-language advertising medium. He also mailed flyers into middle-class Asian neighborhoods. Ron's father had been a salesman and had encouraged his young son to sell almost everything door-to-door. Remembering the advice of his father, Ron sent his salesmen out into the streets of the city to visit shops and hangouts frequented by Asians.

27   However, bringing Asian customers into the car showroom was the easy part. Persuading them to buy was where the real challenge began. It was here that he benefited from his experience with the Asian culture.

penchant: strong like or desire

28   Greenspan understood the Chinese penchant for tough bargaining over prices. To the Chinese, this is simply a normal part of the business culture. "When the guy comes in here and makes a ridiculous offer on a car, you don't get mad," Greenspan instructed his salesmen. "You come back with something equally ridiculous and have a good laugh. Then start your real negotiation."

negotiation: act of talking with another person in order to come to an agreement

29   Another part of Greenspan's "Asian Sensitivity Training" focused on dealing with the family. The Chinese prefer shopping in large family groups, with decisions usually made by the family elders. Greenspan explained to his salesmen that although the car might be for a teenage schoolgirl or a middle-aged engineer, the successful sales pitch may have to be directed to the grandfather or elderly uncle. To help things along, 75-year-old Nat Greenspan is often on hand to make the generational connection. "I introduce the father to my father, and there's an immediate bond there," Greenspan explains.

30   You may think all this is fairly obvious, but Greenspan's Chinese customers appreciate the special considerations he makes. Largely as a result of sales to Asian-Americans, Greenspan has now boosted car sales from only 20 a month to more than 100. In 1984 and 1985, Greenspan's dealership ranked second in the nation in terms of Volkswagen sales. In 1986, it was sixth.

HARRIET NICKOLAUS

31   It's true what they say: if you direct your company openly to minority consumers, some of your traditional Anglo customers may go somewhere else.
However, it is also true that marketing to minorities can have just the opposite
effect. In other words, minority marketing can sometimes be an effective and
inexpensive key to a more mainstream market group. That's the way it worked
out for Harriet Nickolaus.

32   A dance teacher from Connecticut, Nickolaus came up with the idea of a
homemade muscle pain-relieving lotion. Later, several friends tried and liked
her mixture of water, herbs, and spices, and it was only then that she began to
think of selling it to the public.

33   Her idea was to market her homemade lotion as a "natural" muscle pain
reliever. The logical market, she thought, was New York health food stores,
which were frequented mostly by mainstream Anglo shoppers. However, for
two years, Muscle Medic moved very slowly on the store shelves, in need of the
kind of advertising Nickolaus could not afford. In 1985, sales barely reached
$48,000.

34   Then, on the advice she had received from a few Haitian friends, she
placed Muscle Medic in some local bodegas, small local markets that cater to
Hispanics. In contrast to the health food stores, the bodegas seemed able to sell
the product to Hispanics because Hispanics have traditionally been enthusiastic
customers for a variety of homemade remedies.

35   Nickolaus soon decided to move to Miami. "I realized that Miami was a
large Latin market with a lot of local media," she explained. "It was a market we
could really reach." She invested $200,000 in advertising on Spanish-language
television, appearing herself before the camera to explain her product. Her ads
were as homemade as her product—she had taught herself just enough Spanish

remedies: cures; treatments

media: newspapers, television, and radio

to make the TV ads. Despite her awkward presentation, Hispanic viewers seemed to respond favorably to an Anglo woman attempting to sell to them.

36   By the summer of 1986, she was selling more product in a month than she had sold in a year through New York City health food stores. At the same time, visitors from Latin America—who number in the millions each year—started picking up the product, and orders soon began arriving from places like Guatemala, Panama, and Costa Rica.

37   The response from the Hispanic market was quite favorable. Even more favorable were the calls that began to come in from large Anglo-owned stores. Managers of these stores had seen the ads and heard of the customer response. Today Nickolaus counts among her customers 150 Anglo stores, some of which are located outside Hispanic neighborhoods.

38   "I never expected it, but our success with the Latins in Miami opened everything up for us," says Nickolaus, who now reports sales of $400,000. "It was the Latins who led us to the Anglo market."

39   Is this simply a case of good luck? If you ask the business owners themselves, the answer is: "No."

40   Take the case of grocer Mark Roth in El Monte, where our story first began. Although Roth's Mars Market continues to be profitable, he finds that he is facing increasing competition these days from large supermarket chains. These supermarkets have begun to use the same strategies that he has long used to attract Hispanic shoppers. They now have large quantities of Mexican-style meats and produce. Some have hired Spanish-speaking employees. A few have even installed their own tortillerias.

chains: group of connected stores

41   In the long run, Roth believes that he will not be able to compete against these large supermarket chains. So he has found a way to turn this negative point to his advantage. Instead of remaining a competitor to the chains, Roth has decided to become their wholesale supplier.

42   It all started several years ago. When celebrating the opening of his new tortilleria, Roth asked one of his employees to make a little salsa sauce to go with the corn chips. The response of the customers was so enthusiastic that he started selling the salsa sauce at his store. Later, he happened to bring some of the salsa sauce to a meeting of area grocers. The grocers ate it all—and left him with orders for their stores. That's how he became a wholesaler.

43   Soon the workers in the backroom of Mars Market were making not only the original hot salsa sauce, but other Mexican specialties. He began to package these products under his own brand name—*El Burrito*. Now, with sales last year close to $1 million and doubling annually, Roth is already making more money on his packaged foods than he is from the grocery market. He has moved much of his production to a separate food plant several miles away. He counts among his customers supermarkets as far away as Montreal and as close as El Monte.

44   All this started from an interest Roth and other grocers had in serving a growing Hispanic market. It has now gone far beyond that. To Roth's surprise, the largest orders for *El Burrito* packaged foods are not coming from stores in predominately Hispanic sections of L.A. or San Antonio—they're coming from Anglo grocers serving mostly Anglo shoppers. Roth estimates that Anglos now count for 70 percent of the market for his packaged Mexican foods. By setting

out to sell to Hispanics, he has found himself in the center of the latest American food craze—Mexican food.

It is, of course, a familiar story. It is the story of pizza and pita bread, of the bagel and the croissant, of sushi and chop suey. It is a story of minorities that become majorities, of Ukrainians and Mexicans and Cantonese who constantly define and redefine what it is to be American. On the back of the dollar bill, the American eagle carries the message: *E pluribus unum*—from the many, one. For more than 200 years, these words have been the motto of American democracy. Now this motto translates nicely into a marketing strategy for American business.

motto: short sentence or a
few words taken as a guid-
ing principle

READING CHECK

A. Marginal Notes

Look over the following ten marginal notes and write them in the margin of the reading next to the paragraph that relates to the marginal note. If the marginal note relates to more than one paragraph, draw an arrow down (↓) to indicate this. Not all paragraphs will have notes. The notes are listed in random order.

MARGINAL NOTES

the 3 entrepreneurs: 2 things in common

Greenspan's 3 strategies to attract Asians

response of original owner of Mars Market to newly arrived Mexicans

reason Nickolaus changed market focus to bodegas

Roth's 4 strategies to attract Hispanics

favorable Hispanic response opened doors to Anglo market

Asians & Hispanics: fastest-growing markets

favorable Hispanic response to TV ads

Asian Sensitivity Training: 2 things salesmen learn

reason Roth became a wholesaler

B. Guessing the Meaning from Context

Look carefully at the context of the underlined words. Try to guess their meaning. Identify the context clue(s) and be prepared to explain your answer. If necessary, refer to **Appendix 2**.

1. Los Angeles, once an ethnically <u>homogenous</u> city, now is a city of diverse ethnic and racial minorities who together easily outnumber its residents of European descent. (**P6**)

   HOMOGENEOUS _____

   context clue(s):

2. Like many suburban communities of Los Angeles, El Monte was changing rapidly from a predominately white community to one that was predominately Hispanic. To the owner of the local Mars Market, it was a <u>transformation</u> he wanted no part of. (**P9**)

   TRANSFORMATION _____

   context clue(s):

3. The majority population in Belfield—German, Dutch, and Scandinavian in origin—generally <u>looked down on</u> the newly arrived Ukrainians and kept them at a distance. Roth's father's grocery store was one of the few places where the Ukrainian immigrants felt welcomed. (**P11**)

   LOOKED DOWN ON _____

   context clue(s):

4. Greenspan explained to his salesmen that although the car might be for a teenage schoolgirl or a middle-aged engineer, the successful sales pitch may have to be directed to the grandfather or elderly uncle. To help things along, 75-year-old Nat Greenspan is often on hand to make the generational connection. "I introduce the father to my father, and there's an immediate <u>bond</u> there," Greenspan explains. (**P29**)

   BOND _____

   context clue(s):

5. On the advice Nickolaus had received from a few Haitian friends, she placed Muscle Medic in some local <u>bodegas</u>, small local markets that cater to Hispanics. (**P34**)

   BODEGAS _____

   context clue(s):

READ THE SELECTION: SECOND TIME

Read more carefully to get a better understanding of each section. Use the dictionary, only if necessary.

A. True or False

Write true or false and the number of the paragraph(s) that supports your answer. Be prepared to explain your answer.

_____ /_____   **1.** In some U.S. cities, Hispanics and Asians outnumber Anglos.

_____ /_____   **2.** Sociologist Nathan Glazer views the U.S. immigration pattern from a negative perspective.

_____ /_____   **3.** When the population of El Monte changed, the original owner of Mars Market adapted his business to meet the needs of the new residents.

_____ /_____   **4.** Mark Roth learned about the importance of serving the needs of newly arrived immigrants from a college business course.

_____ /_____   **5.** Roth represents the traditional side of marketing to minorities: selling traditional foods and other such goods to ethnic groups.

_____ /_____   **6.** Ron Greenspan took over an auto dealership that was failing because of a change in consumers' taste.

_____ /_____   **7.** Greenspan represents a less traditional, and more difficult, side of selling to ethnic groups because although Asians need cars, they don't necessarily need German cars.

_____ /_____   **8.** Like other auto dealers, Greenspan waits for customers to come into his showroom.

_____ /_____   **9.** Harriet Nickolaus redirected her pain reliever to Hispanics because of their preference for natural, homemade treatments.

_____ /_____   **10.** For both Nickolaus and Roth, marketing to minorities has eventually opened the doors to a larger, more mainstream market.

B. Listing

Make three lists to show how these important points in the reading are developed or explained. Be as brief as possible. Include a heading with each list.

1. When Mark Roth took over Mars Market, he adopted four marketing strategies to attract Hispanics. List these strategies.

   (Heading) _____

   _____

2. When Ron Greenspan took over the Volkswagen dealership, he adopted three marketing strategies to attract Asians. List these strategies.

   (Heading) _____

   _____

   _____

   _____

   _____

3. Greenspan's salesmen take part in an Asian Sensitivity Training program. List two important things that they learn about the Asian business culture.

   (Heading) _____

   _____

   _____

   _____

C. Chart

The chart lists the stages in the marketing of Harriet Nickolaus' natural pain reliever—Muscle Medic. Complete the chart. Then answer the question below.

MARKETING OF MUSCLE MEDIC

Stage 1   Marketed product in New York health food stores frequented mostly by mainstream Anglo shoppers. Product moved slowly because _____ _____.

Stage 2   Changed market focus to bodegas because _____ _____.

Stage 3   Changed location of marketing to Miami because _____ _____.

Stage 4   Expanded into an export business, marketing to _____ _____.

Stage 5   Expanded marketing to Anglo-owned stores both in and outside Hispanic neighborhoods because store managers _____ _____.

■   Although Nickolaus' initial attempt to sell her product in the Anglo market did not succeed, today it is selling well in this market. For Nickolaus, what was the key that opened up the door to this more mainstream market?

_____

_____

_____

TOPICS FOR DISCUSSION AND WRITING

1. Every culture has its own unique way of conducting business. In the American business culture, bargaining over prices is not very common but offering sales and allowing customers to buy with credit is. Can you think of ways in which your business culture differs from the American business culture?

2. Describe several things Roth learned from his grocer father about selling to newly arrived immigrants. What do you think Greenspan learned from his father, who was a door-to-door salesman?

3. Roth started as a retail grocer, but today he is also a wholesaler of Mexican specialty foods. One might say that he got the idea of becoming a wholesaler quite by accident. Explain. What made him realize that becoming a wholesaler would be a good business decision?

4. Compare the three entrepreneurs in this reading. Write at least four statements that show how they are similar or different. Here are two examples.

    Example 1 Roth, Greenspan, and Nickolaus all became successful by marketing to minorities.

    Example 2 In terms of business, Roth and Greenspan were strongly influenced by their fathers, but Nickolaus wasn't.

5. Entrepreneurs have a unique ability to turn current and even future needs into a business opportunity. Go to the library and look through current issues of *Entrepreneur, Inc., Entrepreneurial Woman,* or other business magazines. Find an article about a current or future business trend and take notes. Be prepared to report to the class what you have learned.

VOCABULARY EXERCISES

A. Word Forms

Choose the correct word form that completes each sentence. The base form of the word is in **bold**. For nouns, use singular or plural forms. For verbs, use appropriate verb tenses and passive voice where necessary.

(P1)   1. supply, supplier *n*   **to supply** *v*

   a. Mark Roth is both a retail grocer and a wholesale
       _____ of Mexican specialties.

   b. He _____ Mexican specialties under the
       brand name *El Burrito.*

   c. _____ of Harriet Nickolaus' Muscle Medic are exported
       to Latin America.

(P2)   **2.** transformation *n*   **to transform** *v*

    a. A change in market focus _____
    Nickolaus' business into a highly profitable business which includes an
    export market.

    b. Greenspan's dealership has experienced a dramatic
    _____. It was ranked near the bottom of
    Volkswagen dealerships in sales, but now it is ranked near the top.

(P3)   **3.** advertising, advertisement *n*   **to advertise** *v*

    a. Does _____ on television influence consumers'
    buying habits?

    b. Why does Ron Greenspan place _____ in
    the *Asian Yellow Pages* ?

    c. Nickolaus decided that she would _____ her own
    product on television.

(P5)   **4.** consumption, consumer *n*   **to consume** *v*

    a. Hispanic _____ spend about $20 more per week on
    food than other consumers.

    b. If Hispanic families _____ lower-priced meats than
    other families, why is their weekly grocery bill higher?

    c. If you want to lose weight, you'll have to reduce your _____
    of fat.

    5. persuasion *n*   **to persuade** *v*   persuasive *adj*
(P27)

    a. Good salespeople know how to _____
    potential customers to buy without appearing pushy.

    b. To be _____, salespeople must have an
    understanding of human psychology and knowledge of the merchan-
    dise they are selling.

    c. Car salesmen usually take a training course in which they learn that
    _____ is both an art and a skill.

B. Other Useful Words

Complete the sentences with an appropriate word from the list. Use the same form of the word.

business culture (**P28**)   mainstream (**P31**)
elders (**P29**)   wholesale (**P1**)
extended family (**P16**)
Hispanics (**P5**)
sales pitch (**P29**)

1. The student from Jamaica has a _____ business. He buys large supplies of reggae records and sells them to retail music stores.

2. The marketing class held a contest to determine which group of students had the most effective _____.

3. In the American _____, tipping is a common practice.

4. In the Asian business culture, why is the sales pitch usually directed at the family _____?

5. The fastest-growing consumer group in the United States is _____.

6. In some cultures, the _____ may not only live together but also run a business together.

7. Pita bread used to be consumed by mostly Arab-Americans, but this specialty food is now very popular among more _____ consumers.

C. Vocabulary Oral Practice

Practice using the underlined words by answering the questions below.

1. One way to market a product is to give away <u>complimentary</u> samples. For example, a shampoo company might send <u>complimentary</u> samples of its new product in the mail. What kinds of products have you gotten <u>complimentary</u> samples of? Is this marketing technique better than TV advertising? Explain. (**P17**)

2. Some marketing experts believe that a better and even less expensive way to <u>market</u> a product or service is through customer satisfaction. Do you agree? How can customer satisfaction help a business get new customers? (**P31**)

3. What is a popular fashion or music <u>craze</u> in the United States at this time? What do you think of this <u>craze</u>? (**P44**)

4. You and a friend plan to share a two-bedroom apartment. One bedroom is much smaller than the other one. How will the two of you <u>negotiate</u> who will get the larger bedroom? (**P28**)

5. Describe some ways in which TV <u>advertising</u> in this country is different from TV <u>advertising</u> in your country. Which system do you like better and why? (**P3**)

6. One important development which <u>transformed</u> the way people shop is the creation of the department store. What are some more recent developments which have <u>transformed</u> the way people shop? (**P2**)

D. Dictation

Study the spelling of the words in the previous vocabulary exercises. You will have a dictation of sentences that contain these words.

JOURNAL WRITING

You have read about a current business trend in the United States: minority marketing. In your journal, describe a business trend that has emerged in your country in recent years. Also explain the factors that have led to this trend.

LECTURE | An Interview with Entrepreneur Frank Meeks

In this unit, you have read about risk-taking entrepreneurs and their products and services. Now, you have the opportunity to actually meet one. His name is Frank Meeks and he is in the pizza delivery business. In fact, he is the franchisee of over 40 Domino's Pizza stores throughout the Washington, D.C., area. In this interview, you will hear the story of his success.

Entrepreneur Frank Meeks often helps out at the many Domino's Pizza stores he owns.

LISTENING STRATEGY

Frank Meeks first talks about the background of Tom Monaghan, the founder of Domino's Pizza Delivery, and Domino's expansion into a franchise business. Meeks talks about how he first became involved in this franchise and about his early years as a franchisee. Then he talks about his employees and his customers. Toward the end of the interview, he talks about risk taking, the costs of success, his future goals, and his definition of success.

TERMS USED IN THE LECTURE*

orphan	brand-loyal
pizzeria	30-minute delivery or $3.00 off
intern on Capitol Hill	customer questionnaire
incentive bonuses	23-minute delivery or free
to walk the talk	pre-made
a resume	to be cynical about someone
to go on gut instincts	to run off the competition honorably

* These terms are defined or made clear from context in the lecture.

1. Listen to the interview. Follow the questions below as you listen. Do not write anything at this time.

2. Listen again and take notes on the responses to the questions. Write only key words and phrases. After the interview, compare your notes with a classmate's. You may want to listen to the interview again to confirm any points that you missed.

3. After completing your notes, discuss them with the class.

Interview with Entrepreneur Frank Meeks

1. People are always interested in how a business first got started. How did Domino's Pizza first get started and was it always a pizza delivery service?

   Founded by Tom Monaghan in 1960 (21 yr old)

   Orphan—never went to college or took business course

   Had only $300 and broken down VW

   Bought out struggling pizzeria—changed name to Domino's

   Stopped selling spaghetti, etc.—only pizza delivery

2. When did Domino's expand into a franchise business? And how many stores are there in the franchising system?

   1969 sold 1st franchise; '80s—fast growth

   Today—5,600 stores in U.S. and 26 foreign countries

3. I read that you got involved in Domino's Pizza quite by accident.

   _____

   _____

   _____

4. Since you were quite young at the time, how did you manage to get all of the money together to start your own store?

   _____

   _____

5. You're from Mississippi, but you opened up your first Domino's in the Washington, D.C., area? Why in Washington and why not in Mississippi?

_____

_____

_____

6. Certainly when you opened up your first store, you faced a few problems. What were these problems?

■   Educating public they could get good meal delivered by a quality company—food delivery—foreign to Wash. market at that time

■   _____

_____

_____

7. It's hard to believe that in a little over ten years, you now have over 40 stores. With that many stores, you must have hundreds of employees. But you don't call them employees. What do you call them and why do you call them that?

_____

_____

8. You told me that you try to create an atmosphere of friendly competition among your 40 stores or over 40 stores. Why do you do this and can you give an example of this friendly competition?

■   Why: to build a company where managers compete w/other pizza companies and w/fellow managers; builds motivation

■   Example of competition: _____

_____

_____

9. With so many stores, how do you keep in touch with your team members?

■ _____

■ "Walks the talk"—does same things he asks team members to do

Examples: _____

_____

10. Some of our students might be interested in knowing what you look for in hiring your store managers.

■ What's not important: _____

_____

■ What is:_____

_____

11. Let's talk about your customers. Who are your biggest consumers?

_____

_____

12. We know that in business it's important to show customers that you care about them. How do you show your customers that you care?

■ Puts money behind guarantee of great service:

30-minute delivery or $3.00 off,

satisfaction guarantee or money back

Better to lose some money than a customer

■ _____

_____

13. We've read in our readings on entrepreneurs that they tend to be real risk takers. Can you give some examples of the risks you've taken: both the ones that have worked and the ones that haven't?

■ One that worked: _____

_____

■ Two that didn't: _____

_____

_____

_____

14. We've also read that success usually comes at a cost. What has been the cost of success for you?

   ■ _____

   ■ More cynical about new people he meets; no longer has natural trust in everybody

15. Looking toward the future, what are your goals?

   ■ _____

   ■ To run off the competition honorably

16. And my final question is this: if you could define success in any way, how would you define it?

   _____

DISCUSSION QUESTIONS

1. What do you like most about Frank Meeks?

2. Frank Meeks seems to be a combination of Marcel Bich and Leone Ackerly. How is he similar to both of these entrepreneurs?

3. What are some questions that you would like to ask Frank Meeks?

READING FOR PLEASURE

POETRY

   In this unit, we have read about several entrepreneurs who have worked hard and done well in business, and in some cases, have made a great fortune and become famous. In other words, these entrepreneurs have been successful. However, success in life can be measured in other ways than success in business.

   The two poems that follow consider the meaning of success from a different perspective than that of the entrepreneur. Read the poems to find out how these two poets have defined the word.

   The first poem is written by Edgar Guest, the same poet who wrote "It Couldn't Be Done."

I hold no dream of fortune vast,
    Nor seek undying fame.
I do not ask when life is past
    That many know my name.

I may not own the skill to rise
    To glory's topmost height,
Nor win a place among the wise,
    But I can keep the right.

And I can live my life on earth
    Contented to the end,
If but a few shall know my worth
    And proudly call me friend.

fame: being famous

contented: satisfied

worth: good qualities

DISCUSSION QUESTIONS

1. Which lines of the poem give the poet's definition of success? In your own words, explain his definition of success.

2. What does the expression "when life is past" mean in the first stanza? What does the expression "to the end" mean in the last stanza?

3. In general, what is the poet telling us in the first seven lines of the poem? In your own words, tell the five specific things he mentions in these lines. Why do you think he begins his poem this way?

4. How does this poem show that Guest is "the poet of the plain people"?

BIOGRAPHICAL SKETCH: RALPH WALDO EMERSON (1803–1882)

Ralph Waldo Emerson was an American philosopher, poet, and essayist. Born in Boston, he entered Harvard College at the age of 14. Later he studied theology and for a period of time served as a church minister. From 1833 on, he spent his life writing and giving lectures. His philosophy toward life emphasized the importance of self-reliance and individual freedom.

POEM

What Is Success?

To laugh often and much;

To win the respect of intelligent people
and the affection of children;

To earn the appreciation of honest critics
and endure the betrayal of false friends;

endure: accept with tolerance
betrayal: act of being disloyal or unfaithful

To appreciate beauty;

To find the best in others;

To leave the world a bit better, whether by
a healthy child, a garden
patch or a redeemed social condition;

redeemed: improved

To know even one life has breathed
easier because you have lived;

This is to have succeeded.

1. How many parts does Emerson have in his definition of success? What repeated structure does he use for each part in order to create rhythm in the poem?

2. What can you infer about Emerson's attitude toward making a fortune in business? How can you infer this?

3. In your opinion, are all of the parts of Emerson's definition of equal importance for you? Or do you think that some are more important than others? If so, which ones do you believe are more important? Why?

4. Now that you have read Guest's and Emerson's definitions of success, think about your own definition of success in life.

A

(to) abolish 49
abuse 212
accurate 81
achievement 170
adolescent 168
(to) adopt policies 144
(to) advance 49
(dis)advantage 100
(to) advertise 252
advertising 254
(to) afford 143
affordable 145
(to) (dis)agree (with) 48
aggressive 120
allowance 169
(to) alter 144
ambiguity 101
Americanization 30
anger 120
annually 188
anxious 119
(to) assist 143
attitude (toward something) 81

B

(to) behave 80
(to) believe (that) 80
(to be) better off (than) 50

bitter 223
(to) blame 101
breakthrough 230
business culture 253

C

capital 212
celebration 30
(to) change one's mind 121
characteristic 212
(to) classify 82
colony 14
(to) combine 99
(to be) (over)committed 169
community service 188
comparison 29
competition 29
competitive 224
(to) complain 168
complimentary 253
concentration 100
conflict 120
consent 16
constructive 120
(to) consume 252
(to) contradict 81
contribution 29
control 29
controversial issue 82
(to) cope with 120
costume 30
craze 254
(to) create 211
(to) criticize 168
crop 49
cultural tradition 30
curiosity 101

D

dedicated 223
demand (for something) 49
demanding 170
(to) demonstrate 15
(to) depend on 14
destructive 120
(to) develop 28
(to) differ 29
(to be) different 29
disabilities 188
(to) discard 213
discrimination 49
diversity 29
divorce 145
(to) dominate 28
(to) donate 188
dramatic 143

E

easy-going 30
effect 80
elders 253
(to) eliminate 82
entrepreneur 210
environmental protection 189
established 224
eventually 15
exception 101
extended family 253
extensive 188

F

factor 49
farsighted 223
favorable 81
favorite 223
federal government 49
fierce 223
first-hand 230
flexible 100
(to) focus on 81
fortunate 188
(to) frustrate 119
funds 145

G

(to) get along with 30
(to) govern 15
(to) grow 28
(to) guarantee 50

H

Hispanics 253

I

ideal 101
(to) imagine 211
(to) imitate 82
incentive 170
inevitable 121
inflation 144
(to) influence 81
(to) inherit 82
initially 30
initiative 189
innovation 212
intensive 169
intergenerational 169

intuition 101
(to) invent 211
(to) invest 145

K

(to) keep in touch with 230
(to) keep up with 169
key 230

L

labor 212
lack (of something) 100
lasting 81
leading citizen 213
(to) lend a hand 230
(to) level off 144
luxury 169

M

mainstream 253
major 29
(to) make a fortune (in) 212
(to) make up one's mind 121
(to) manage 211
(to) market 254
(to) mass produce 212
merchant 15
military occupation 15
minority 50
mixture 29
modernization 49
modest 144
(to) motivate 99

N

necessary 143
needy 188
(to) negotiate 254

O

obsession 213
obstacle 121
(to) oppose 49
optimistic 81
(to) organize 15
origin 29
outstanding 188
(to) overcome 121

P

Parliament 15
(to) participate 142
persistence 100
(to) persuade 252
pessimistic 81
(to) place a greater emphasis on 169
(to) play a key role 213
(to) predict 99
preservation movement 49
(to) prevent 100
primary responsibility 145
private 223
productive 145
profile 212
(to) profit from 169
(to) prohibit 49
(to) protest 15
public service 188
(to) punish 16

Q

quality 145

R

rarely 100
(to) react 119
recession 144
record 145
(to) recover 144
(to) recruit 188
relative 121
reliable 100
(to) relieve 120
(to) represent 14
(to) resent 15
(to) resolve 121
(to) respond to 80
(to) restore 15
(to) restrict 48
(to) retain 144
(in) retrospect 213
revolution 15
role model 188
routine 169

S

sacrifice 212
sales pitch 253
(to) seek opportunities 212
self-centered 213
self-made 230
sense of security 82
(to) settle 15
shortcomings 121
significant 100
single-parent family 144
slave labor 49
(to) slow down 169
source of strength 50
(to) stagnate 144
standard of living 144
stubborn 224
success 99
(to) supply 251
symbol 16

T

(to) take risks 100
task 230
territory 15
tip 230

(to) tolerate 81
top priority 170
trait 100
(to) transform 252, 254
transition 170
two-income family 144

U

ultimately 100
unique 29
unruly 15
unsung hero 212

V

(to) vacillate 120
vast 29
volunteer 188

W

(to) warn 16
wholesale 253
(to) withdraw 120
worldwide 224

VOCABULARY STRATEGIES FOR UNFAMILIAR WORDS

When you read English books, magazine and newspaper articles, and other material, you undoubtedly find some words you do not know. What do you do when this happens? Do you stop reading each time and look up the unfamiliar word in the dictionary? This will take much time, and while you are looking up the word, you might forget what you are reading. To be a more successful reader, you must know other strategies to deal with unfamiliar words. The dictionary should be your last strategy in understanding a word.

SEQUENCE OF VOCABULARY STRATEGIES FOR UNFAMILIAR WORDS

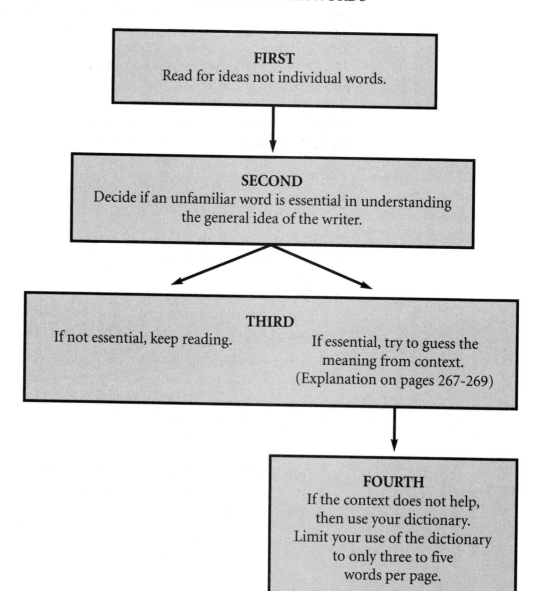

FIRST
Read for ideas not individual words.

SECOND
Decide if an unfamiliar word is essential in understanding the general idea of the writer.

THIRD
If not essential, keep reading.

If essential, try to guess the meaning from context.
(Explanation on pages 267-269)

FOURTH
If the context does not help, then use your dictionary.
Limit your use of the dictionary to only three to five words per page.

Do you use these strategies in your own language?

Think about how you read in your own language. Do you read for ideas (not words) in your own language? If you find a word that you don't know, do you continue reading if its meaning is not essential? Do you sometimes guess the meaning of an unfamiliar word from its context? In your own language, do you use the dictionary only when necessary?

You probably answered "yes" to these questions. Good! So when you read in English, you should try to use these same strategies.

To help you, this book will give you practice with one strategy in particular, *guessing the meaning from context*. You will find that most chapters in the book include an exercise on guessing the meaning from context. Below is an explanation of this strategy.

HOW TO GUESS THE MEANING FROM CONTEXT

First of all, it is important to note that this strategy will give you *only the general meaning* of an unfamiliar word. It will not give you the specific meanings found in the dictionary. In most cases, the general meaning is sufficient to help you understand the key ideas of the writer.

To understand an unfamiliar word from its context, you must analyze the *context clues* in the sentence in which the word is found or in the surrounding sentences. The unfamiliar word may have more than one context clue, so *use as many clues as possible* to guess its meaning. Sometimes it is also helpful to know the part of speech (noun/verb/adjective/adverb) of the unfamiliar word.

Common Context Clues

Here are nine common context clues. In the example sentence for each type of clue, the unfamiliar word(s) is underlined.

1. **Familiar Situation**
    Your own knowledge and experience of the situation described in the context help you understand the meaning of the unfamiliar word.

    Example: What was everyday life like in colonial times? What did the colonists do for food? There were no grocery stores in early colonial times, so the early settlers planted vegetables and fruit seeds that came all the way from Europe. Also, in the nearby forests, they gathered nuts and hunted <u>game</u> for food.

2. **Sufficient Explanation/Examples/Description [SEED]**
    The writer provides sufficient explanation, examples, or description of the situation to help you understand the meaning of the unfamiliar word.

    Example: During the colonial period, customs were quite different from today. Women and girls kept their hair covered all the time—

even in the house. They wore hats and <u>hoods or kerchiefs</u>. In those days, men and boys had long hair. To keep a proper appearance, men in upper-class families often wore <u>wigs</u> over their hair. They put white powder on the <u>wigs</u> to keep them looking clean. On a windy day, the powder blew away like snow.

3. **Cause and Effect Relationship**

This type of relationship is expressed by words such as "because," "since," "so," "therefore," and "thus" and also by ideas that show cause and effect.

Example: People in colonial days walked more than people do today, so they <u>wore out</u> their shoes faster. There was always work for the town cobbler. He <u>mended</u> old shoes and made new ones. No one had to worry about left shoes and right shoes because the cobbler made all shoes exactly alike.

4. **Contrasting Relationship**

This type of relationship is expressed by words such as "but," "however," "although," and "on the other hand" and also by ideas that show contrast.

Example: What kinds of medicines were used during colonial times? Plants called herbs were said to cure almost anything. For example, if a child had a stomachache, his mother would give him a drink made from herbs to help him feel better. Every family grew their own herbs in their garden and made their own medicines. Herbs might have been good medicine, but they tasted <u>bitter</u>.

5. **Similar Words**

The writer uses an unfamiliar word but in the surrounding context gives a word or phrase that has a similar meaning to the unfamiliar word. This word or phrase may be stated in a different grammatical form.

Example: Houses in early colonial days were not very warm. In winter-time, a colonial house was so cold that if someone was writing a letter, the ink might freeze in his pen! To make the house warmer, people burned giant <u>logs</u> in the fireplace. In fact, sometimes the wood was so big that it took two horses to pull it into the house.

6. **Reference Words**

The clue is expressed by words such as "other," "another," "this," "that," and "such."

Example: In the countryside, there were mostly farmers; in the towns, there were mostly <u>masons, blacksmiths, carpenters, cabinet-makers,</u> and other skilled workers.

7. Descriptive Words

It can be very difficult to guess the meaning of descriptive words, namely, adjectives and adverbs. Sometimes it is helpful to know only whether the word has a positive or negative meaning.

Example: Most people in the countryside made their own furniture, but people in big towns built <u>fancier</u> houses and wanted <u>fancier</u> furniture. The cabinetmaker made this furniture.

8. Definition Provided by Writer

Writers sometimes give the definition of a word because they believe that the readers will not know its meaning. This kind of definition is often given for more technical or specialized words. Sometimes commas are used to separate the unfamiliar word and its definition.

Example: What did people do on Sunday? Sunday was the Lord's Day. Everyone, both young and old, was expected to go to the <u>meeting-house</u>, which was their word for church, for two hours of prayer in the morning and for two more hours in the afternoon. A watchman called a <u>tithing-man</u> saw that everyone paid attention. The tithing-man carried a long stick. On one end was a furry foxtail. On the other end was a wooden knob. The tithing-man used the wooden knob on the heads of children who fell asleep or talked in church, and he used the furry tail to tickle the nose of old men and women who fell asleep.

9. Word Parts

If you know the meaning of some word parts, you can break the word into its parts to help you guess the meaning.

Example: Ships and shipbuilding kept many men busy during the colonial days. <u>Lumbermen</u> cut down the tall pine trees to make the tall masts for the ships. <u>Carpenters</u> built the wooden parts of the ship. <u>Sailmakers</u> made the ships' sails. <u>Coopers</u> made barrels to hold food and drink for the long voyage. <u>Sailors</u> and captains sailed the ships.

In reading these example sentences, did you find that some unfamiliar words had more than the particular context clue indicated to help you understand the meaning? Can you give an example of this?

To develop your ability to guess the meaning of unfamiliar words from context requires a lot of practice. In time, you will gain more confidence in reading without understanding every word, and you will improve your reading speed. This will help you become a better reader.

GUIDELINES FOR SMALL GROUP DISCUSSIONS

One of the important ways in which you learn is by exchanging ideas with other people. You do this often in everyday conversation. You are likely to learn more, however, when you take part in a special kind of group conversation called a small group discussion. A small group discussion is more orderly than a conversation and generally has a more serious purpose. This purpose may be to share information or solve a problem. The guidelines below will help you to have a more successful discussion.

BE PREPARED

Think about the subject to be discussed ahead of time. Prepare for the discussion by making some notes of the ideas you want to share with the group. Practice expressing your ideas at home. During the discussion, do not read your notes. Use them only as a reminder of what you want to say.

SHARE YOUR IDEAS

Take part in the discussion. Explain your ideas as clearly as possible and give examples when appropriate. Check to make sure the other members of your group understand what you are trying to say. Get feedback from them. For example, ask if they agree or disagree with you or if they have had a similar experience. Be prepared to see your ideas sometimes criticized, but at the same time, have the courage to stand up for an idea or belief that is really important to you.

LISTEN AND THINK

Listen thoughtfully and actively to others. When other members of your group present their ideas, give them appropriate feedback. If you do not understand an idea, it is your responsibility to let them know this. Encourage more quiet members to take part in the discussion.

BE AWARE OF THE TIME

Most discussions have a time limit, so you must learn to use time effectively. Some groups elect a leader whose responsibility is to make sure that the goal of the discussion is reached within the specified time limit and that no one member of the group talks too much or too little. If your group has five questions to discuss, try to spend equal time on each question.

■ **To express an opinion or surprise**

I agree that the taxes were unfair because....
I understand your point, but I don't feel the same way as you because....
Really? You don't have any taxes in your country?

■ **To ask for clarification or a restatement**

I'm sorry, I can't understand what you're trying to say? Can you give an
example?
I'm sorry, but what did you say about the Boston Massacre?

■ **To ask others' opinion or encourage others to take part in the discussion**

Ahmed, what do you think caused the soldiers to fire?
Ahmed, don't you think the taxes were unfair?

■ **To signal an irrelevant point or the need to move on**

I think we're getting off the subject. Let's try to stay on the topic.
I think we need to move on and begin discussing the next topic.

■ **To check if others understand**

Do you understand what I'm trying to say?
Do you know what I mean?

CHAPTER 3

For "Merry-Go-Round" poem
From *Selected Poems* by Langston Hughes. Copyright 1942 by Langston Hughes and renewed 1970 by Arna Bontemps and George Houston Bass. Reprinted by permission of Alfred A. Knopf, Inc.

For "I, too, sing America" poem
From *Selected Poems* by Langston Hughes. Copyright 1926 by Alfred A. Knopf, Inc., and renewed 1954 by Langston Hughes. Reprinted by permission of the publisher.

CHAPTER 4

For "Attitudes" reading selection
Personal Psychology for Life and Work, 3rd Edition, by Rita K. Baltus. Copyright 1988, Glencoe/McGraw-Hill. Used by permission of the Glencoe Division of the Macmillan/McGraw-Hill School Publishing Company.

For "The Tiger's Whisker"
The Tiger's Whisker and Other Tales and Legends from Asia and the Pacific, © 1959, 1987 by Harold Courlander. Reprinted by permission of Harcourt Brace Jovanovich, Inc.

CHAPTER 5

For "Language-Learner Traits" reading selection
How to Be a More Successful Language Learner by Joan Rubin and Irene Thompson. Copyright 1982, Heinle & Heinle Publishers, Inc.

CHAPTER 6

For "Frustration" reading selection
Adapted excerpts from *Psychology: An Introduction,* Third Edition, by Jerome Kagan and Ernest Havemann. Copyright © 1976 by Harcourt Brace Jovanovich, Inc. Reprinted by permission of the publisher.

For Journal Writing
From the book *Ann Landers Says...Truth Is Stranger...*by Ann Landers © 1968, used by permission of the publisher: Prentice Hall/A Division of Simon & Schuster, Englewood Cliffs, N.J.

For "Stonecutter"
Author unknown.

CHAPTER 7

For "Mothers at Work: The New American Family" reading selection
"Mothers at Work: The New American Family" by Marguerite Connerton, Director of Public Policy for the Service Employees International Union, reprinted by permission of the author.

For "Fatherhood"
From *Fatherhood* by Bill Cosby. Copyright © 1986 by William H. Cosby, Jr., used by permission of Doubleday, a division of Bantam Doubleday Dell Publishing Group, Inc.

CHAPTER 8

For "When Teenagers Work" reading selection
Excerpts from *When Teenagers Work* by Ellen Greenberger and Laurence Steinberg. Copyright © 1986 by Basic Books, Inc., reprinted by permission of Basic Books, a division of HarperCollins Publishers.

For "A Mother's Advice: Make Something of Yourself"
Reprinted from *Growing Up* by Russell Baker. Copyright © 1982. Used with permission of Congdon & Weed, Chicago.

CHAPTER 9

For "The New Volunteers" reading selection (two sources)
"The New Volunteers" and "A Salute to Everyday Heroes," from *Newsweek*, July 10, 1989, copyright © 1989, Newsweek, Inc. All rights reserved. Reprinted by permission.

CHAPTER 10

For "The American Entrepreneur: A Historical Perspective" reading selection
The Entrepreneurs: An American Adventure by Robert Sobel and David B. Sicilia, copyright 1986, Houghton Mifflin Company. Used with permission of The Karpfinger Agency.

For "It Couldn't Be Done" poem
Reprinted from *The Collected Verse of Edgar A. Guest* by Edgar A. Guest, copyright © 1934. Used with permission of Contemporary Books, Inc., Chicago.

CHAPTER 11

For "Marcel Bich" reading selection
Adapted with permission of G. K. Hall Reference, a Division of Macmillan, Inc., from *Entrepreneurs: The Men and Women Behind Famous Brand Names and How They Made It* by Joseph J. Fucini and Suzy Fucini. Copyright © 1985 by G. K. Hall & Co.

For "Leone Ackerly" reading selection
From *The Service Edge* by Ron Zemke and Dick Schaaf. Copyright © 1989 by
Ron Zemke and Dick Schaaf. Used by permission of New American Library, a
division of Penguin Books USA Inc.

For Journal Writing
Reprinted by permission of Chung Hyowon, 1992.

CHAPTER 12

For "Selling to the New America" reading selection
"Selling to the New America." Reprinted with permission, *Inc.* magazine,
(July 1987). Copyright © 1987 by Goldhirsh Group Inc., 38 Commercial.

For "Success" poem
Reprinted from *The Collected Verse of Edgar A. Guest* by Edgar A. Guest.
Copyright © 1934. Used with permission of Contemporary Books, Inc., Chicago.

PHOTO AND ILLUSTRATION CREDITS

Facing page 1: Michael Dwyer/Stock, Boston (*upper left*), Bob Daemmrich/ Image Works (*upper right*), Peter Menzel/Stock, Boston (*lower left*), Franklin Jay Viola/Comstock (*lower right*).

Pages 6 and 7: Courtesy of The Bostonian Society.

Pages 21, 32, and 174: Granger Collection.

Page 22: Joseph Schuyler/Stock, Boston.

Page 37: Franklin Jay Viola/Comstock.

Page 38: Image Works.

Page 51: AP/Wide World Photos.

Page 62: Rhoda Sidney/Image Works (*top*), Peter Menzel/Stock, Boston (*center*), Comstock (*bottom*).

Pages 64 and 181: Bob Daemmrich/Image Works.

Page 70: Mike Lajoie.

Page 88: Jeffry Myers/Stock, Boston (*left*), Mike Lajoie (*right*).

Page 107: Mike Lajoie.

Pages 111 and 155: Courtesy of Monchai Mankongcharoen (EFL student from Thailand).

Page 129: Courtesy of Brian Potts, *Wheeling News Register*, Wheeling, West Virginia.

Page 130: Peter Sickles/Stock, Boston.

Page 132: Courtesy of Clare Iacobelli.

Page 142: Reprinted with special permission of King Features Syndicate.

Page 152: UPI/Bettman.

Page 158: Elizabeth Crews/Stock, Boston.

Page 159: John Lei/Stock, Boston.

Page 179: Nina Winter/Image Works.

Page 191: Courtesy of Philip Fahy.

Page 196: Richard Heinzen/Superstock (*top*), courtesy of the Gillette Company (*bottom*).

Page 198: Mike Lajoie.

Page 202: Alan Carey/Image Works.

Pages 216 and 224: Courtesy of Mini Maid, Marietta, Georgia.

Page 218: Beth Bridge. BIC® is a registered trademark of Bic Corporation.

Pages 224 and 242: Blake Little.

Pages 237, 238, and 240: "Selling to the New America." Reprinted with permission, *Inc.* magazine (July 1987). Copyright © 1987 by Goldhirsh Group Inc., 38 Commercial.

Page 244: Red Morgan.

Page 255: Courtesy of Domino's Pizza, Washington, D.C.